SAS® Programming 1: Essentials

Course Notes

SAS® Programming 1: Essentials Course Notes was developed by Charlot Bennett, Michele Ensor, and Kathy Passarella. Additional contributions were made by Davetta Dunlap, Susan Farmer, Ted Meleky, Linda Mitterling, and Theresa Stemler. Editing and production support was provided by the Curriculum Development and Support Department.

SAS® Programming 1: Essentials Course Notes

Book code E2795, course code LWPG1/PG1, prepared date 20Mar2015.   LWPG1_001

ISBN 978-1-62959-735-5

Table of Contents

Course Description

This course is for users who want to learn how to write SAS programs. It is the entry point to learning SAS programming and is a prerequisite to many other SAS courses. If you do not plan to write SAS programs and you prefer a point-and-click interface, you should attend the SAS® Enterprise Guide® 1: Querying and Reporting course.

To learn more...

For information about other courses in the curriculum, contact the SAS Education Division at 1-800-333-7660, or send e-mail to training@sas.com. You can also find this information on the web at http://support.sas.com/training/ as well as in the Training Course Catalog.

For a list of other SAS books that relate to the topics covered in this course notes, USA customers can contact the SAS Publishing Department at 1-800-727-3228 or send e-mail to sasbook@sas.com. Customers outside the USA, please contact your local SAS office.

Also, see the SAS Bookstore on the web at http://support.sas.com/publishing/ for a complete list of books and a convenient order form.

Prerequisites

Before attending this course, you should have experience using computer software. Specifically, you should be able to

- understand file structures and system commands on your operating systems

- access data files on your operating systems.

No prior SAS experience is needed. If you do not feel comfortable with the prerequisites or are new to programming and think that the pace of this course might be too demanding, you can take the SAS® Programming Introduction: Basic Concepts course before attending this course. SAS® Programming Introduction: Basic Concepts is designed to introduce you to computer programming and presents a portion of the SAS® Programming 1: Essentials material at a slower pace.

Chapter 1   Introduction

1.1 Overview

Objectives

- Define SAS.
- Describe the functionality of Base SAS.

3

What Is SAS?

SAS is a suite of business solutions and technologies to help organizations solve business problems.

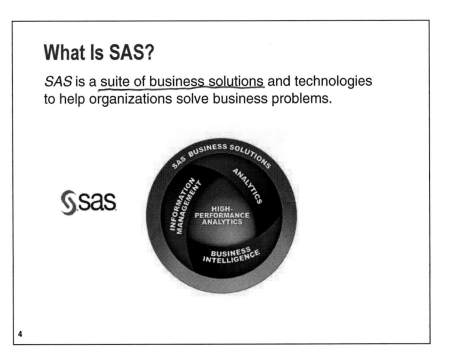

4

Why Use SAS?

SAS enables you to do the following:

- access and manage data across multiple sources
- perform analyses and deliver information across your organization

Base SAS is the primary focus of this course.

5

What Is Base SAS?

Base SAS is the foundation for all SAS software.

Base SAS provides the following:

- a highly flexible, highly extensible, fourth-generation programming language
- a rich library of encapsulated programming procedures
- a choice of programming interfaces

Base SAS

6

1.01 Multiple Choice Poll

What is your programming experience with SAS?
  a. maintaining programs written by others
  b. writing new programs
  c. no experience
  d. other

7

1.2 Course Logistics

Objectives

- Describe the data that is used in the course.
- Specify the naming convention that is used for the course files.
- Define the three levels of exercises.
- Explain the extended learning for this course.

10

Orion Star Sports & Outdoors

This course focuses on a fictitious global sports and outdoors retailer that has traditional stores, an online store, and a catalog business.

11

Orion Star Data

Large amounts of data are stored in various formats.

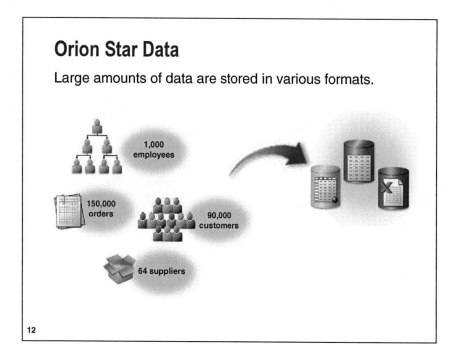

12

Program Naming Conventions

In this course, you use the structure below to retrieve and save SAS programs.

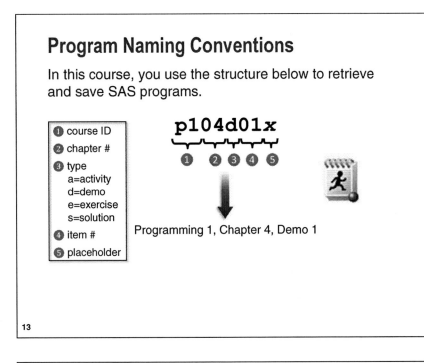

① course ID
② chapter #
③ type
   a=activity
   d=demo
   e=exercise
   s=solution
④ item #
⑤ placeholder

Programming 1, Chapter 4, Demo 1

13

Locating Data Files

In this course, macro variable references are used to give a more flexible approach for locating files.

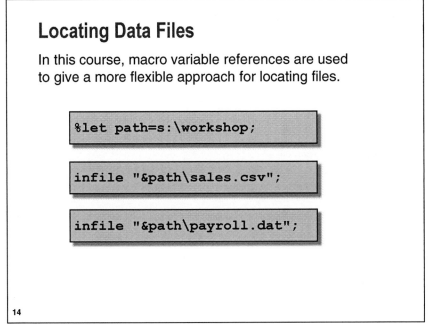

```
%let path=s:\workshop;
```

```
infile "&path\sales.csv";
```

```
infile "&path\payroll.dat";
```

14

Three Levels of Exercises

The course is designed to have you complete only *one* set of exercises. Select the level that is most appropriate for your skill set.

Level 1	Provides step-by-step instructions.
Level 2	Provides less information and guidance.
Challenge	Provides minimal information and guidance. You might need to use SAS Help and documentation.

15

Extending Your Learning

After class, you have access to an extended learning page that was created for this course. The page includes the following:

- course data and program files
- a PDF file of the course notes
- other course-specific resources

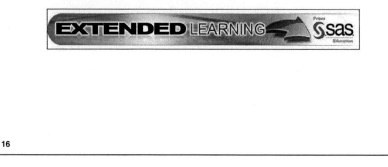

16

Chapter 2   SAS® Programs

2.1 Introduction to SAS Programs

Objectives

- List the components of a SAS program.

3

SAS Programs

A *SAS program* is a sequence of one or more steps.

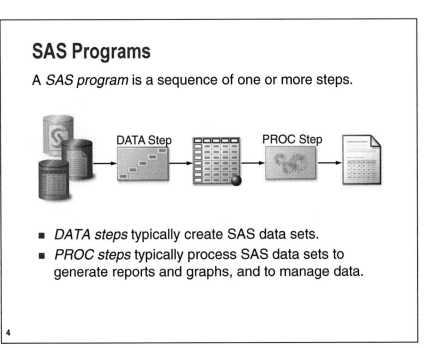

- *DATA steps* typically create SAS data sets.
- *PROC steps* typically process SAS data sets to generate reports and graphs, and to manage data.

4

SAS Program Steps

A *step* is a sequence of SAS statements. This program
has a DATA step and a PROC step.

```
data work.newemps;
   infile "&path\newemps.csv" dlm=',';
   input First $ Last $ Title $ Salary;
run;

proc print data=work.newemps;
run;
```

5

Step Boundaries

SAS steps begin with either of the following:

- a DATA statement
- a PROC statement

SAS detects the end of a step when it encounters
one of the following:

- a RUN statement (for most steps)
- a QUIT statement (for some procedures)
- the beginning of another step (DATA statement
  or PROC statement)

6

2.01 Short Answer Poll

How many steps are in program **p102d01**?

```
data work.newsalesemps;
   length First_Name $ 12
          Last_Name $ 18 Job_Title $ 25;
   infile "&path\newemps.csv" dlm=',';
   input First_Name $ Last_Name $
         Job_Title $ Salary;
run;

proc print data=work.newsalesemps;
run;

proc means data=work.newsalesemps;
   var Salary;
run;
```

7   p102d01

SAS Program Example

This DATA step creates a temporary SAS data set named
work.newsalesemps by reading four fields from a file.

```
data work.newsalesemps;
   length First_Name $ 12
          Last_Name $ 18 Job_Title $ 25;
   infile "&path\newemps.csv" dlm=',';
   input First_Name $ Last_Name $
         Job_Title $ Salary;
run;

proc print data=work.newsalesemps;
run;

proc means data=work.newsalesemps;
   var Salary;
run;
```

9   p102d01

SAS Program Example

This PROC PRINT step lists the **work.newsalesemps** data set.

```
data work.newsalesemps;
   length First_Name $ 12
          Last_Name $ 18 Job_Title $ 25;
   infile "&path\newemps.csv" dlm=',';
   input First_Name $ Last_Name $
         Job_Title $ Salary;
run;

proc print data=work.newsalesemps;
run;

proc means data=work.newsalesemps;
   var Salary;
run;
```

10   p102d01

SAS Program Example

This PROC MEANS step summarizes the **Salary** variable in the **work.newsalesemps** data set.

```
data work.newsalesemps;
   length First_Name $ 12
          Last_Name $ 18 Job_Title $ 25;
   infile "&path\newemps.csv" dlm=',';
   input First_Name $ Last_Name $
         Job_Title $ Salary;
run;

proc print data=work.newsalesemps;
run;

proc means data=work.newsalesemps;
   var Salary;
run;
```

11   p102d01

Idea Exchange

How does SAS detect the end of each step in this program?

```
data work.newsalesemps;
   length First_Name $ 12
          Last_Name $ 18 Job_Title $ 25;
   infile "&path\newemps.csv" dlm=',';
   input First_Name $ Last_Name $
         Job_Title $ Salary;
run;

proc print data=work.newsalesemps;

proc means data=work.newsalesemps;
   var Salary;
```

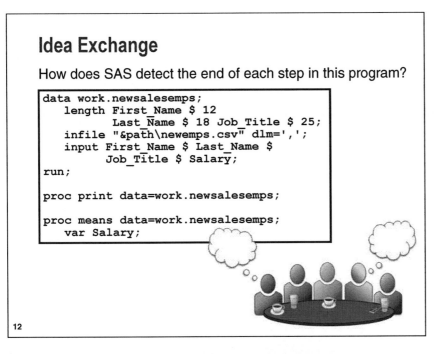

12

2.2 Submitting a SAS Program

Objectives

- Describe various processing modes and SAS interfaces.
- Define the three primary tabs or windows used within a SAS interface.
- Submit a SAS program to create the course data files.
- Submit the SAS program introduced in the previous section.

15

Processing Modes

The following are two possible processing modes for submitting a SAS program:

Interactive Mode	A SAS program is submitted within a SAS interface for foreground processing
Batch Mode	A SAS program is submitted to the operating environment for background processing

✎ In this course, interactive mode is used to process SAS programs.

16

- With foreground processing, the SAS interface coordinates all the work, so you cannot use your SAS interface to do other work while your program is running.
- With background processing, the operating environment coordinates all the work, so you can use your workstation session while your program is running.

SAS Interfaces

There are three possible SAS interfaces for processing a SAS program in interactive mode.

SAS Windowing Environment

SAS Enterprise Guide

SAS Studio

17

SAS Interfaces

Past ← → *Present*

SAS Windowing Environment

SAS Enterprise Guide

SAS Studio

18

---

sas SAS Windowing Environment

The *SAS windowing environment* is an application that is accessed from different operating environments.

The SAS windowing environment provides a full programming interface that can be used to write, edit, and submit SAS code.

19

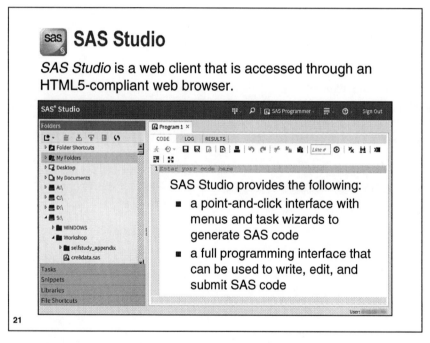

SAS Studio is the interface used in SAS University Edition. For more information about
SAS University Edition, visit **http://www.sas.com/en_us/software/university-edition.html**.

2.02 Multiple Choice Poll

Which interface will you use during this course?

a. SAS Studio
b. SAS Enterprise Guide
c. SAS windowing environment

22

SAS Interface Tabs or Windows

Regardless of the SAS interface that you choose to use, there are three primary tabs or windows.

Editor	Enter, edit, submit, and save a SAS program
Log	Browse notes, warnings, and errors relating to a submitted SAS program
Results	Browse output from reporting procedures

23

SAS Interface Tabs or Windows

Each interface uses specific terms to reference these three primary tabs or windows.

	SAS Studio (tabs)	SAS Enterprise Guide (tabs)	SAS Windowing Environment (windows)
Editor	Code	Program	Enhanced or Program Editor
Log	Log	Log	Log
Results	Results	Results	Results Viewer or Output

24

SAS Interface Tabs or Windows

The following is an example workflow of how a user might use the three primary tabs or windows:

25

Business Scenario

In this section, the following actions are completed:

- Submit a SAS program to create the data files that are needed for the course.
- Submit the SAS program introduced in Section 2.1.

26

Submitting SAS Programs with SAS Studio

 This demonstration is based on SAS Studio 3.3.

Submitting the cre8data Program

1. Start SAS Studio. The main window of SAS Studio consists of a navigation pane on the left and a work area on the right.

2. In the Folders section of the navigation pane, navigate in the file structure to find the **cre8data** program.

3. Double-click **cre8data** to open the program. Instead of double-clicking, you can drag the program into the work area.

4. On the CODE tab for the **cre8data** program, find the %LET statement.

5. If your data files are to be created at a location other than **s:\workshop**, change the value that is assigned to the **path** macro variable to reflect the location. If your data files are created in **s:\workshop**, then no change is needed.

   The **cre8data** program uses forward slashes for portability across operating environments. UNIX and Linux require forward slashes. Windows accepts forward slashes and might convert them to backslashes.

6. On the CODE tab, click ![Run icon] (**Run**) or press F3 to submit the program.

7. On the RESULTS tab, verify that the output contains a list of data files.

Submitting the p102d01 Program

1. In the Folders section of the navigation pane, navigate in the file structure to find the **p102d01** program.

2. Double-click **p102d01** to open the program. Instead of double-clicking, you can drag the program into the work area.

3. On the CODE tab, click (**Run**) or press F3 to submit the program.

4. On the RESULTS tab, view the PROC PRINT and PROC MEANS output.

5. Click the **LOG** tab and verify that no errors or warnings appear.

Submitting SAS Programs with SAS Enterprise Guide

✎ This demonstration is based on SAS Enterprise Guide 7.1.

Submitting the cre8data Program

1. Start SAS Enterprise Guide. Close the Welcome to SAS Enterprise Guide window by clicking the **X** in the right corner of the window. By default, SAS Enterprise Guide contains a Project Tree window and Servers window. They are docked on the left side. A Process Flow window is docked on the right side.

2. Select **File** ⇨ **Open** ⇨ **Program** or click (**Open**) ⇨ **Program**.

3. In the Open Program window, navigate in the file structure to find **cre8data** and click **Open**.

4. On the Program tab for the **cre8data** program, find the %LET statement.

5. If your data files are to be created at a location other than **s:\workshop**, change the value that is assigned to the **path** macro variable to reflect the location. If your data files are created in **s:\workshop**, then no change is needed.

    ✎ The **cre8data** program uses forward slashes for portability across operating environments. UNIX and Linux require forward slashes. Windows accepts forward slashes and might convert them to backslashes.

6. On the Program tab, click **Run** or press F3 to submit the program.

7. On the Results tab, verify that the output contains a list of data files.

Submitting the p102d01 Program

1. Select **File** ⇨ **Open** ⇨ **Program** or click (**Open**) ⇨ **Program**.

2. In the Open Program window, navigate in the file structure to find **p102d01** and click **Open**.

3. On the Program tab, click **Run** or press F3 to submit the program.

4. On the Results tab, view the PROC PRINT and PROC MEANS output.

5. Click the **Log** tab and verify that no errors or warnings appear.

Submitting SAS Programs in the SAS Windowing Environment

✎   This demonstration is based on SAS 9.4M2.

Submitting the cre8data Program

1. Start the SAS windowing environment. If you see a pop-up window that references a change notice or getting started with SAS, click **Close**. By default, the SAS windowing environment consists of a left pane containing the Results and Explorer windows and a right pane containing the Output, Log, and Editor windows.

2. Click 📂 (**Open**) when the Editor window is the active window or select **File ⇨ Open Program**.

3. In the Open window, navigate in the file structure to find **cre8data** and click **Open**.

4. In the Editor window for the **cre8data** program, find the %LET statement.

5. If your data files are to be created at a location other than **s:\workshop**, change the value that is assigned to the **path** macro variable to reflect the location. If your data files are created in **s:\workshop**, then no change is needed.

   ✎   The **cre8data** program uses forward slashes for portability across operating environments. UNIX and Linux require forward slashes. Windows accepts forward slashes and might convert them to backslashes.

6. Click 🏃 (**Submit**) or press F3 to submit the program.

7. In the Results Viewer window, verify that the output contains a list of data files.

8. Go to the Log window and click 🗋 (**New**) or select **Edit ⇨ Clear All** to clear the Log window.

Submitting the p102d01 Program

1. Click 📂 (**Open**) when the Editor window is the active window or select **File ⇨ Open Program**.

2. In the Open window, navigate in the file structure to find **p102d01** and click **Open**.

3. Click 🏃 (**Submit**) or press F3 to submit the program.

4. In the Results Viewer window, view the PROC PRINT and PROC MEANS output.

5. Go to the Log window and verify that no errors or warnings appear. Be sure to scroll up to see all messages.

Exercises

All of the exercises in this chapter are self-guided. No solutions are needed.

SAS Studio

⚠️   You **must** complete this exercise to create the course data files. If you do not create the data files, the majority of programs in this course will fail.

1. **Creating Course Data with SAS Studio**

    a. Start SAS Studio. The main window of SAS Studio consists of a navigation pane on the left and a work area on the right.

    b. In the Folders section of the navigation pane, navigate in the file structure to find the **cre8data** program.

    c. Double-click **cre8data** to open the program. Instead of double-clicking, you can drag the program into the work area.

    d. On the CODE tab for the **cre8data** program, find the %LET statement shown below.

```
15
16 %let path=s:/workshop;
17
18
                                    Line 20, Column 21
```

    e. If your data files are to be created at a location other than **s:\workshop**, change the value that is assigned to the **path** macro variable to reflect the location. If your data files are created in **s:\workshop**, then no change is needed.

✎   The **cre8data** program uses forward slashes for portability across operating environments. UNIX and Linux require forward slashes. Windows accepts forward slashes and might convert them to backslashes.

f. On the CODE tab, click Run (**Run**) or press F3 to submit the program.

g. On the RESULTS tab, verify that the output contains a list of data files.

h. Close the program tab for **cre8data** by clicking the **X** next to the name.

2. **Exploring SAS Studio**

Using the Primary Interface Tabs

a. On the CODE tab of the Program 1 tab, enter the PROC PRINT step shown below.

```
1 proc print data=sashelp.class;
2 run;
```

b. On the CODE tab, click Run (**Run**) or press F3 to submit the program. If the program runs successfully, the RESULTS tab automatically opens and shows the PROC PRINT output.

1) Click the **LOG** tab and check the log for the two notes below. If you see any warnings or errors, return to the CODE tab, fix any mistakes, and rerun the program.

```
NOTE: There were 19 observations read from the data set SASHELP.CLASS.
NOTE: PROCEDURE PRINT used (Total process time):
```

2) Click the **RESULTS** tab. Notice that the PROC PRINT output contains an **Obs** column.

Obs	Name	Sex	Age	Height	Weight
1	Alfred	M	14	69.0	112.5
2	Alice	F	13	56.5	84.0
3	Barbara	F	13	65.3	98.0
4	Carol	F	14	62.8	102.5
5	Henry	M	14	63.5	102.5

c. Click the **CODE** tab and add the NOOBS option to eliminate the **Obs** column.

```
1 proc print data=sashelp.class noobs;
2 run;
```

✎   The NOOBS option is in the PROC PRINT statement before the semicolon.

1) On the CODE tab, click 🏃 (**Run**) or press F3 to submit the program.

2) View the new information on the RESULTS tab and the LOG tab.

d. Create another program. In the Folders section of the navigation pane, click [➕▾] (**New**) ⇨ **SAS Program (F4)** or press F4.

Folders

SAS Program (F4)
Query
Folder
Folder Shortcut

1) On the CODE tab of the Program 2 tab, enter the PROC PRINT step and the PROC MEANS step shown below.

*Program 1 ×   *Program 2 ×

CODE   LOG   RESULTS

```
1 proc print data=sashelp.class;
2 run;
3 proc means data=sashelp.class;
4 run;
```

2) On the CODE tab, click 🏃 (**Run**) or press F3 to submit the program. If the program runs successfully, the RESULTS tab automatically opens and shows the PROC PRINT and PROC MEANS output.

3) Click the **LOG** tab. Check the log for notes. If you see any warnings or errors, return to the CODE tab, fix any mistakes, and rerun the program.

4) Click the **CODE** tab and click 🔲 (**Save As**) to save the program.

5) In the Save As window, choose a file location such as **s:\workshop**, name the file **MyProgram**, and click **Save**.

Save As	✕
Location:	📷
▷ 🖥 Desktop	
▷ 🗂 My Documents	
▷ 💾 A:\	
▷ 💾 C:\	
▷ 💾 D:\	
▲ 💾 S:\	
▷ 📁 WINDOWS	
▲ 📁 Workshop	
Name:	MyProgram.sas
Save as type:	SAS Program (*.SAS) ▾
	Save Cancel

6) Notice that the Program 2 tab now appears with the program name. Close the program tab for **MyProgram** by clicking the **X** next to the name.

✏️   An asterisk (*) in front of a filename means that the program was not saved.

e. Open the program that you saved and closed. In the Folders section of the navigation pane, navigate to the file location for **MyProgram.sas**.

Folders	
📄▾ 🗑 ⬇ ⬆ ☰ ↺	
▲ 💾 S:\	
▷ 📁 WINDOWS	
▲ 📁 Workshop	
▷ 📁 selfstudy_appendix	
📄 cre8data.sas	
📄 custcaus.xls	
📄 custfm.xls	
📄 MyProgram.sas	

1) Double-click **MyProgram.sas** to open the program. Instead of double-clicking, you can drag the program into the work area.

2) Submit a portion of the program. On the CODE tab, highlight the PROC MEANS step (two lines of code) and click ![Run icon] (**Run**) or press F3 to submit the highlighted code.

3) View the RESULTS tab and the LOG tab. Notice that the information on the tabs pertains only to the PROC MEANS step.

Using the CODE Tab Features

f. On the CODE toolbar, click ![Maximize icon] (**Maximize View**) to maximize the work area and hide the navigation pane.

   After you maximize the window, click ![Exit Maximize icon] (**Exit Maximize View**) to unhide the navigation pane.

g. In the Folders section of the navigation pane, click ![New icon] (**New**) ⇨ **SAS Program (F4)** or press F4 to start a new program.

1) On the CODE tab of Program 2, start to enter a PROC PRINT step. Notice the autocomplete feature as you type. The autocomplete feature gives you a window of possible keywords that might come next in your program. For example, after you enter **proc print**, a pop-up window appears. The window contains procedure options that pertain to the PRINT procedure.

   ✏ To navigate to the desired keyword in the window, scroll through the list by using the up and down arrow keys, the Page Up or Page Down keys, or drag the scroll bar with your mouse pointer. To add the keyword to your program, double-click the keyword or press the Enter key.

2) Start to enter the DATA= option. Syntax Help appears as you narrow the list of keywords. Syntax Help also appears if you right-click a keyword in the program and select **Syntax Help**.

3) Complete the PROC PRINT step. Notice the autocomplete feature and Syntax Help as you type.

```
proc print data=sashelp.class;
run;
```

You can also access Syntax Help by positioning the mouse pointer on a valid keyword in your program, if you enable the feature in the editor preferences. To enable the option, click ☰ (**More Application Options**) on the main toolbar.

4) Select **Preferences** ⇨ **Editor** and notice the list of editor preferences.

5) Select the **Enable hint** check box and click **Save**.

6) Position your mouse pointer on the word **print** in your program to see the Syntax Help.

Using RESULTS Tab Features

h. On the CODE tab of Program 2, click ![Run icon] (**Run**) or press F3 to submit the PROC PRINT step. If the program runs successfully, the RESULTS tab automatically opens and shows the PROC PRINT output.

i. By default, the results created on the RESULTS tab are HTML5 output. On the RESULTS toolbar, click ![icon] (**Open In A New Browser Tab**) to open the HTML5 output on another browser tab.

j. After viewing the output in the new browser tab, close the browser tab.

✎   PDF output and RTF output are created by default in addition to HTML5 output. PDF output and RTF output are not displayed on the RESULTS tab. You can download the HTML5, PDF, and RTF output to a file by clicking the appropriate button.

k. Click ![icon] (**Download Results As A PDF File**) or ![icon] (**Download Results As An RTF File**) to download the PDF or RTF output. Follow the prompts to open the file. After viewing the file, close the file.

l. You can change results preferences in the Preferences window. To access the results preferences, click ![icon] (**More Application Options**).

1) Select **Preferences** ⇨ **Results** and notice the list of results preferences.

2) Click **Cancel** to close the Preferences window.

3. **Accessing Help and Documentation**

    a. You can access SAS Help and documentation from the main toolbar.

    b. Click [?] ⇨ **SAS Studio Help** to be directed to the SAS Studio documentation web page. This web page is useful for assistance with navigating the SAS Studio interface. After you view the web page, close the window.

✎   External address to the SAS Studio page:
http://support.sas.com/software/products/sasstudio/

c. Click ⊙⌄ ⇨ **SAS Product Documentation** to be directed to the SAS Products & Solutions web page. This web page is useful for learning information about a SAS product.

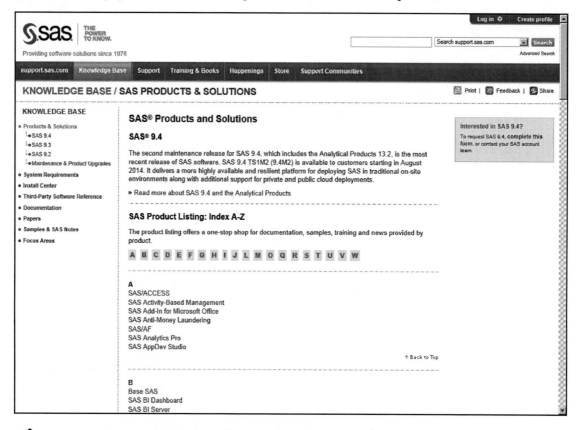

✎   External address to the SAS Products page: **http://support.sas.com/software/**

d. From the above web page, select **Documentation** in the KNOWLEDGE BASE navigation pane.

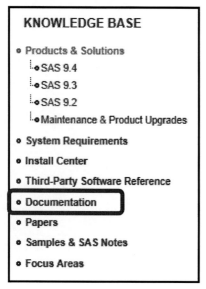

e. The SAS Product Documentation web page appears. This web page is useful for viewing the syntax documentation related to a SAS product.

 External address to the SAS Product Documentation page:
http://support.sas.com/documentation/

f. From this web page, select **Programmer's Bookshelf**. Then select the link for your version of SAS.

 The Programmer's Bookshelf contains selected documentation for SAS products such as Base SAS.

g. Browse the Programmer's Bookshelf web page. Close the window when you are finished browsing.

SAS Enterprise Guide

⚠️ You *must* complete this exercise to create the course data files. If you do not create the data files, the majority of programs in this course will fail.

4. **Creating Course Data with SAS Enterprise Guide**

a. Start SAS Enterprise Guide. Close the Welcome to SAS Enterprise Guide window by clicking the **X** in the right corner of the window. By default, SAS Enterprise Guide contains a Project Tree window and a Servers window. They are docked on the left side. The Process Flow window is docked on the right side.

b. Select **File** ⇨ **Open** ⇨ **Program** or click ![icon] (**Open**) ⇨ **Program**.

c. In the Open Program window, navigate to the file location to find **cre8data** and click **Open**.

d. On the Program tab for the **cre8data** program, find the %LET statement shown below.

e. If your data files are to be created at a location other than **s:\workshop**, change the value that is assigned to the **path** macro variable to reflect the location. If your data files are created in **s:\workshop**, then no change is needed.

🖉 The **cre8data** program uses forward slashes for portability across operating environments. UNIX and Linux require forward slashes. Windows accepts forward slashes and might convert them to backslashes.

1) On the Program tab, click **Run** or press F3 to submit the program.

2) On the Results tab, verify that the output contains a list of data files.

cre8data ▾   ✕

🔲 Program | 📄 Log | 📋 Results

🔄 Refresh | Export ▾ Send To ▾ Create ▾ Publish | 📇 Properties

The CONTENTS Procedure

Directory	
Libref	ORION
Engine	V9
Physical Name	s:\workshop
Filename	s:\workshop

#	Name	Member Type	File Size	Last Modified
1	CHARITIES	DATA	131072	01/26/2015 11:33:25
2	CONSULTANTS	DATA	131072	01/26/2015 11:33:25

3) Remove **cre8data** from the project. Right-click **cre8data** in the Project Tree window and select **Delete**. Click **Yes** to delete all the items when you are prompted.

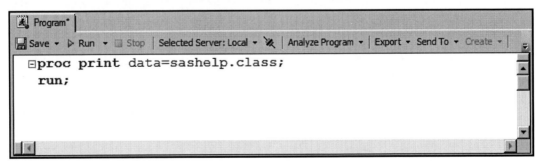

5. **Exploring SAS Enterprise Guide**

Using the Primary Interface Tabs

a. Start a new program by selecting **File** ⇨ **New** ⇨ **Program** or by clicking ▤▾ (**New**) ⇨ **Program**.

1) On the Program tab, enter the PROC PRINT step shown below.

```
proc print data=sashelp.class;
  run;
```

2) On the Program tab, click **Run** or press F3 to submit the program. If the program runs successfully, the Results tab automatically opens and shows the PROC PRINT output.

3) Click the **Log** tab and check the log for the two notes shown below. If you see any warnings or errors, return to the Program tab, fix any mistakes, and rerun the program.

```
NOTE: There were 19 observations read from the data set SASHELP.CLASS.
NOTE: PROCEDURE PRINT used (Total process time):
```

4) Click the **Results** tab. Notice that the PROC PRINT output contains an **Obs** column.

Obs	Name	Sex	Age	Height	Weight
1	Alfred	M	14	69.0	112.5
2	Alice	F	13	56.5	84.0
3	Barbara	F	13	65.3	98.0
4	Carol	F	14	62.8	102.5
5	Henry	M	14	63.5	102.5

5) Click the **Program** tab and add the NOOBS option to eliminate the **Obs** column.

```
proc print data=sashelp.class noobs;
  run;
```

✎ The NOOBS option is in the PROC PRINT statement before the semicolon.

6) On the Program tab, click the **Run** button or press F3 to submit the program.

7) Click **Yes** to replace the results from the previous run.

SAS Enterprise Guide

Do you want to replace the results from the previous run?

Choosing "No" will save the changes to a new task, named "Program (2)".

[Yes]   [No]   [Cancel]

8) View the new information on the Results tab and the Log tab.

b. Create another program. Select **File** ⇨ **New** ⇨ **Program** or click 📄▾ (**New**) ⇨ **Program**.

1) On the new Program tab, enter the PROC PRINT step and the PROC MEANS step as shown.

```
proc print data=sashelp.class;
  run;
proc means data=sashelp.class;
  run;
```

✎ An asterisk (*) after the word **Program** on the Program tab means that the program was not saved.

2) On the Program tab, click the **Run** button or press F3 to submit the program. If the program runs successfully, the Results tab automatically opens and shows the PROC PRINT and PROC MEANS output.

3) Click the **Log** tab. Check the log for notes. If you see any warnings or errors, return to the Program tab, fix any mistakes, and rerun the program.

4) Click the **Program** tab. Select **File** ⇨ **Save Program (2) As** or click the **Save** button and then select **Save As** to save the program.

5) In the Save window, choose a file location such as **s:\workshop**, name the file **MyProgram**, and click **Save**.

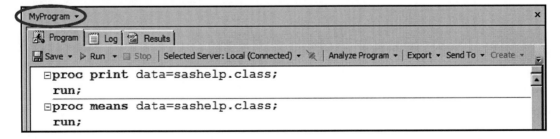

6) Notice that the workspace area contains the program name above the Program, Log, and Results tabs.

7) Remove **MyProgram** from the project. Right-click **MyProgram** in the Project Tree window and select **Delete**. Click **Yes** to delete all the items when you are prompted.

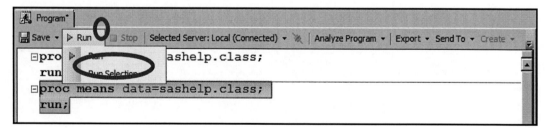

This action deletes the program from the project. However, the program still exists.

c. Open the program that you saved and removed. Select **File** ⇨ **Open** ⇨ **Program** or click [icon] (**Open**) ⇨ **Program**.

1) In the Open Program window, navigate to the file location to find **MyProgram**. Click **Open**.

2) Submit a portion of the program. On the Program tab, highlight the PROC MEANS step (two lines of code). Click the drop-down arrow next to the Run button and select **Run Selection** or press F3 to submit the highlighted code.

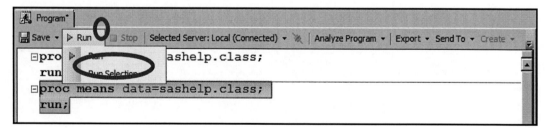

3) View the Results tab and the Log tab. Notice that the information on the tabs pertains only to the PROC MEANS step.

Using Program Tab Features

d. Select **View** ⇨ **Maximize Workspace** to maximize the Program window and hide the Project Tree and Servers windows.

To unhide the Project Tree and Servers windows, select **View** ⇨ **Maximize Workspace** again.

e. Click the **Program** tab for **MyProgram**.

1) The appearance and functionality of the Program tab can be customized. To customize it, select **Tools** ⇨ **Options** ⇨ **SAS Programs**. Then click **Editor Options**.

2) In the Enhanced Editor Options window, four tabs contain editor options. On the Appearance tab, increase the font size and click **OK**. Click **OK** to close the Options window. Notice the change in the text's font size on the Program tab.

f. Start a new program. Select **File** ⇨ **New** ⇨ **Program** or click (New) ⇨ **Program**.

1) On the Program tab, start entering a PROC PRINT step. Notice the autocomplete feature as you type. The autocomplete feature gives you a window of possible keywords that can come next in your program. For example, after you enter **proc print**, a pop-up window appears with procedure options that pertain to the PRINT procedure.

✏️ To navigate to the desired keyword in the window, scroll through the list by using the up and down arrow keys, the Page Up or Page Down keys, or the scroll bar. To add a keyword to a program, double-click the keyword or press the Enter key or the spacebar.

2) In addition to displaying possible keywords, autocomplete can display libraries, data sets, and variables.

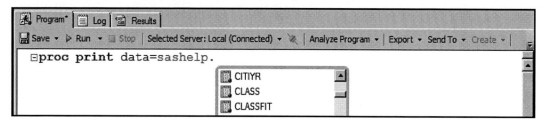

3) Complete the PROC PRINT step. Notice the autocomplete feature as you type.

```
proc print data=sashelp.class;
run;
```

g. You can access syntax Help by positioning the mouse pointer on a valid keyword in your program. Position your mouse pointer on the word **print** in the program to see the syntax Help.

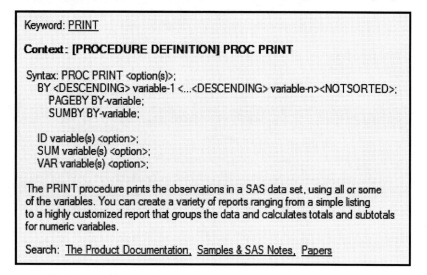

Customizing Results

h. On the Program tab, click the **Run** button or press F3 to submit the program. If the program runs successfully, the Results tab automatically opens and shows the PROC PRINT output.

1) By default, the results that are created on the Results tab are SAS Report output. SAS Report output is an XML file, which can be viewed within SAS applications.

2) In addition to creating SAS Report output, other output types can be created. Select **Tools** ⇨ **Options** ⇨ **Results General**.

3) A check mark already appears in front of SAS Report. Select the **HTML, PDF, RTF**, and **Text output** check boxes. Click **OK**.

i. Submit the PROC PRINT step. Click **Yes** to replace the results from the previous run. Five Results tabs appear.

j. Click each tab to view the results. When you click the PDF tab, the PDF output opens in an Adobe product such as Adobe Reader. When you click the RTF tab, the RTF output opens in a word processing application such as Microsoft Word. After you click the PDF and RTF tabs, the tabs disappear because the files are opened outside of SAS. The Listing tab contains the text output.

k. Select **Tools** ⇨ **Options** ⇨ **Results General**. Clear the **HTML, PDF**, and **RTF** check boxes. Do *not* change the SAS Report and Text output check boxes. Click **OK**.

6. **Accessing Help and Documentation**

   SAS Help and documentation can be accessed from the Help drop-down menu.

a. Select **Help** ⇨ **SAS Enterprise Guide Help** to be directed to a window that displays help for SAS Enterprise Guide. This window is useful for assistance with navigating the SAS Enterprise Guide interface. After you view the Help window, close the window

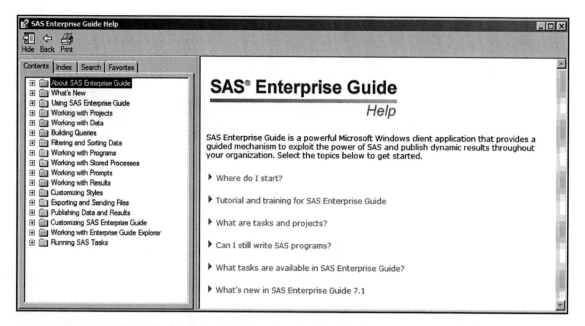

b. Select **Help** ⇨ **SAS on the Web** ⇨ **SAS Product Documentation** to be directed to the SAS Product Documentation web page. This web page is useful for viewing the syntax documentation related to a SAS product.

   ✎   External address to the SAS Product Documentation page:
        http://support.sas.com/documentation/

c. On this web page, select **Programmer's Bookshelf**. Then select the link for the appropriate SAS version.

   ✎   The Programmer's Bookshelf contains selected documentation for SAS products such as Base SAS.

d. Browse the Programmer's Bookshelf web page. Close the window after browsing it.

SAS Windowing Environment

⚠   You **must** complete this exercise to create the course data files. If you do not create the data files, the majority of programs in this course will fail.

7. **Creating Course Data in the SAS Windowing Environment**

    a. Start the SAS windowing environment. If you see a pop-up window that references a change notice or getting started with SAS, click **Close**. By default, the SAS windowing environment consists of a left pane containing the Results and Explorer windows and a right pane containing the Output, Log, and Editor windows.

    b. Click [icon] (**Open**) when the Editor window is the active window or select **File** ⇨ **Open Program**.

    c. In the Open window, navigate to the file location to find **cre8data** and click **Open**.

    d. In the Editor window for the **cre8data** program, find the %LET statement shown below.

    e. If your data files are to be created at a location other than **s:\workshop**, change the value that is assigned to the **path** macro variable to reflect the location. If your data files are created in **s:\workshop**, then no change is needed.

       🖊 The **cre8data** program uses forward slashes for portability across operating environments. UNIX and Linux require forward slashes. Windows accepts forward slashes and might convert them to backslashes.

    f. Click [icon] (**Submit**) or press F3 to submit the program.

    g. In the Results Viewer window, verify that the output contains a list of data files.

Results Viewer - SAS Output

The SAS System

The CONTENTS Procedure

Directory	
Libref	ORION
Engine	V9
Physical Name	s:\workshop
Filename	s:\workshop

#	Name	Member Type	File Size	Last Modified
1	CHARITIES	DATA	131072	01/26/2015 11:42:34
2	CONSULTANTS	DATA	131072	01/26/2015 11:42:34

h. Go to the Log window and click ☐ (**New**) or select **Edit** ⇨ **Clear All** to clear the Log window.

i. Close the Editor window for **cre8data** by clicking the **X** in the right corner of the window.

cre8data.sas

8. Exploring the SAS Windowing Environment

Using the Primary Interface Windows

a. Select **View** ⇨ **Enhanced Editor** to open a new Editor window.

   1) In the Editor window, enter the PROC PRINT step shown below.

```
Editor - Untitled2 *
proc print data=sashelp.class;
run;
```

   ✎   The Enhanced Editor is used when you use the Editor window.

   2) Click 🏃 (**Submit**) or press F3 to submit the program. If the program runs successfully, the Results Viewer window automatically appears and shows the PROC PRINT output.

   3) Go to the Log window and check the log for the two notes below. If you see any warnings or errors, return to the Editor window, fix any mistakes, and rerun the program.

```
NOTE: There were 19 observations read from the data set SASHELP.CLASS.
NOTE: PROCEDURE PRINT used (Total process time):
```

4) Return to the Results Viewer window. Notice that the PROC PRINT output contains an **Obs** column.

The SAS System

Obs	Name	Sex	Age	Height	Weight
1	Alfred	M	14	69.0	112.5
2	Alice	F	13	56.5	84.0
3	Barbara	F	13	65.3	98.0
4	Carol	F	14	62.8	102.5
5	Henry	M	14	63.5	102.5

5) Return to the Editor window and add the NOOBS option to eliminate the **Obs** column.

```
Editor - Untitled2 *
proc print data=sashelp.class noobs;
run;
```

The NOOBS option is in the PROC PRINT statement before the semicolon.

6) Click ⚡ (**Submit**) or press F3 to submit the program.

7) View the information in the Results Viewer window and the Log window. Notice that the information in these windows is cumulative. The most recent information is added at the bottom.

8) Close the Log window by clicking the **X** in the right corner of the window. Select **View** ⇨ **Log** to reopen the log. The Log window still contains the information from the previous two submissions.

9) To clear the Log window, click 📄 (**New**) when the Log window is the active window. You can also select **Edit** ⇨ **Clear All** to clear the Log window.

b. Create another program. Click 📄 (**New**) from an existing Editor window or select **View** ⇨ **Enhanced Editor**.

1) In the new Editor window, enter the PROC PRINT step and PROC MEANS step shown below.

```
Editor - Untitled3 *
proc print data=sashelp.class;
run;
proc means data=sashelp.class;
run;
```

An asterisk (*) at the end of a filename means that the program was not saved.

2) Click (**Submit**) or press F3 to submit the program. If the program runs successfully, the Results Viewer window automatically appears and shows the PROC PRINT and PROC MEANS output. Do not forget that the Results Viewer is cumulative. The most recent information is added at the bottom.

3) Go to the Log window. Check the log for notes. If you see any warnings or errors, return to the Editor window, fix any mistakes, and rerun the program.

4) Return to the Editor – Untitled3 window. Click (**Save**) or select **File ⇨ Save As** to save the program.

5) In the Save As window, choose a file location such as **s:\workshop**, name the file **MyProgram**, and click **Save**.

6) Notice that the Editor window now appears with the program name. Close the Editor window for **MyProgram** by clicking the **X** in the right corner of the window.

```
proc print data=sashelp.class;
run;
proc means data=sashelp.class;
run;
```

c. Open the program that you saved and closed. To open a program, click (**Open**) when the Editor window is the active window or select **File ⇨ Open Program**.

1) In the Open window, navigate to the file location to find **MyProgram** and click **Open**.

2) Submit a portion of the program. In the Editor window, highlight the PROC MEANS step
(two lines of code). Click Submit (**Submit**) or press F3 to submit the highlighted code.

3) View the Results Viewer window and the Log window. Notice that the last submission
submitted only the PROC MEANS step.

Customizing the Enhanced Editor

d. Return to the Editor window for **MyProgram**. If you want, click the **Maximize** button in the top
right corner of the window to maximize the window.

e. The appearance and functionality of the Enhanced Editor can be customized. To customize the
Enhanced Editor, select **Tools** ⇨ **Options** ⇨ **Enhanced Editor** from the main toolbar.

1) In the Enhanced Editor Options window, two tabs contain editor options. On the Appearance
tab, increase the font size and click **OK**. Notice the change of the text's font size in the Editor
window.

2) To browse a list of the function key definitions for the windowing environment, select **Tools**
⇨ **Options** ⇨ **Keys** to access the Keys window. Notice the following key definitions:

- F1 is help.

- F3 is end.

- F6 is log.

- F8 is zoom off and submit.

      The End command is an alias for the Submit command when it is initiated in the
      Editor window.

3) The function key definitions can be customized. For example, F12 can be set to clear the log and submit the program. This function key is used in an Editor window. Enter the following command in the Definition column for F12:

```
clear log; submit
```

4) Close the Keys window by clicking the **X** in the right corner of the window or by pressing F3.

f. Return to the Editor window for **MyProgram**. Press F12. Confirm that the Log window contains only the messages for the PROC PRINT and PROC MEANS steps that were submitted.

Customizing Results

g. By default, the results created in the Results Viewer window are cumulative HTML4 output. To clear the previous output, you can add ODS statements to the program to close the existing output and start new output. Add the following two ODS statements to the beginning of **MyProgram**:

```
ods html close; ods html;
```

h. Click ⚡ (**Submit**) or press F3 to submit the modified program. Verify that the Results Viewer window contains only one PROC PRINT output and one PROC MEANS output.

i. In addition to creating HTML4 output in the Results Viewer window, you can create text output in the Output window.

1) Select **Tools** ⇨ **Options** ⇨ **Preferences** and click the **Results** tab. The Create HTML check box is already selected.

2) Select the **Create listing** check box to create text output. Click **OK**.

j. Submit the program.

1) Verify that the Results Viewer window contains PROC PRINT and PROC MEANS output. The Results Viewer window is not cumulative when you submit the two ODS statements.

2) In addition, verify that the PROC PRINT and PROC MEANS output is also visible in the Output window as text output. The Output window is cumulative. The most recent information is added at the bottom.

3) The Results window is used to navigate the results. The window contains bookmarks that you can expand and collapse.

Results

```
Results
 ⊞ Print:  The SAS System
 ⊞ Print:  The SAS System
 ⊞ Print:  The SAS System
 ⊞ Means:  The SAS System
 ⊞ Means:  The SAS System
 ⊞ Print:  The SAS System
 ⊞ Means:  The SAS System
 ⊞ Print:  The SAS System
 ⊞ Means:  The SAS System
 ⊞ Print:  The SAS System
 ⊞ Means:  The SAS System
```

k. Select the last **Means** node in the Results window.

   1) Click the plus sign in front of **Means** to expand the node.

   2) Click the plus sign in front of **Summary statistics** to expand it. Each report bookmark contains an icon that indicates the file type, such as HTML or LISTING (text output).

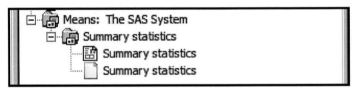

   3) Double-click one of the report bookmarks to view the corresponding report in the appropriate window.

l. The previously defined F12 key can be modified to clear the Log window, clear the Output window, and clear the Results window.

   1) To modify F12, select **Tools ⇨ Options ⇨ Keys** to access the Keys window.

   2) Enter the following command in the Definition column for F12:

```
clear log; clear output; odsresults; clear;
```

   3) Close the Keys window by clicking the **X** in the right corner of the window or by pressing F3.

   4) Press F12. Confirm that the Log, Output, and Results windows are cleared.

m. Return to the Editor window for **MyProgram** and click 💾 (**Save**) or select **File ⇨ Save** to save the program.

n. Close the Editor window for **MyProgram** by clicking the **X** in the right corner of the window.

9. Accessing Help and Documentation

SAS Help and SAS documentation can be accessed from the **Help** drop-down menu.

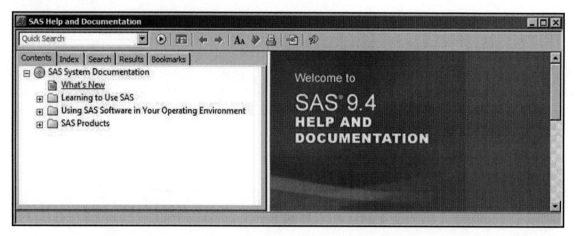

a. Click **Help** ⇨ **SAS Help and Documentation** to be directed to a window that displays SAS Help and documentation.

b. To view the syntax documentation for a specific product, expand **SAS Products** on the **Contents** tab. Choose the desired product, such as Base SAS, to view the product documentation. Close the window when you are finished browsing.

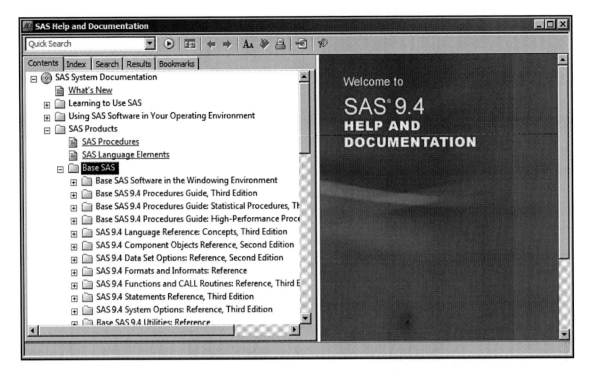

c. Alternatively, you can access the documentation for a SAS product directly from the following SAS Product Documentation web page: **http://support.sas.com/documentation/**.

d. From this web page, select **Programmer's Bookshelf**. Then choose the link for the appropriate version of SAS.

The Programmer's Bookshelf contains selected documentation for SAS products such as Base SAS.

e. Browse the Programmer's Bookshelf web page. Close the window after browsing it.

2.3 SAS Program Syntax

Objectives

- Identify the characteristics of SAS statements.
- Define SAS syntax rules.
- Document a program using comments.
- Diagnose and correct a program with errors.

32

Business Scenario

Well-formatted, clearly documented SAS programs are an industry best practice.

33

SAS Syntax Rules: Statements

SAS statements

- usually begin with an ***identifying keyword***
- always end with a ***semicolon***.

```
data work.newsalesemps;
   length First_Name $ 12
          Last_Name $ 18 Job_Title $ 25;
   infile "&path\newemps.csv" dlm=',';
   input First_Name $ Last_Name $
         Job_Title $ Salary;
run;

proc print data=work.newsalesemps;
run;

proc means data=work.newsalesemps;
   var Salary;
run;
```

34   p102d01

2.03 Short Answer Poll

How many statements make up this DATA step?

```
data work.newsalesemps;
   length First_Name $ 12
          Last_Name $ 18 Job_Title $ 25;
   infile "&path\newemps.csv" dlm=',';
   input First_Name $ Last_Name $
         Job_Title $ Salary;
run;
```

35

SAS Program Structure

SAS code is free format.

```
data work.newsalesemps;
length First_Name $ 12
Last_Name $ 18 Job_Title $ 25;
infile "&path\newemps.csv" dlm=',';
input First_Name $ Last_Name $
Job_Title $ Salary;run;
proc print data=work.newsalesemps; run;
   proc means data  =work.newsalesemps;
var Salary;run;
```

This program is syntactically correct but difficult to read.

37   **p102d02**

SAS Program Structure

Rules for SAS Statements
- Statements can begin and end in any column.
- A single statement can span multiple lines.
- Several statements can appear on the same line.
- Unquoted values can be lowercase, uppercase, or mixed case.

unconventional formatting

```
data work.newsalesEmps;
length First_Name $ 12
Last_Name $ 18 Job_Title $ 25;
infile "&path\newemps.csv" dlm=',';
input First_Name $ Last_Name $
Job_Title $ Salary;run;
proc print data=work.newsalesemps; run;
   proc means data  =work.newsalesemps;
var Salary;run;
```

38

Recommended Formatting

- Begin each statement on a new line.
- Use white space to separate words and steps.
- Indent statements within a step.
- Indent continued lines in multi-line statements.

```
data work.newsalesemps;
   length First_Name $ 12
          Last_Name $ 18 Job_Title $ 25;
   infile "&path\newemps.csv" dlm=',';
   input First_Name $ Last_Name $
         Job_Title $ Salary;
run;

proc print data=work.newsalesemps;
run;

proc means data=work.newsalesemps;
   var Salary;
run;
```

conventional formatting

39

White space can be blanks, tabs, and new lines. Add them to increase the readability of the code.

Program Documentation

You can embed comments in a program as explanatory text.

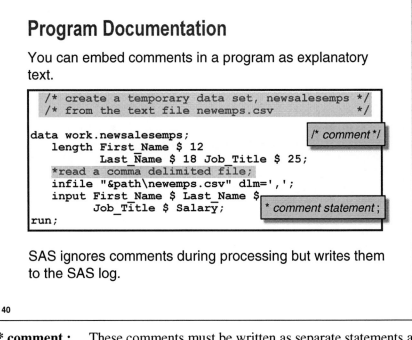

```
/* create a temporary data set, newsalesemps */
/* from the text file newemps.csv            */

data work.newsalesemps;
   length First_Name $ 12
          Last_Name $ 18 Job_Title $ 25;
   *read a comma delimited file;
   infile "&path\newemps.csv" dlm=',';
   input First_Name $ Last_Name $
         Job_Title $ Salary;
run;
```

/* comment */

* comment statement;

SAS ignores comments during processing but writes them to the SAS log.

40

* comment ;   These comments must be written as separate statements and cannot contain internal semicolons.

/* comment */   These comments can be any length and can contain semicolons. They cannot be nested.

SAS Comments

This program contains four comments.

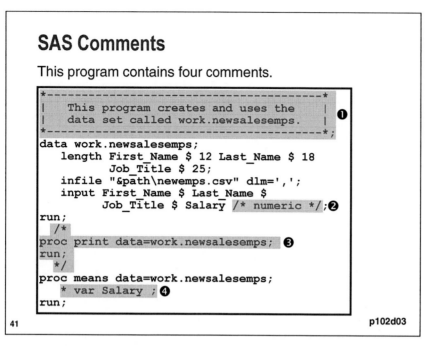

```
*----------------------------------------*
|    This program creates and uses the   |
|    data set called work.newsalesemps.  |      ❶
*----------------------------------------*;
data work.newsalesemps;
   length First_Name $ 12 Last_Name $ 18
          Job_Title $ 25;
   infile "&path\newemps.csv" dlm=',';
   input First_Name $ Last_Name $
         Job_Title $ Salary /* numeric */;  ❷
run;
   /*
proc print data=work.newsalesemps;  ❸
run;
   */
proc means data=work.newsalesemps;
   * var Salary ;  ❹
run;
```

41   p102d03

- To comment out a block of code using the /* */ technique in the SAS interfaces, you can highlight the code and then press the Ctrl key and the / (forward slash) key simultaneously.

- To uncomment a block of code in SAS Studio, highlight the block and then press the Ctrl key and the / key simultaneously.

- To uncomment a block of code in SAS Enterprise Guide and the SAS windowing environment, highlight the block and then press the Ctrl key, the Shift key, and the / key simultaneously.

2.04 Short Answer Poll

Open and examine **p102a01**. Based on the comments, which steps do you think are executed and what output is generated?

Submit the program. Which steps were executed?

42

Business Scenario

Orion Star programmers must be able to identify and correct syntax errors in a SAS program.

45

Syntax Errors

A *syntax error* is an error in the spelling or grammar of a SAS statement. SAS finds syntax errors as it compiles each SAS statement, before execution begins.

Examples of syntax errors:
- misspelled keywords
- unmatched quotation marks
- missing semicolons
- invalid options

46

2.05 Short Answer Poll

This program includes three syntax errors. One is an invalid option. What are the other two syntax errors?

```
daat work.newsalesemps;
   length First_Name $ 12
          Last_Name $ 18 Job_Title $ 25;
   infile "&path\newemps.csv" dlm=',';
   input First_Name $ Last_Name $
         Job_Title $ Salary;
run;

proc print data=work.newsalesemps
run;

                                        invalid option
proc means data=work.newsalesemps average min;
   var Salary;
run;
```

47   p102d04

Syntax Errors

Syntax errors in a SAS program can possibly be detected based on the color of the syntax on the Editor tab or in the window.

49

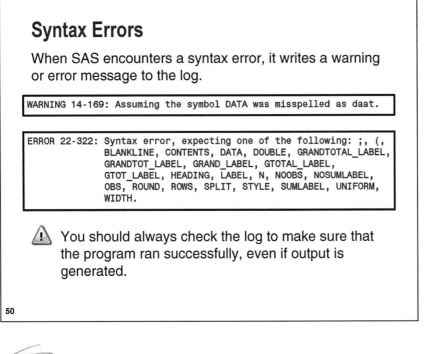

Syntax Errors

When SAS encounters a syntax error, it writes a warning or error message to the log.

```
WARNING 14-169: Assuming the symbol DATA was misspelled as daat.
```

```
ERROR 22-322: Syntax error, expecting one of the following: ;, (,
              BLANKLINE, CONTENTS, DATA, DOUBLE, GRANDTOTAL_LABEL,
              GRANDTOT_LABEL, GRAND_LABEL, GTOTAL_LABEL,
              GTOT_LABEL, HEADING, LABEL, N, NOOBS, NOSUMLABEL,
              OBS, ROUND, ROWS, SPLIT, STYLE, SUMLABEL, UNIFORM,
              WIDTH.
```

⚠ You should always check the log to make sure that the program ran successfully, even if output is generated.

50

Diagnosing and Correcting Syntax Errors

p102d04

1. Open and submit **p102d04**.

2. Go to the log and view the notes, warnings, and errors.

Partial SAS Log

```
15    daat work.newsalesemps;
      ----
      14
WARNING 14-169: Assuming the symbol DATA was misspelled as daat.

16       length First_Name $ 12
17             Last_Name $ 18 Job_Title $ 25;
18       infile "&path\newemps.csv" dlm=',';
19       input First_Name $ Last_Name $
20             Job_Title $ Salary;
21    run;

NOTE: The infile "s:\workshop\newemps.csv" is:
      Filename=s:\workshop\newemps.csv,

NOTE: 71 records were read from the infile "s:\workshop\newemps.csv".
NOTE: The data set WORK.NEWSALESEMPS has 71 observations and 4 variables.

22
23    proc print data=work.newsalesemps
24    run;
      ---
      22
      202
ERROR 22-322: Syntax error, expecting one of the following: ;, (, BLANKLINE, CONTENTS, DATA,
              DOUBLE, GRANDTOTAL_LABEL, GRANDTOT_LABEL, GRAND_LABEL, GTOTAL_LABEL,
GTOT_LABEL,
              HEADING, LABEL, N, NOOBS, NOSUMLABEL, OBS, ROUND, ROWS, SPLIT, STYLE, SUMLABEL,
              UNIFORM, WIDTH.
ERROR 202-322: The option or parameter is not recognized and will be ignored.
25

NOTE: The SAS System stopped processing this step because of errors.

26    proc means data=work.newsalesemps average min;
                                         -------
                                         22
                                         202
ERROR 22-322: Syntax error, expecting one of the following: ;, (, ALPHA, CHARTYPE, CLASSDATA,
              CLM, COMPLETETYPES, CSS, CV, DATA, DESCEND, DESCENDING, DESCENDTYPES, EXCLNPWGT,
              EXCLNPWGTS, EXCLUSIVE, FW, IDMIN, KURTOSIS, LCLM, MAX, MAXDEC, MEAN, MEDIAN, MIN,
              MISSING, MODE, N, NDEC, NMISS, NOLABELS, NONOBS, NOPRINT, NOTHREADS, NOTRAP, NWAY,
              ORDER, P1, P10, P20, P25, P30, P40, P5, P50, P60, P70, P75, P80, P90, P95, P99,
              PCTLDEF, PRINT, PRINTALL, PRINTALLTYPES, PRINTIDS, PRINTIDVARS, PROBT, Q1, Q3,
              QMARKERS, QMETHOD, QNTLDEF, QRANGE, RANGE, SKEWNESS, STACKODS, STACKODSOUTPUT,
              STDDEV, STDERR, SUM, SUMSIZE, SUMWGT, T, THREADS, UCLM, USS, VAR, VARDEF.
ERROR 202-322: The option or parameter is not recognized and will be ignored.
27       var Salary;
28    run;

NOTE: The SAS System stopped processing this step because of errors.
NOTE: The SAS System stopped processing this step because of errors.
```

The log indicates that SAS did the following:

- assumed that the keyword DATA was misspelled, issued a warning, and executed the DATA step

- interpreted the word RUN as an option in the PROC PRINT statement (because of a missing semicolon), so the PROC PRINT step did not execute
- did not recognize the word AVERAGE as a valid option in the PROC MEANS statement, so the PROC MEANS step did not execute

3. Return to the program and edit the program.

   a. Correct the spelling of DATA.

   b. Put a semicolon at the end of the PROC PRINT statement.

   c. Change the word AVERAGE to MEAN in the PROC MEANS statement.

```
data work.newsalesemps;
   length First_Name $ 12
          Last_Name $ 18 Job_Title $ 25;
   infile "&path\newemps.csv" dlm=',';
   input First_Name $ Last_Name $
         Job_Title $ Salary;
run;

proc print data=work.newsalesemps;
run;

proc means data=work.newsalesemps mean min;
   var Salary;
run;
```

4. Submit the program. Verify that it executes without warnings or errors and produces results.

5. Save the corrected program.

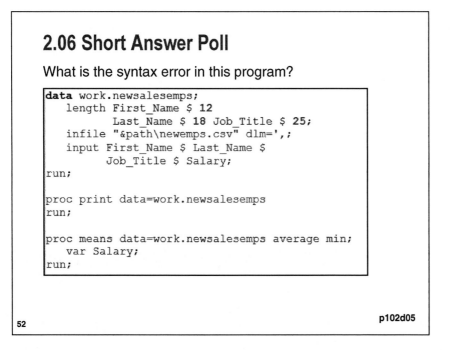

2.06 Short Answer Poll

What is the syntax error in this program?

```
data work.newsalesemps;
   length First_Name $ 12
          Last_Name $ 18 Job_Title $ 25;
   infile "&path\newemps.csv" dlm=',';
   input First_Name $ Last_Name $
         Job_Title $ Salary;
run;

proc print data=work.newsalesemps
run;

proc means data=work.newsalesemps average min;
   var Salary;
run;
```

52   p102d05

Exercises

SAS Studio

10. Correcting Quotation Marks with SAS Studio

   a. In SAS Studio, in the navigation pane, navigate in the file structure of the Folders section to find the **p102e10** program.

   b. Double-click **p102e10** to open the program. Notice that the closing quotation mark for the DLM= option in the INFILE statement is missing.

   c. On the CODE tab, click 🏃 (**Run**) or press F3 to submit the program.

   d. On the LOG tab, notice that there are no messages following each step in the log. The absence of messages often indicates unbalanced quotation marks.

   Partial SAS Log

```
71        data work.newsalesemps;
72           length First_Name $ 12
73                 Last_Name $ 18 Job_Title $ 25;
74           infile "&path\\newemps.csv" dlm=',;
75           input First_Name $ Last_Name $
76                 Job_Title $ Salary;
77        run;
78
79        proc print data=work.newsalesemps;
80        run;
81
82        proc means data=work.newsalesemps;
83           var Salary;
84        run;
```

   e. Return to the program. Add a closing quotation mark to the DLM= option in the INFILE statement to correct the program.

```
       infile "&path\newemps.csv" dlm=',';
```

   f. On the CODE tab, click 🏃 (**Run**) or press F3 to submit the program.

   g. On the RESULTS tab, view the PROC PRINT and PROC MEANS output.

   h. On the LOG tab, verify that no errors or warnings appear.

   i. On the CODE tab, click 💾 (**Save Program**) to save the program.

11. Diagnosing Errors with SAS Studio

   a. In the Folders section of the navigation pane, click 📄▾ (**New**) ⇨ **SAS Program (F4)** or press F4 to start a new program.

   b. On the CODE tab, enter the following program with the formatting as shown:

```
proc print data=  sashelp.class; run; proc  means
data=sashelp.class; run;
```

c. On the CODE toolbar, click ⊞ (**Format Code**) to make your program easier to read. This button automatically formats your code by adding line breaks and indenting at appropriate nesting levels.

d. Add two mistakes to the program. Remove the letter **o** from the first PROC step and remove the semicolon after the last reference to **sashelp.class**.

```
prc print data=sashelp.class;
run;
proc means data=sashelp.class
run;
```

e. On the CODE tab, click 🏃 (**Run**) or press F3 to submit the program. The Program tab shows an icon in front of the program name if the program contains errors, warnings, or both.

Errors or Errors and Warnings:	⊗ *Program 3 ✕
Warnings with no Errors:	⚠ *Program 3 ✕

f. On the RESULTS tab, notice that there is PROC PRINT output but no PROC MEANS output.

g. On the LOG tab, scroll through the log. Notes appear as blue text, warnings as green text, and errors as red text.

h. Expand the Errors, Warnings, and Notes sections to view the messages at the beginning of the Log window.

> ◢ Errors, Warnings, Notes
>   ◢ ⊗ Errors (2)
>   ERROR 22-322: Syntax error, expecting one of the following: ;, (, ALPHA, CHARTYPE, CLASSDATA, CLM,
>   ERROR 202-322: The option or parameter is not recognized and will be ignored.
>   ◢ ⚠ Warnings (1)
>   WARNING 14-169: Assuming the symbol PROC was misspelled as prc.

i. Click on a message in an Errors, Warnings, or Notes section. The message is highlighted in the log farther down.

▲ Errors, Warnings, Notes

   ▲ ⊗ Errors (2)

      ERROR 22-322: Syntax error, expecting one of the following: ;, (, ALPHA, CHARTYPE, CLASSDATA, CLM,

      ERROR 202-322: The option or parameter is not recognized and will be ignored.

   ▲ ⚠ Warnings (1)

      WARNING 14-169: Assuming the symbol PROC was misspelled as prc.

```
1          OPTIONS NONOTES NOSTIMER NOSOURCE NOSYNTAXCHECK;
57
58         prc print data=sashelp.class;

           ____
           14
WARNING 14-169: Assuming the symbol PROC was misspelled as prc.
59         run;

NOTE: There were 19 observations read from the data set SASHELP.CLASS.
```

j. Return to the CODE tab and fix the two mistakes. Submit the program and verify that there are no errors or warnings in the log.

k. In the log, notice the OPTIONS statement at the beginning and ending of the program. SAS Studio automatically includes these statements before and after your program. In addition, SAS Studio includes supplemental code before and after your program. By default, this code is not visible in the log.

l. To view the complete program executed by SAS, including the generated code, click ▤ (**More Application Options**) ⇨ **Preferences** ⇨ **General**.

m. Select the **Show generated code in the SAS log** check box and click **Save**.

Preferences   ✕

General

    ☑ Show generated code in the SAS log

Editor

Results   ☐ Include a "Show Details" button in error messages

Tasks   ☐ Start new programs in interactive mode

     Time-out interval: 1 ⬍ hours

     SAS variable name policy: ANY   ▾

     Default text encoding: UTF-8   ▾

                             Reset to Defaults

                       Save   Cancel

n. Submit the program and view the supplemental code in the log.

o. Return to the Preferences window and clear the **Show generated code in the SAS log** check box. Click **Save**.

SAS Enterprise Guide

12. Correcting Quotation Marks with SAS Enterprise Guide

a. In SAS Enterprise Guide, select **File** ⇨ **Open** ⇨ **Program** or click ⬚ (**Open**) ⇨ **Program**.

b. In the Open Program window, navigate in the file structure to find **p102e12** and click **Open**. Notice that the closing quotation mark for the DLM= option in the INFILE statement is missing.

c. On the Program tab, click **Run** or press F3 to submit the program.

d. On the Log tab, notice that there are no messages following each step in the log. The absence of messages often indicates unbalanced quotation marks.

Partial SAS Log

```
71      data work.newsalesemps;
72         length First_Name $ 12
73                Last_Name $ 18 Job_Title $ 25;
74         infile "&path\\newemps.csv" dlm=',;
75         input First_Name $ Last_Name $
76               Job_Title $ Salary;
77      run;
78
79      proc print data=work.newsalesemps;
80      run;
81
82      proc means data=work.newsalesemps;
83         var Salary;
84      run;
```

e. Return to the program. Add a closing quotation mark to the DLM= option in the INFILE statement to correct the program.

```
infile "&path\newemps.csv" dlm=',';
```

f. On the Program tab, click **Run** or press F3 to submit the program. Click **Yes** to replace the results.

g. On the Results tab, view the PROC PRINT and PROC MEANS output.

h. On the Log tab, verify that no errors or warnings appear.

i. On the Program tab, click **Save** to save the program.

13. Diagnosing Errors with SAS Enterprise Guide

a. Select **File** ⇨ **New** ⇨ **Program** or click ⬚ (**New**) ⇨ **Program** to start a new program.

b. On the Program tab, enter the following program with the formatting as shown below.

```
proc print data=sashelp.class;
run; proc means data=sashelp.class;    run;
```

c. Click **Edit** ⇨ **Format Code** so that your program is easier to read. This selection automatically formats your code by adding line breaks and indenting at appropriate nesting levels.

d. Add two mistakes to the program. Remove the letter **o** from the first PROC step and remove the semicolon after the last reference to **sashelp.class**.

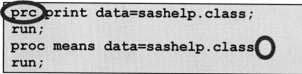

```
prc print data=sashelp.class;
run;
proc means data=sashelp.class
run;
```

e. On the Program tab, click the **Run** button or press F3 to submit the program. The Program tab shows a special icon in front of the program name if the program contains errors, warnings, or both.

Errors or Errors and Warnings:	[icon] Program*
Warnings with no Errors:	[icon] Program*

f. On the Results tab, notice that there is PROC PRINT output but no PROC MEANS output.

g. On the Log tab, scroll through the log. Notes appear as green text, warnings as light blue text, and errors as red text. Use the Up and Down arrows on the Log tab to find the previous or next warning or error.

```
Program*  Log  Results - SAS Report  Results - Listing
Export ▾  Send To ▾  Create ▾  ↑  ↓  | Log Summary  Project Log  Properties

              14
    WARNING 14-169: Assuming the symbol PROC was misspelled as prc.
    25        run;
```

h. Go to the Log Summary window, which is located below the Log tab. The log summary lists all the errors, warnings, and notes that were generated when the program ran, as well as related line numbers and a sample of the affected code. By default, all types of messages are displayed. You can filter the messages by selecting or deselecting the tab for the type of message.

Log Summary

⊗ Errors (2)   ⚠ Warnings (1)   ⓘ Notes (6)

	Description	Line	Affected Code
ⓘ	NOTE: Writing TAGSETS.SASREPORT13(EGSR) Body file: EGSR	24	options(rolap="on")
⚠	WARNING 14-169: Assuming the symbol PROC was misspelled as prc.	32	prc print data=sashelp.class;
ⓘ	NOTE: There were 19 observations read from the data set SASHELP.CLASS.	35	run;
ⓘ	NOTE: The PROCEDURE PRINT printed page 1.	36	run;
ⓘ	NOTE: PROCEDURE PRINT used (Total process time):	37	run;
⊗	ERROR 22-322: Syntax error, expecting one of the following: :, (, ALPHA, CHARTYPE, CL...	48	run;
⊗	ERROR 202-322: The option or parameter is not recognized and will be ignored.	54	run;
ⓘ	NOTE: The SAS System stopped processing this step because of errors.	66	;*';*";*/;quit;
ⓘ	NOTE: PROCEDURE MEANS used (Total process time):	67	;*';*";*/;quit;

i. In the Log Summary window, click a message description and view the message on the Log tab.

j. Click the **Program** tab and fix the two mistakes. Submit the program and click **Yes** to replace the results from the previous run. Verify that there are no errors or warnings in the log.

k. In the log, notice that SAS Enterprise Guide includes supplemental code before and after your program. This generated wrapper code is included in the log by default.

l. To hide the generated wrapper code in the log, select **Tools** ⇨ **Options** ⇨ **Results General**. Clear the **Show generated wrapper code in SAS log** check box and click **OK**.

m. Submit the program and view the log. Notice that the majority of the generated wrapper code is hidden.

SAS Windowing Environment

14. Correcting Quotation Marks in the SAS Windowing Environment

   a. In the SAS windowing environment, click [≝] (**Open**) when the Editor window is the active window or select **File ⇨ Open Program**.

   b. In the Open window, navigate in the file structure to find **p102e14** and click **Open**. Notice that the closing quotation mark for the DLM= option in the INFILE statement is missing.

   c. Click [🏃] (**Submit**) or press F3 to submit the program.

   d. In the Log window, notice that there are no messages following each step in the log. The absence of messages often indicates unbalanced quotation marks.

   Partial SAS Log

   ```
   71      data work.newsalesemps;
   72         length First_Name $ 12
   73                Last_Name $ 18 Job_Title $ 25;
   74         infile "&path\\newemps.csv" dlm=',;
   75         input First_Name $ Last_Name $
   76                Job_Title $ Salary;
   77      run;
   78
   79      proc print data=work.newsalesemps;
   80      run;
   81
   82      proc means data=work.newsalesemps;
   83         var Salary;
   84      run;
   ```

   e. In the Log window, click [🗋] (**New**) or select **Edit ⇨ Clear All** to clear the Log window.

   f. Return to the program. Notice the "DATA STEP running" message in the banner of the Editor window. This message appears because the RUN statement was viewed as part of the character literal and not as a step boundary.

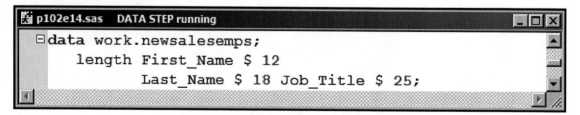

   g. To stop the DATA step from running, click [⊘] (**Break**) or press the Ctrl and Break keys.

   h. Select the **1. Cancel Submitted Statements** radio button in the Tasking Manager window. Click **OK**.

i. Select the **Y to Cancel submitted statements.** radio button. Click **OK**.

BREAK -> Submit

Press

     Y to cancel submitted statements,

     N to continue.

         OK

j. Add a closing quotation mark to the DLM= option in the INFILE statement to correct the program.

```
infile "&path\newemps.csv" dlm=',';
```

k. Click ![Submit] (**Submit**) or press F3 to submit the program.

l. In the Results Viewer window, view the PROC PRINT and PROC MEANS output.

m. In the Log window, verify that no errors or warnings appear.

n. Click ![New] (**New**) or select **Edit** ⇨ **Clear All** to clear the Log window.

o. In the Editor window, click ![Save] (**Save**) to save the program.

15. **Diagnosing Errors in the SAS Windowing Environment**

a. Click ![Open] (**Open**) when the Editor window is the active window or select **File** ⇨ **Open Program** to open a program.

b. In the Open window, navigate in the file structure to find **MyProgram**. Click **Open**.

c. Add two mistakes to the program. Remove the letter **o** from the first PROC step and remove the semicolon after the last reference to **sashelp.class**.

```
ods html close; ods html;
prc print data=sashelp.class;
run;
proc means data=sashelp.class
run;
```

d. Click (**Submit**) or press F3 to submit the program.

e. In the Results Viewer and Output windows, notice that there is PROC PRINT output, but no PROC MEANS output.

f. In the Log window, scroll through the log. Notes appear as blue text, warnings as green text, and errors as red text.

```
Log - (Untitled)                                                        _ □ ×
30    ods html close; ods html;
NOTE: Writing HTML Body file: sashtml16.htm
31    prc print data=sashelp.class;
      ---
      14
WARNING 14-169: Assuming the symbol PROC was misspelled as prc.
32    run;

NOTE: There were 19 observations read from the data set SASHELP.CLASS.
NOTE: PROCEDURE PRINT used (Total process time):
      real time            0.04 seconds
      cpu time             0.03 seconds


33    proc means data=sashelp.class
34    run;
      ---
      22
      202
ERROR 22-322: Syntax error, expecting one of the following: ;, (, ALPHA, CHARTYPE, CLASSDATA, CLM,
              COMPLETETYPES, CSS, CV, DATA, DESCEND, DESCENDING, DESCENDTYPES, EXCLNPWGT, EXCLNPWGTS,
              EXCLUSIVE, FW, IDMIN, KURTOSIS, LCLM, MAX, MAXDEC, MEAN, MEDIAN, MIN, MISSING, MODE, N,
              NDEC, NMISS, NOLABELS, NONOBS, NOPRINT, NOTHREADS, NOTRAP, NWAY, ORDER, P1, P10, P20,
              P25, P30, P40, P5, P50, P60, P70, P75, P80, P90, P95, P99, PCTLDEF, PRINT, PRINTALL,
              PRINTALLTYPES, PRINTIDS, PRINTIDVARS, PROBT, Q1, Q3, QMARKERS, QMETHOD, QNTLDEF,
              QRANGE, RANGE, SKEWNESS, STACKODS, STACKODSOUTPUT, STDDEV, STDERR, SUM, SUMSIZE,
              SUMWGT, T, THREADS, UCLM, USS, VAR, VARDEF.

ERROR 202-322: The option or parameter is not recognized and will be ignored.▮
```

g. Return to the Editor window. Notice the text on the title bar that states "PROC MEANS running."

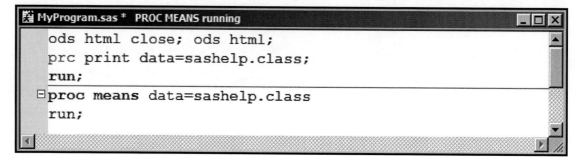

h. To stop the step from running, click (**Break**) or press the Ctrl and Break keys.

i. Select the **1. Cancel Submitted Statements** radio button in the Tasking Manager window. Click **OK**.

j. Select the **Y to cancel submitted statements.** radio button. Click **OK**.

k. The program is no longer running, so fix the two mistakes. Clear the log, submit the program, and verify that there are no errors or warnings in the log.

2.4 Solutions

Solutions to Student Activities (Polls/Quizzes)

2.01 Short Answer Poll – Correct Answer

How many steps are in program **p102d01**? **three**

```
data work.newsalesemps;
   length First_Name $ 12
          Last_Name $ 18 Job_Title $ 25;
   infile "&path\newemps.csv" dlm=',';
   input First_Name $ Last_Name $
         Job_Title $ Salary;
run;

proc print data=work.newsalesemps;
run;

proc means data=work.newsalesemps;
   var Salary;
run;
```

DATA Step

PROC Step

PROC Step

8   p102d01

2.03 Short Answer Poll – Correct Answer

How many statements make up this DATA step?

```
data work.newsalesemps;
   length First_Name $ 12
          Last_Name $ 18 Job_Title $ 25;
   infile "&path\newemps.csv" dlm=',';
   input First_Name $ Last_Name $
         Job_Title $ Salary;
run;
```

This DATA step has five statements.

36

2.04 Short Answer Poll – Correct Answer

Open and examine **p102a01**. Based on the comments, which steps do you think are executed and what output is generated?

Submit the program. Which steps were executed?

- **The DATA step executes and creates an output data set.**
- **The PROC PRINT step executes and produces a report.**
- **The PROC MEANS step is "commented out," and therefore, does not execute.**

43

2.05 Short Answer Poll – Correct Answer

This program includes three syntax errors. One is an invalid option. What are the other two syntax errors?

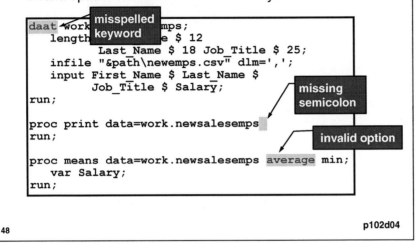

```
daat work        mps;         misspelled keyword
    length        e $ 12
            Last_Name $ 18 Job_Title $ 25;
    infile "&path\newemps.csv" dlm=',';
    input First_Name $ Last_Name $
            Job_Title $ Salary;
run;

proc print data=work.newsalesemps        missing semicolon
run;
                                          invalid option
proc means data=work.newsalesemps average min;
    var Salary;
run;
```

48   p102d04

2.06 Short Answer Poll – Correct Answer

What is the syntax error in this program?

```
data work.newsalesemps;
    length First_Name $ 12
            Last_Name $ 18 Job_Title $ 25;
    infile "&path\newemps.csv" dlm=',;
    input First_Name $ Last_Name $
            Job_Title $ Salary;
run;

proc print data=work.newsalesemps
run;

proc means data=work.newsalesemps average min;
    var Salary;
run;
```

The program contains unbalanced quotation marks in the DLM= option in the INFILE statement.

53   p102d05

Chapter 3   Accessing Data

3.1 Examining SAS Data Sets

Objectives

- Define the components of a SAS data set.
- Use the CONTENTS procedure to browse the descriptor portion of a SAS data set.
- Use the PRINT procedure to browse the data portion of a SAS data set.
- Define a SAS variable.
- Define a missing value.
- Define a SAS date value.

3

Business Scenario

Many SAS data sets related to the Orion Star project already exist. The programmers need to know how to display the structure and contents of the data sets.

SAS Data Set   Report

4

What Is a SAS Data Set?

A *SAS data set* is a specially structured data file that SAS creates and that only SAS can read. A SAS data set is a table that contains observations and variables.

5

SAS Data Set Terminology

SAS Terminology	Database Terminology
SAS Data Set ⟷	Table
Observation ⟷	Row
Variable ⟷	Column

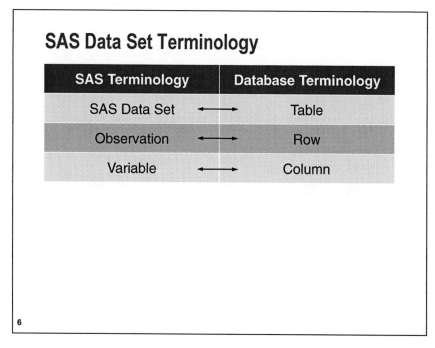

6

SAS Data Set Terminology

A SAS data set contains a descriptor portion
and a data portion.

7

Descriptor Portion

The *descriptor portion* contains the following metadata:

- general properties (such as data set name and
  number of observations)
- variable properties (such as name, type, and length)

Partial **work.newsalesemps**

Data Set Name	WORK.NEWSALESEMPS			
Engine	V9			
Created	Mon, Feb 27, 2012 01:28 PM			
Observations	71			
Variables	4			
...				

general properties

First_Name	Last_Name	Job_Title	Salary
$ 12	$ 18	$ 25	N 8

variable properties

8

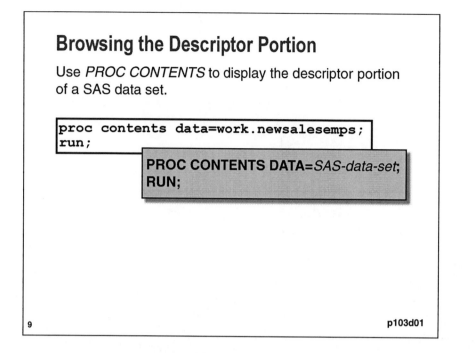

Browsing the Descriptor Portion

Use *PROC CONTENTS* to display the descriptor portion of a SAS data set.

```
proc contents data=work.newsalesemps;
run;
```

PROC CONTENTS DATA=SAS-data-set;
RUN;

9   p103d01

Viewing the Output

Partial PROC CONTENTS Output

```
                    The CONTENTS Procedure

Data Set Name    WORK.NEWSALESEMPS          Observations          71
Member Type      DATA                        Variables             4
Engine           V9                          Indexes               0
Created          Mon, Feb 27, 2012 01:28:51 PM   Observation Length    64
Last Modified    Mon, Feb 27, 2012 01:28:51 PM   Deleted Observations  0
Protection                                   Compressed           NO
Data Set Type                                Sorted               NO


              Engine/Host Dependent Information
                          ...


          Alphabetic List of Variables and Attributes

              #    Variable    Type    Len

              1    First_Name  Char     12
              3    Job_Title   Char     25
              2    Last_Name   Char     18
              4    Salary      Num       8
```

10

The default PROC CONTENTS report has three parts:

- general data set properties
- engine/host information
- variable properties

3.01 Short Answer Poll

Open program **p103a01**. Add a PROC CONTENTS step after the DATA step to view **work.donations**. Submit the program and review the results. How many observations are in the data set **work.donations**?

11

Data Portion

The *data portion* of a SAS data set contains the data values, which are either character or numeric.

Partial **work.newsalesemps**

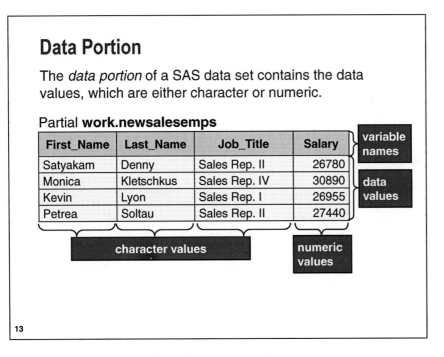

13

Variable names are part of the descriptor portion, not the data portion.

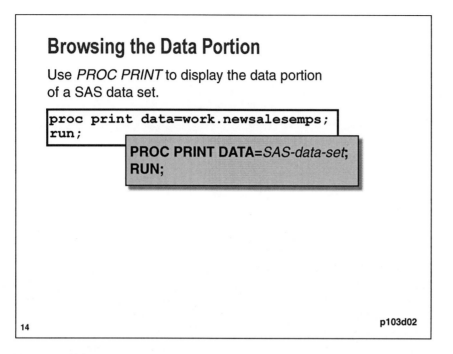

Browsing the Data Portion

Use *PROC PRINT* to display the data portion
of a SAS data set.

```
proc print data=work.newsalesemps;
run;
```

PROC PRINT DATA=*SAS-data-set*;
RUN;

14   p103d02

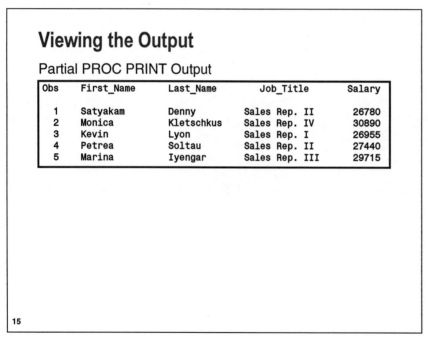

Viewing the Output

Partial PROC PRINT Output

Obs	First_Name	Last_Name	Job_Title	Salary
1	Satyakam	Denny	Sales Rep. II	26780
2	Monica	Kletschkus	Sales Rep. IV	30890
3	Kevin	Lyon	Sales Rep. I	26955
4	Petrea	Soltau	Sales Rep. II	27440
5	Marina	Iyengar	Sales Rep. III	29715

15

SAS Variable Names

SAS variable names
- can be 1 to 32 characters long.
- must start with a letter or underscore. Subsequent characters can be letters, underscores, or numerals.
- can be uppercase, lowercase, or mixed case.
- are not case sensitive.

Salary	_score2_

cust_ID	month1	FirstName

16

The same naming rules apply to SAS data set names.

3.02 Multiple Answer Poll

Which variable names are invalid?

a. data5mon
b. 5monthsdata
c. data#5
d. five months data
e. five_months_data
f. FiveMonthsData
g. fivemonthsdata

17

A variable name can contain special characters if you place the name in quotation marks and immediately follow it with the letter N (for example, **'Flight#'n**). This is called a *SAS name literal*. In order to use SAS name literals as variable names, the VALIDVARNAME= option must be set to ANY.

```
options validvarname=any;
```

This setting is the default in SAS Enterprise Guide and SAS Studio.

Data Types

A SAS data set supports two types of variables.

Character variables

- can contain any value: letters, numerals, special characters, and blanks
- range from 1 to 32,767 characters in length
- have 1 byte per character.

Numeric variables

- store numeric values using floating point or binary representation
- have 8 bytes of storage by default
- can store 16 or 17 significant digits.

19

Missing Data Values

Missing values are valid values in a SAS data set.

Partial **work.newsalesemps**

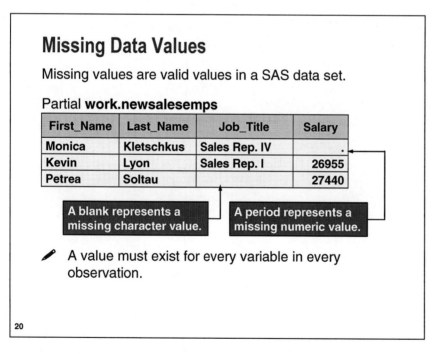

First_Name	Last_Name	Job_Title	Salary
Monica	Kletschkus	Sales Rep. IV	.
Kevin	Lyon	Sales Rep. I	26955
Petrea	Soltau		27440

A blank represents a missing character value.

A period represents a missing numeric value.

✎ A value must exist for every variable in every observation.

20

By default, a period is printed for missing numeric values. This default can be altered with the MISSING= system option.

SAS Date Values

SAS stores calendar dates as numeric values.

A *SAS date value* is stored as the number of days between January 1, 1960, and a specific date.

21

SAS can perform calculations on dates starting from 1582 A.D. SAS can read either two- or four-digit year values. If SAS encounters a two-digit year, the YEARCUTOFF= system option is used to specify to which 100-year span the two-digit year should be attributed. For example, by setting the YEARCUTOFF= option to 1950, the 100-year span from 1950 to 2049 is used for two-digit year values.

3.03 Short Answer Poll

Submit program **p103a02**. View the output to retrieve the current date as a SAS date value (that is, a numeric value referencing January 1, 1960). What is the numeric value for today's date?

22

Exercises

If you restarted your SAS session since the last exercise, open and submit the **libname** program found in the data folder so that you can set the value of the macro variable, **path**.

Level 1

1. **Examining the Data Portion of a SAS Data Set**

   a. Retrieve the starter program **p103e01**.

   b. After the PROC CONTENTS step, add a PROC PRINT step to display all observations, all variables, and the Obs column for the data set named **work.donations**.

   c. Submit the program to create the PROC PRINT report below. The results contain 124 observations.

   Partial PROC PRINT Output

Obs	Employee_ ID	Qtr1	Qtr2	Qtr3	Qtr4	Total
1	120265	.	.	.	25	25
2	120267	15	15	15	15	60
3	120269	20	20	20	20	80
...						
123	121145	35	35	35	35	140
124	121147	10	10	10	10	40

Level 2

2. **Examining the Descriptor and Data Portions of a SAS Data Set**

   a. Retrieve the starter program **p103e02**.

   b. After the DATA step, add a PROC CONTENTS step to display the descriptor portion of **work.newpacks**.

   c. Submit the program and answer the following questions:

   How many observations are in the data set? _____

   How many variables are in the data set? _____

   What is the length (byte size) of the variable **Product_Name**? _____

   d. After the PROC CONTENTS step, add a PROC PRINT to display the data portion of **work.newpacks**.

Submit the program to create the following PROC PRINT report:

```
                        Supplier_
  Obs    Supplier_Name    Country    Product_Name

    1    Top Sports          DK       Black/Black
    2    Top Sports          DK       X-Large Bottlegreen/Black
    3    Top Sports          DK       Comanche Women's 6000 Q Backpack. Bark
  ...
   12    Luna sastreria S.A. ES       Hammock Sports Bag
   13    Miller Trading Inc  US       Sioux Men's Backpack 26 Litre.
```

Challenge

3. **Working with Times and Datetimes**

   a. Retrieve and submit the starter program **p103e03**.

   b. Notice the values of **CurrentTime** and **CurrentDateTime** in the PROC PRINT output.

   c. Use the SAS Help facility or product documentation to investigate how times and datetimes are stored in SAS.

   d. Complete the following sentences:

      A SAS time value represents the number of _____.

      A SAS datetime value represents the number of _____.

   ✎ The remaining exercises in this chapter are self-guided, so no solutions are provided.

3.2 Accessing SAS Libraries

Objectives

- Explain the concept of a SAS library.
- State the difference between a temporary library and a permanent library.
- Use a LIBNAME statement to assign a library reference name to a SAS library.
- Investigate a SAS library programmatically and interactively.

27

Business Scenario

Orion Star programmers need to access existing
SAS data sets, so they need to understand how the
data sets are stored in SAS.

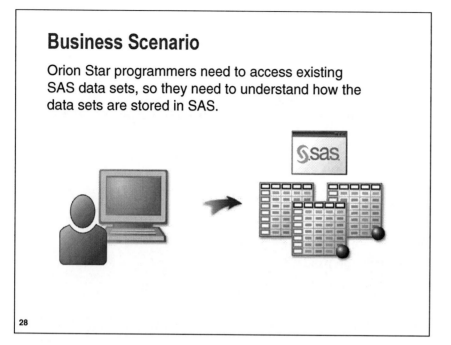

28

SAS Libraries

SAS data sets are stored in *SAS libraries*. A SAS library
is a collection of SAS files that are referenced and stored
as a unit.

A file can be stored in a temporary or permanent library.

29

How SAS Libraries Are Defined

When a SAS session starts, SAS creates one temporary and at least one permanent SAS library. These libraries are open and ready to be used.

You refer to a SAS library by a logical name called a library reference name, or *libref*.

30

Temporary Library

Work is a temporary library where you can store and access SAS data sets for the duration of the SAS session. It is the default library.

⚠ SAS deletes the **Work** library and its contents when the session terminates.

31

Permanent Libraries

Sashelp is a permanent library that contains sample
SAS data sets you can access during your SAS session.

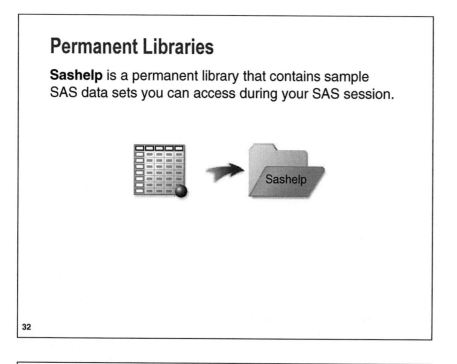

32

Accessing SAS Data Sets

All SAS data sets have a two-level name that consists of
the libref and the data set name, separated by a period.

When a data set is in the temporary **Work** library, you can
use a one-level name (for example, **newsalesemps**).

33

Business Scenario

Orion Star programmers need to access and view SAS data sets that are stored in a permanent user-defined library.

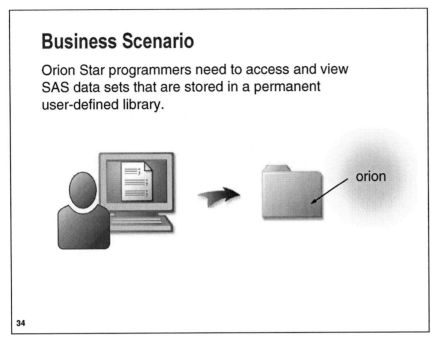

orion

34

User-Defined Libraries

A user-defined library

- is created by the user.
- is permanent. Data sets are stored until the user deletes them.
- is not automatically available in a SAS session.
- is implemented within the operating environment's file system.

35

User-Defined Libraries

Operating Environment	A SAS library is...	Example
Microsoft Windows	a folder	s:\workshop
UNIX	a directory	~/workshop
z/OS (OS/390)	a sequential file	*userid*.workshop.sasdata

The user must submit a SAS LIBNAME statement to associate a libref with the physical location of the library.

36

LIBNAME Statement

The SAS LIBNAME statement is a *global* SAS statement.

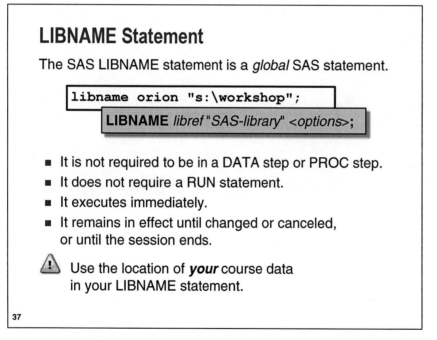

```
libname orion "s:\workshop";
```

LIBNAME *libref* "*SAS-library*" *<options>*;

- It is not required to be in a DATA step or PROC step.
- It does not require a RUN statement.
- It executes immediately.
- It remains in effect until changed or canceled, or until the session ends.

⚠ Use the location of *your* course data in your LIBNAME statement.

37

- In the Microsoft Windows environment, an existing folder is used as a SAS library. The LIBNAME statement cannot create a new folder.
- In the UNIX environment, an existing directory is used as a SAS library. The LIBNAME statement cannot create a new directory.
- In the z/OS environment, a sequential file is used as a SAS library. z/OS (OS/390) users can use a SAS LIBNAME statement, a DD statement, or a TSO ALLOCATE command. These statements and commands can create a new library.

LIBNAME Statement

Partial SAS Log

```
47   libname orion "s:\workshop";
NOTE: Libref ORION was successfully assigned as follows:
      Engine:        V9
      Physical Name: s:\workshop
```

SAS files in **s:\workshop** are referenced using the **orion** libref.

orion.*data-set-name*

38

Changing or Canceling a Libref

A libref remains in effect until you change or cancel it, or until you end your SAS session.

To change a libref, submit a LIBNAME statement with the same libref but a different path.

```
libname orion "c:\myfiles";
```

To cancel a libref, submit a LIBNAME statement with the CLEAR option.

```
libname orion clear;
```

39

3.04 Multiple Choice Poll

Which of the following correctly assigns the libref **myfiles** to a SAS library in the **c:\mysasfiles** folder?

a. libname orion myfiles "c:\mysasfiles";

b. libname myfiles "c:\mysasfiles";

c. libref orion myfiles "c:\mysasfiles";

d. libref myfiles "c:\mysasfiles";

40

Browsing a Library

You can browse a library

- programmatically using the CONTENTS procedure
- interactively in SAS Studio, SAS Enterprise Guide, or the SAS windowing environment.

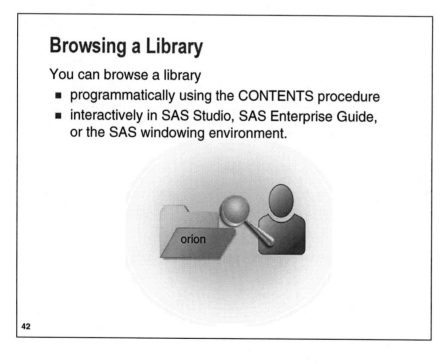

42

Browsing a Library Programmatically

Use PROC CONTENTS with the _ALL_ keyword
to generate a list of all SAS files in a library.

```
proc contents data=orion._all_ nods;
run;
```

PROC CONTENTS DATA=*libref*._ALL_ NODS;
RUN;

- _ALL_ requests all the files in the library.
- The NODS option suppresses the individual data set descriptor information.
- NODS can be used only with the keyword _ALL_.

p103d03

43

Viewing the Output

Partial PROC CONTENTS Output

```
                      The CONTENTS Procedure

                            Directory

                  Libref          ORION
                  Engine          V9
                  Physical Name   S:\workshop
                  Filename        S:\workshop


                           Member    File
          #   Name         Type      Size   Last Modified

          1   CHARITIES    DATA      9216   23Aug12:15:58:39
          2   CONSULTANTS  DATA      5120   23Aug12:15:58:39
          3   COUNTRY      DATA     17408   13Oct10:19:04:39
              COUNTRY      INDEX    17408   13Oct10:19:04:39
          4   CUSTOMER     DATA     33792   04Nov11:09:52:27
          5   CUSTOMER_DIM DATA     33792   04Nov11:09:52:27
```

44

A member type of DATA indicates a standard SAS data set. The INDEX member type indicates a file that enables SAS to access observations in the SAS data set quickly and efficiently.

 Browsing a SAS Library Programmatically

libname, p103d03

1. Open the **libname** program and add the LIBNAME statement shown below.

```
%let path=s:/workshop;
libname orion "s:/workshop";
```

The %LET statement creates a macro variable named **path** and assigns it a full path to the course data folder. The LIBNAME statement associates the libref, **orion**, with the same data location.

      The **libname** program is generated by the **cre8data** program. The code uses forward slashes for portability across operating environments. UNIX and Linux require forward slashes. Windows accepts forward slashes and can convert them to backslashes.

2. Submit the program.

3. Check the log to confirm that the **orion** libref was successfully assigned. The physical name reflects the location of your SAS data files and might differ from the name shown below.

```
43          %let path=s:/workshop;
44          libname orion "s:/workshop";
NOTE: Libref ORION was successfully assigned as follows:
      Engine:         V9
      Physical Name: s:\workshop
```

4. Save the **libname** program. This overwrites the previous version.

      When you work with the course data and programs, be sure to run the **libname** program at the start of every SAS session to set the **path** variable and assign the **orion** libref.

5. Use the CONTENTS procedure to explore the **orion** library programmatically. Open and submit the **p103d03** program to generate a list of library members. Partial output is shown below.

```
proc contents data=orion._all_ nods;
run;
```

```
                    The CONTENTS Procedure

                          Directory

                 Libref          ORION
                 Engine          V9
                 Physical Name   s:\workshop
                 Filename        s:\workshop

                          Member    File
      #  Name            Type      Size   Last Modified

      1  CHARITIES       DATA      9216   23Aug12:15:58:39
      2  CONSULTANTS     DATA      5120   23Aug12:15:58:39
      3  COUNTRY         DATA     17408   13Oct10:19:04:39
         COUNTRY         INDEX    17408   13Oct10:19:04:39
      4  CUSTOMER        DATA     33792   04Nov11:09:52:27
```

6. Start a new program. Then enter and submit the following statement to clear the **orion** libref:

```
libname orion clear;
```

7. Check the log to verify that the **orion** libref was deassigned.

```
15          libname orion clear;
NOTE: Libref ORION has been deassigned.
```

Exercises

Using your preferred SAS interface, complete Exercise 4 and one additional exercise.
These exercises are self-guided, so no solutions are provided.

4. **Assigning and Browsing a Library Programmatically**

   a. Open the **libname** program and add the LIBNAME statement shown below.

   ```
   %let path=s:/workshop;
   libname orion "s:/workshop";
   ```

   > The **libname** program is generated by the **cre8data** program. The code uses forward
   > slashes for portability across operating environments. UNIX and Linux require forward
   > slashes. Windows accepts forward slashes and can convert them to backslashes.

   b. Submit the program.

   c. Check the log to confirm that the **orion** libref was successfully assigned. The physical name
      reflects the location of your SAS data files and might differ from the name shown below.

   ```
   43          %let path=s:/workshop;
    44           libname orion "s:/workshop";
   NOTE: Libref ORION was successfully assigned as follows:
          Engine:        V9
          Physical Name: s:\workshop
   ```

   d. Save the **libname** program. This overwrites the previous version.

   e. Use the CONTENTS procedure to explore the **orion** library programmatically. Start a new
      program. Enter the following PROC CONTENTS step and a LIBNAME statement to clear
      the libref:

   ```
   proc contents data=orion._all_ nods;
   run;

   libname orion clear;
   ```

   f. Submit the program. Partial output is shown below.

   ```
                         The CONTENTS Procedure

                              Directory

                       Libref         ORION
                       Engine         V9
                       Physical Name  s:\workshop
                       Filename       s:\workshop

                          Member    File
        #   Name          Type      Size   Last Modified

        1   CHARITIES     DATA       9216  23Aug12:15:58:39
        2   CONSULTANTS   DATA       5120  23Aug12:15:58:39
        3   COUNTRY       DATA      17408  13Oct10:19:04:39
            COUNTRY       INDEX     17408  13Oct10:19:04:39
        4   CUSTOMER      DATA      33792  04Nov11:09:52:27
   ```

g. Check the log to verify that the **orion** libref was deassigned.

```
15          libname orion clear;
NOTE: Libref ORION has been deassigned.
```

✎   When you work with the course data and programs, be sure to run the **libname** program at the start of every SAS session to set the **path** variable and assign the **orion** libref.

5. **Assigning and Browsing a Library Interactively with SAS Studio**

   a. In the Navigation pane, navigate to the **Libraries** section.

   > Folders
   > Tasks
   > Snippets
   > **Libraries**
   >
   > ▷ My Libraries

   b. Click the arrow in front of My Libraries to expand the folder. Observe the libraries that are assigned automatically in your SAS Studio session.

   c. Click 🗄 (**New Library**) to assign a new library.

   d. In the New Library window, enter **orion** in the **Name** field, and enter **s:/workshop** or the path to your data folder in the **Path** field. Selecting the check box causes SAS to re-create the library at the start of each SAS Studio session. Click **OK**.

   > **New Library**   ✕
   >
   > To create a library for this session, specify these values:
   >
   > Name:
   > `orion`
   >
   > Path:
   > `s:/workshop`
   >
   > Options:
   > *LIBNAME options (separated by spaces)*
   >
   > ☐ Re-create this library at start-up
   >   (adds the library to the SAS autoexec file)
   >
   >   OK   Cancel

The **orion** library is displayed in the Libraries section.

e. Expand **orion** to see the list of data sets that it contains.

f. Double-click the **COUNTRY** data set to open it. The data is displayed in a data grid in the workspace. The columns are listed in the Columns section to the left of the data grid. All columns are selected by default.

Columns	Total rows: 7 Total columns: 6					Rows 1-7
☑ Select all		Country	Country_Name	Population	Country_ID	Continent_ID	Country_FormerN
☑ Country	1	AU	Australia	20,000,000	160	96	
☑ Country_Name	2	CA	Canada	.	260	91	
☑ Population	3	DE	Germany	80,000,000	394	93	East/West Germany
☑ Country_ID	4	IL	Israel	5,000,000	475	95	
☑ Continent_ID	5	TR	Turkey	70,000,000	905	95	
☑ Country_FormerName	6	US	United States	280,000,000	926	91	
	7	ZA	South Africa	43,000,000	801	94	

g. Clear **Select all**, and then select the **Country_Name** check box. The column properties are displayed below the Columns list. Only the selected column appears in the data grid.

h. Click ▤ in the View toolbar to display the table properties. The SAS Table Properties dialog box lists the general properties. Click the **Columns** tab to display column properties.

i. Click **Close** to close the SAS Table Properties dialog box.

j. Click ⊠ on the **orion.country** tab to close the data grid.

6. Assigning and Browsing a Library Interactively with SAS Enterprise Guide

a. In the Servers pane, select **Servers** ⇨ **Local** ⇨ **Libraries**. Observe the libraries that are assigned automatically in your SAS Enterprise Guide session.

b. Select **Tools** ⇨ **Assign Project Library**.

c. In the Assign Project Library Wizard, do the following:

- Step 1: Enter **orion** in the **Name** field, and click **Next**.
- Step 2: Accept the default engine and engine type. Click the **Browse** button and navigate to **s:\workshop**, or to the location of your data folder. Click **OK**. The path is displayed. Click **Next**.
- Step 3: Click **Next**.
- Step 4: Click **Finish**.

d. In the Servers pane, select **Libraries** and click **Refresh** or right-click **Libraries** and select **Refresh**.

e. Verify that the **orion** library is displayed in the list of active libraries.

f. Expland the **orion** library.

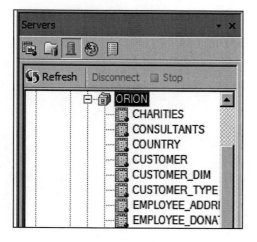

g. Double-click the **COUNTRY** data set in the **orion** library to open it. The data is displayed in a data grid in the workspace. Move the mouse pointer over a column name to see the column properties. Click ☒ to close the data grid.

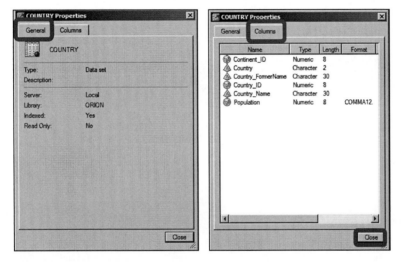

h. Right-click the **COUNTRY** data set in the **orion** library to display the data set properties. The **General** tab is displayed by default. Click the **Columns** tab to see column properties. Click **Close** to close the COUNTRY Properties dialog box.

7. Assigning and Browsing a Library Interactively in the SAS Windowing Environment

a. Select **Tools** ⇨ **New Library**, or click 🗊 (**Add New Library**). The New Library dialog box is displayed.

b. Enter **orion** in the **Name** field. Click **Browse** and navigate to **s:\workshop** or to the location of your data folder, and click **OK**. The path is displayed in the dialog box. Selecting the **Enable at startup** check box causes SAS to re-create the library at the start of each session.

c. Click **OK**.

d. In the Explorer window, double-click **Libraries**.

e. Verify that the **Orion** library is displayed in the list of active libraries.

f. Double-click the **Orion** library. Verify that the data sets contained in the **Orion** library are displayed.

g. Double-click the **Country** data set in the **Orion** library to open it. The data is displayed in a viewtable. Column labels are displayed by default.

	Country Abbreviation	Current Name of Country	Population (approx.)	Country ID	Numeric Rep. for Continent	Former Name of Country
1	AU	Australia	20,000,000	160	96	
2	CA	Canada	.	260	91	
3	DE	Germany	80,000,000	394	93	East/West Germany
4	IL	Israel	5,000,000	475	95	
5	TR	Turkey	70,000,000	905	95	
6	US	United States	280,000,000	926	91	
7	ZA	South Africa	43,000,000	801	94	

h. Click **View** ⇨ **Column Names** on the toolbar to display column names instead of labels. Click [×] to close the viewtable.

		VIEWTABLE: Orion.Country				_ □ ×
	Country	Country_Name	Population	Country_ID	Continent_ID	Country_FormerName
1	AU	Australia	20,000,000	160	96	
2	CA	Canada	.	260	91	
3	DE	Germany	80,000,000	394	93	East/West Germany
4	IL	Israel	5,000,000	475	95	
5	TR	Turkey	70,000,000	905	95	
6	US	United States	280,000,000	926	91	
7	ZA	South Africa	43,000,000	801	94	

i. Right click the **Country** data set in the **Orion** library, and select **Properties**. The data set properties are displayed with the **General** tab selected by default. Click the **Columns** tab to see column properties. Click [×] or **OK** to close the Orion.Country Properties dialog box.

Orion.Country Properties (General tab)

General | Details | Columns | Indexes | Integrity | Passwords

Country

Type:	TABLE
Default Action:	VIEWTABLE %8b."%s".DATA
Location:	Orion.Country
Engine:	V9
Rows:	7
Columns:	6
Created:	21Jan2015:15:54:15
Modified:	21Jan2015:15:54:17

Description:

OK   Cancel   Help

Orion.Country Properties (Columns tab)

General | Details | Columns | Indexes | Integrity | Passwords

Find column name: [   ]   Find

Column Name	Type	Length	Format	Informat
Country	Text	2		
Country_Name	Text	30		
Population	Number	8	COMMA12.	
Country_ID	Number	8		
Continent_ID	Number	8		
Country_Form...	Text	30		

OK   Cancel   Help

3.3 Solutions

Solutions to Exercises

1. **Examining the Data Portion of a SAS Data Set**

```
data work.donations;
   infile "&path\donation.dat";
   input Employee_ID Qtr1 Qtr2 Qtr3 Qtr4;
   Total=sum(Qtr1,Qtr2,Qtr3,Qtr4);
run;


proc contents data=work.donations;
run;


proc print data=work.donations;
run;
```

2. **Examining the Descriptor and Data Portions of a SAS Data Set**

```
data work.newpacks;
   input Supplier_Name $ 1-20 Supplier_Country $ 23-24
         Product_Name $ 28-70;
   datalines;
Top Sports          DK     Black/Black
Top Sports          DK     X-Large Bottlegreen/Black
   ...
Miller Trading Inc  US     Sioux Men's Backpack 26 Litre.
;

proc contents data=work.newpacks;
run;

proc print data=work.newpacks noobs;
   var Product_Name Supplier_Name;
run;
```

- How many observations are in the data set? **13**
- How many variables are in the data set? **3**
- What is the length (byte size) of the variable **Product_Name**? **43**

3. **Working with Times and Datetimes**

- A SAS time value represents the number of **seconds since midnight of the current day**.
- A SAS datetime value represents the number of **seconds between midnight January 1, 1960, and an hour/minute/second within a specified date**.

Solutions to Student Activities (Polls/Quizzes)

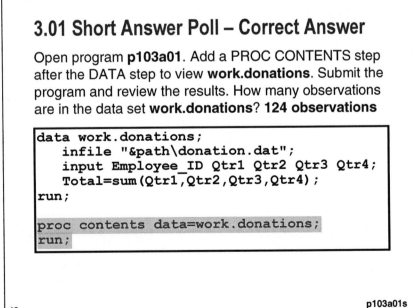

3.01 Short Answer Poll – Correct Answer

Open program **p103a01**. Add a PROC CONTENTS step after the DATA step to view **work.donations**. Submit the program and review the results. How many observations are in the data set **work.donations**? **124 observations**

```
data work.donations;
   infile "&path\donation.dat";
   input Employee_ID Qtr1 Qtr2 Qtr3 Qtr4;
   Total=sum(Qtr1,Qtr2,Qtr3,Qtr4);
run;

proc contents data=work.donations;
run;
```

12   p103a01s

3.02 Multiple Answer Poll – Correct Answer

Which variable names are invalid?

a. data5mon
b. 5monthsdata
c. data#5
d. five months data
e. five_months_data
f. FiveMonthsData
g. fivemonthsdata

18

3.03 Short Answer Poll – Correct Answer

Submit program **p103a02**. View the output to retrieve the current date as a SAS date value (that is, a numeric value referencing January 1, 1960). What is the numeric value for today's date?

The answer depends on the current date.

Example: If the current date is February 27, 2012, the numeric value is 19050.

23

3.04 Multiple Choice Poll – Correct Answer

Which of the following correctly assigns the libref **myfiles** to a SAS library in the **c:\mysasfiles** folder?

a. libname orion myfiles "c:\mysasfiles";
b. libname myfiles "c:\mysasfiles";
c. libref orion myfiles "c:\mysasfiles";
d. libref myfiles "c:\mysasfiles";

41

Chapter 4   Producing Detail Reports

4.1 Subsetting Report Data

Objectives

- Create a default PROC PRINT report.
- Select variables with a VAR statement.
- Calculate totals with a SUM statement.
- Select observations with a WHERE statement.
- Define a date constant.
- Identify observations with an ID statement.

3

Business Scenario

Orion Star management wants a report that displays the names, salaries, and a salary total for all sales employees.

Obs	Last_Name	First_Name	Salary
1	XXXXXXX	XXXXXXXXXX	99999
2	XXXXXXX	XXXXXXXXXX	99999
3	XXXXXXX	XXXXXXXXXX	99999

			99999

4

PRINT Procedure

By default, PROC PRINT displays all observations,
all variables, and an Obs column on the left side.

```
proc print data=orion.sales;
run;
```

Partial PROC PRINT Output

Obs	Employee_ID	First_Name	Last_Name	Gender	Salary	Job_Title	Country	Birth_Date	Hire_Date
1	120102	Tom	Zhou	M	108255	Sales Manager	AU	3510	10744
2	120103	Wilson	Dawes	M	87975	Sales Manager	AU	-3996	5114
3	120121	Irenie	Elvish	F	26600	Sales Rep. II	AU	-5630	5114
4	120122	Christina	Ngan	F	27475	Sales Rep. II	AU	-1984	6756
5	120123	Kimiko	Hotstone	F	26190	Sales Rep. I	AU	1732	9405

Statements and options can be added to the
PRINT procedure to modify the default behavior.

5   p104d01

The columns are listed, left to right, in the order in which the variables are stored in the data set.

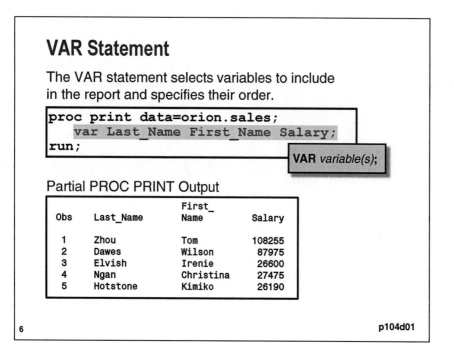

VAR Statement

The VAR statement selects variables to include
in the report and specifies their order.

```
proc print data=orion.sales;
    var Last_Name First_Name Salary;
run;
```

VAR *variable(s)*;

Partial PROC PRINT Output

Obs	Last_Name	First_Name	Salary
1	Zhou	Tom	108255
2	Dawes	Wilson	87975
3	Elvish	Irenie	26600
4	Ngan	Christina	27475
5	Hotstone	Kimiko	26190

6   p104d01

SUM Statement

The *SUM statement* calculates and displays report totals for the requested **numeric** variables.

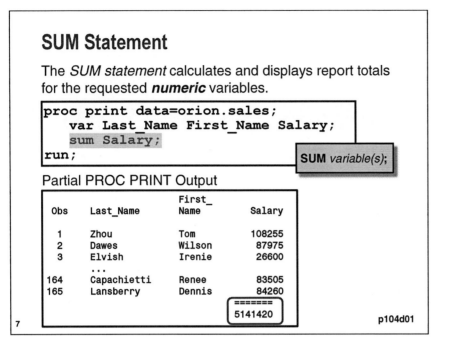

Partial PROC PRINT Output

```
                    First_
   Obs   Last_Name    Name      Salary

    1    Zhou         Tom       108255
    2    Dawes        Wilson     87975
    3    Elvish       Irenie     26600
         ...
  164    Capachietti  Renee      83505
  165    Lansberry    Dennis     84260
                                =======
                                5141420
```

p104d01

7

Viewing the Log

Partial SAS Log

```
84    proc print data=orion.sales;
85       var Last_Name First_Name Salary;
86       sum salary;
87    run;

NOTE: There were 165 observations read from the data set ORION.SALES.
```

✎ The order of statements in a SAS procedure is usually not important.

8

Business Scenario

Orion Star management wants a report that displays the names and salaries of the sales employees who earn less than $25,500. Suppress the Obs column.

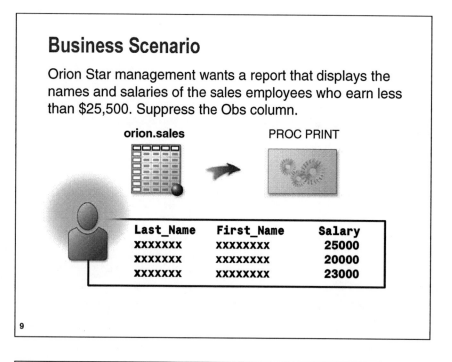

9

WHERE Statement

The *WHERE statement* selects observations that meet the criteria specified in the WHERE expression.

```
proc print data=orion.sales;
    var Last_Name First_Name Salary;
    where Salary<25500;
run;
```

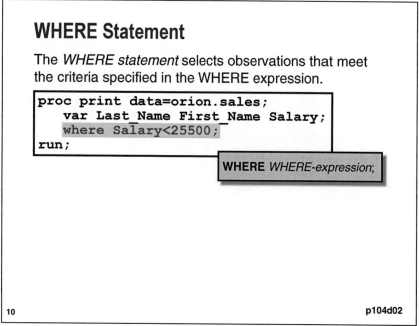

WHERE *WHERE-expression*;

10   p104d02

Viewing the Log

Only 7 of the 165 observations from **orion.sales** were
selected by the WHERE statement.

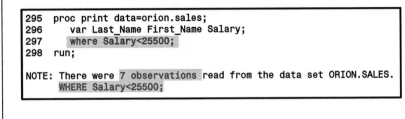

```
295  proc print data=orion.sales;
296     var Last_Name First_Name Salary;
297     where Salary<25500;
298  run;

NOTE: There were 7 observations read from the data set ORION.SALES.
      WHERE Salary<25500;
```

11

Viewing the Output

PROC PRINT Output

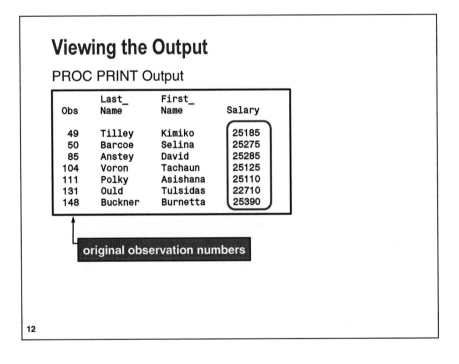

Obs	Last_Name	First_Name	Salary
49	Tilley	Kimiko	25185
50	Barcoe	Selina	25275
85	Anstey	David	25285
104	Voron	Tachaun	25125
111	Polky	Asishana	25110
131	Ould	Tulsidas	22710
148	Buckner	Burnetta	25390

original observation numbers

12

Suppressing the Obs Column

Use the NOOBS option in the PROC PRINT statement
to suppress the Obs column.

```
proc print data=orion.sales noobs;
   var Last_Name First_Name Salary;
   where Salary<25500;
run;
```

PROC PRINT DATA=SAS-data-set **NOOBS;**

PROC PRINT Output

Last_ Name	First_ Name	Salary
Tilley	Kimiko	25185
Barcoe	Selina	25275
Anstey	David	25285
Voron	Tachaun	25125
Polky	Asishana	25110
Ould	Tulsidas	22710
Buckner	Burnetta	25390

13   p104d02

WHERE Statement

The WHERE expression defines the condition (or
conditions) for selecting observations.

WHERE *WHERE-expression;*

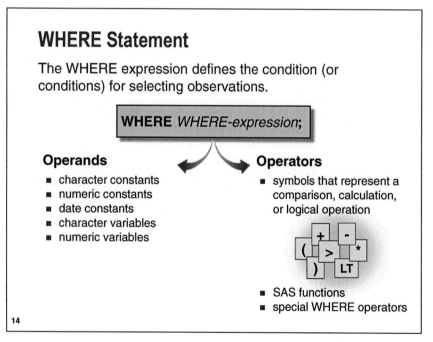

Operands
- character constants
- numeric constants
- date constants
- character variables
- numeric variables

Operators
- symbols that represent a
  comparison, calculation,
  or logical operation

- SAS functions
- special WHERE operators

14

Operands

Constants are fixed values.

- Character values are enclosed in quotation marks and are case sensitive.
- Numeric values do not use quotation marks or special characters.

Variables must exist in the input data set.

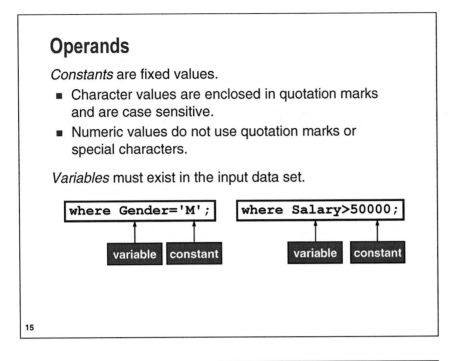

15

SAS Date Constant

A *SAS date constant* is a date written in the following form: **'ddmmm<yy>yy'd**

Examples
'01JAN2000'd
'31Dec11'D
'1jan04'd
'06NOV2000'D

SAS automatically converts a date constant to a SAS date value.

16

Comparison Operators

Comparison operators compare a variable with a value or with another variable.

Symbol	Mnemonic	Definition
=	EQ	Equal to
^= ¬= ~=	NE	Not equal to
>	GT	Greater than
<	LT	Less than
>=	GE	Greater than or equal
<=	LE	Less than or equal
	IN	Equal to one of a list

17

The caret (^), tilde (~), and the not sign (¬) indicate a logical *not*. Use the character available on your keyboard, or use the mnemonic equivalent.

Comparison Operators

Examples
`where Gender eq ' ';`
`where Salary ne .;`
`where Salary>=50000;`
`where Hire_Date<'01Jan2000'd;`
`where Country in ('AU','US');`
`where Country in ('AU' 'US');`
`where Order_Type in (1,2,3);`

The value list in the IN operator must be enclosed in parentheses and separated by either commas or blanks. Character values must be enclosed in quotation marks.

18

Setup for the Poll

Program **p104a01** contains two WHERE statements.
Open and submit the program.

19

4.01 Multiple Choice Poll

Which of the following is true?

a. The program executes, and applies both WHERE
   conditions successfully.
b. The program fails and an error message is written
   to the log.
c. The program executes, but only the first WHERE
   condition is applied.
d. The program executes, but only the second WHERE
   condition is applied.

20

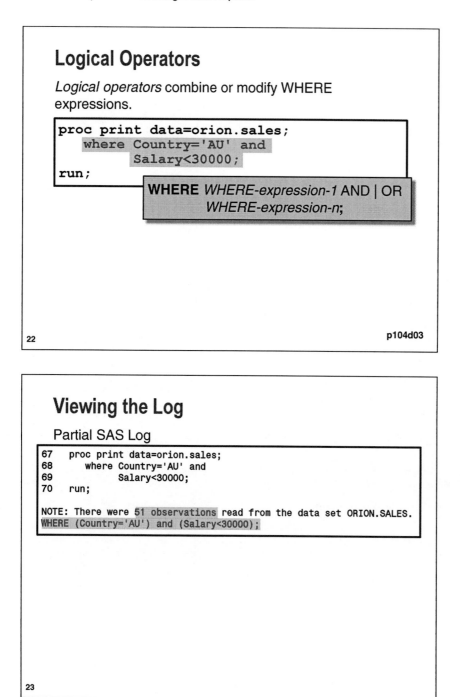

Logical Operator Priority

The operators can be written as symbols or mnemonics, and parentheses can be added to modify the order of evaluation.

Symbol	Mnemonic	Priority
^ ¬ ~	NOT	I
&	AND	II
|	OR	III

The NOT operator modifies a condition by finding the complement of the specified criteria.

```
where City not in ('London','Rome','Paris');
```

24

- NOT modifies a condition by finding the complement of the specified criteria. Use the character that is available on your keyboard, or use the mnemonic equivalent.
- AND finds observations that satisfy both conditions.
- OR finds observations that satisfy one or both conditions.

Logical Operators

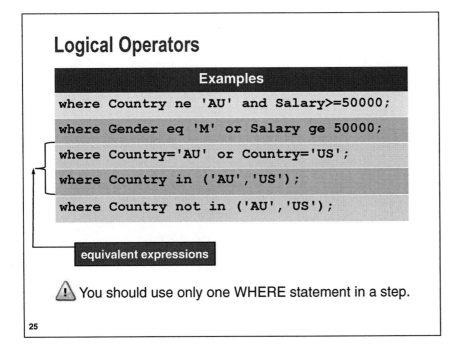

Examples
`where Country ne 'AU' and Salary>=50000;`
`where Gender eq 'M' or Salary ge 50000;`
`where Country='AU' or Country='US';`
`where Country in ('AU','US');`
`where Country not in ('AU','US');`

equivalent expressions

⚠ You should use only one WHERE statement in a step.

25

4.02 Short Answer Poll

Which WHERE statement correctly subsets the numeric values for May, June, or July and missing character names?

a.
```
where Month in (5-7)
      and Names=.;
```

b.
```
where Month in (5,6,7)
      and Names=' ';
```

c.
```
where Month in ('5','6','7')
      and Names='.';
```

26

Business Scenario

Orion Star management wants a report that lists only the Australian sales representatives.

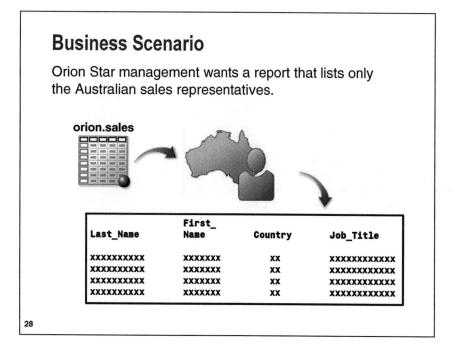

orion.sales

Last_Name	First_Name	Country	Job_Title
XXXXXXXXXX	XXXXXXX	XX	XXXXXXXXXXXX
XXXXXXXXXX	XXXXXXX	XX	XXXXXXXXXXXX
XXXXXXXXXX	XXXXXXX	XX	XXXXXXXXXXXX
XXXXXXXXXX	XXXXXXX	XX	XXXXXXXXXXXX

28

Exploring the Data

```
proc print data=orion.sales noobs;
   var Last_Name First_Name Country
       Job_Title;
run;
```

Partial PROC PRINT Output

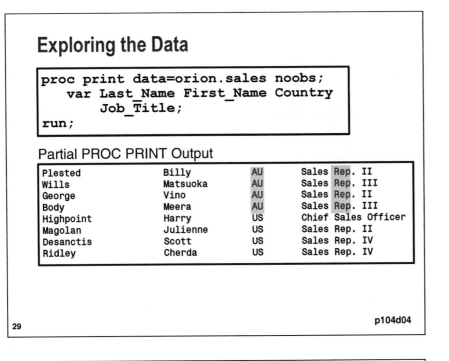

Plested	Billy	AU	Sales Rep. II
Wills	Matsuoka	AU	Sales Rep. III
George	Vino	AU	Sales Rep. II
Body	Meera	AU	Sales Rep. III
Highpoint	Harry	US	Chief Sales Officer
Magolan	Julienne	US	Sales Rep. II
Desanctis	Scott	US	Sales Rep. IV
Ridley	Cherda	US	Sales Rep. IV

29   p104d04

Subsetting in a PROC PRINT Step

Include a WHERE statement to subset by **Country**
and **Job_Title**.

```
proc print data=orion.sales noobs;
   var Last_Name First_Name Country
       Job_Title;
   where Country='AU' and
         Job_Title contains 'Rep';
run;
```

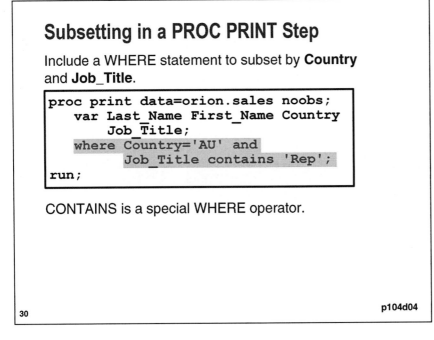

CONTAINS is a special WHERE operator.

30   p104d04

CONTAINS Operator

The *CONTAINS operator* selects observations
that include the specified substring.

Equivalent Statements
where Job_Title contains 'Rep';
where Job_Title ? 'Rep';

- ? can be used instead of the mnemonic.
- The position of the substring within the variable's values is not important.
- Comparisons made with the CONTAINS operator are case sensitive.

31

Viewing the Output

Partial PROC PRINT Output

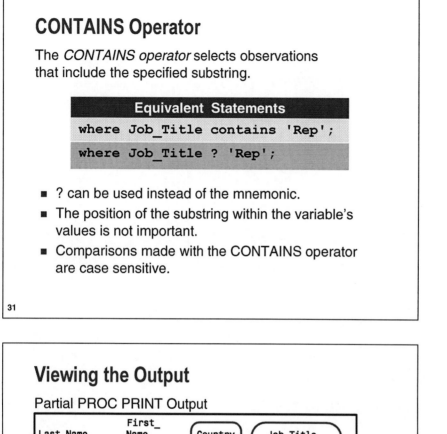

```
                First_
Last_Name       Name          Country     Job_Title

Elvish          Irenie          AU         Sales Rep. II
Ngan            Christina       AU         Sales Rep. II
Hotstone        Kimiko          AU         Sales Rep. I
Daymond         Lucian          AU         Sales Rep. I
Hofmeister      Fong            AU         Sales Rep. IV
```

32

Special WHERE Operators

Special WHERE operators are operators
that can be used only in WHERE expressions.

Operator	Definition	Char	Num
CONTAINS	Includes a substring	x	
BETWEEN-AND	An inclusive range	x	x
WHERE SAME AND	Augment a WHERE expression	x	x
IS NULL	A missing value	x	x
IS MISSING	A missing value	x	x
LIKE	Matches a pattern	x	

33

Special WHERE operators cannot be used in IF-THEN or subsetting IF statements.

BETWEEN-AND Operator

The *BETWEEN-AND operator* selects observations in
which the value of a variable falls within an inclusive
range of values.

Examples
where salary between 50000 and 100000;
where salary not between 50000 and 100000;
where Last_Name between 'A' and 'L';
where Last_Name between 'Baker' and 'Gomez';

34

BETWEEN-AND Operator

Equivalent Statements
`where salary between 50000 and 100000;`
`where salary>=50000 and salary<=100000;`
`where 50000<=salary<=100000;`

35

WHERE SAME AND Operator

Use the *WHERE SAME AND operator* to add more
conditions to an existing WHERE expression.

```
proc print data=orion.sales;
   where Country='AU' and Salary<30000;
   where same and Gender='F';
   var First_Name Last_Name Gender
       Salary Country;
run;
```

The WHERE SAME AND condition **augments** the original
condition.

36   p104d05

Viewing the Log

Partial SAS Log

```
22    proc print data=orion.sales;
23        where Country='AU'  and Salary<30000;
24        where same and Gender='F';
NOTE: WHERE clause has been augmented.
25        var First_Name Last_Name Gender Salary Country;
26    run;

NOTE: There were 23 observations read from the data set ORION.SALES.
      WHERE (Country='AU') and (Gender='F') and (Salary<30000);
```

37

Viewing the Output

Partial PROC PRINT Output

Obs	First_Name	Last_Name	Gender	Salary	Country
3	Irenie	Elvish	F	26600	AU
4	Christina	Ngan	F	27475	AU
5	Kimiko	Hotstone	F	26190	AU
9	Sharryn	Clarkson	F	28100	AU
14	Fancine	Kaiser	F	28525	AU
15	Petrea	Soltau	F	27440	AU
19	Marina	Iyengar	F	29715	AU
20	Shani	Duckett	F	25795	AU
21	Fang	Wilson	F	26810	AU
23	Amanda	Liebman	F	27465	AU

Country='AU'
Gender='F'
Salary<30000

38

4.03 Short Answer Poll

Open **p104a01b**. Change WHERE SAME AND to WHERE ALSO. Submit the program and view the log. What message is written to the log?

39

IS NULL Operator

The *IS NULL operator* selects observations in which a variable has a missing value.

Examples
`where Employee_ID is null;`
`where Employee_ID is not null;`

IS NULL can be used for both character and numeric variables, and is equivalent to the following statements:

```
where employee_ID=' ';
```

```
where employee_ID=.;
```

41

IS MISSING Operator

The *IS MISSING operator* selects observations
in which a variable has a missing value.

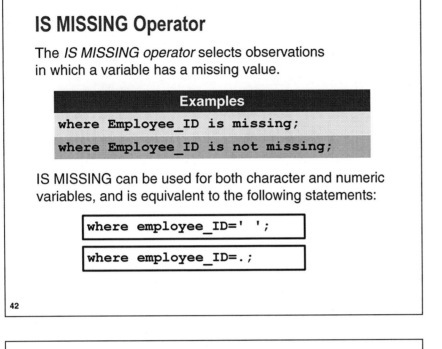

Examples
`where Employee_ID is missing;`
`where Employee_ID is not missing;`

IS MISSING can be used for both character and numeric
variables, and is equivalent to the following statements:

```
where employee_ID=' ';
```

```
where employee_ID=.;
```

42

LIKE Operator

The *LIKE operator* selects observations by comparing
character values to specified patterns. Two special
characters are used to define a pattern.

- A percent sign (%) specifies that ***any number***
  of characters can occupy that position.
- An underscore (_) specifies that ***exactly one***
  character must occupy that position.

Examples
`where Name like '%N';`
`where Name like 'T_m';`
`where Name like 'T_m%';`

43

When you use the LIKE operator, be aware of the following:

- Consecutive underscores can be specified.
- A percent sign and an underscore can be specified in the same pattern.
- The operator is case sensitive.

4.04 Short Answer Poll

Which WHERE statement returns all the observations that have a first name starting with the letter M for the given values?

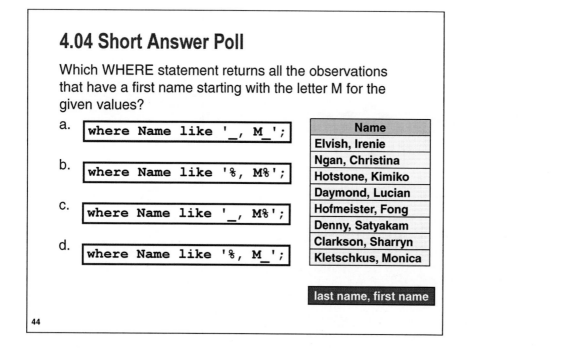

a.
```
where Name like '_, M_';
```

b.
```
where Name like '%, M%';
```

c.
```
where Name like '_, M%';
```

d.
```
where Name like '%, M_';
```

Name
Elvish, Irenie
Ngan, Christina
Hotstone, Kimiko
Daymond, Lucian
Hofmeister, Fong
Denny, Satyakam
Clarkson, Sharryn
Kletschkus, Monica

last name, first name

44

Business Scenario

The Sales Manager wants a report that includes only the customers who are 21 years old.

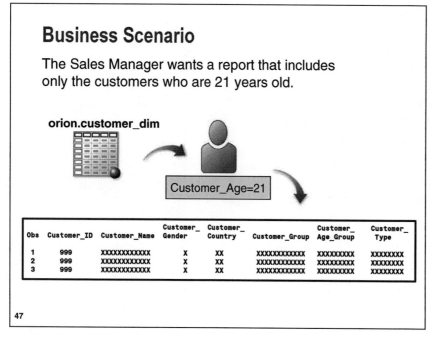

orion.customer_dim

Customer_Age=21

Obs	Customer_ID	Customer_Name	Customer_ Gender	Customer_ Country	Customer_Group	Customer_ Age_Group	Customer_ Type
1	999	XXXXXXXXXXXX	X	XX	XXXXXXXXXXXX	XXXXXXXX	XXXXXXXX
2	999	XXXXXXXXXXXX	X	XX	XXXXXXXXXXXX	XXXXXXXX	XXXXXXXX
3	999	XXXXXXXXXXXX	X	XX	XXXXXXXXXXXX	XXXXXXXX	XXXXXXXX

47

Subsetting the Data Set

Display the required rows and variables.

```
proc print data=orion.customer_dim;
    where Customer_Age=21;
    var Customer_ID Customer_Name
        Customer_Gender Customer_Country
        Customer_Group Customer_Age_Group
        Customer_Type;
run;
```

🖈 The subsetting variable does not need to be included in the report.

p104d06

48

Viewing the Output

In this output, two lines are used for each observation.

PROC PRINT Output

Obs	Customer_ID	Customer_Name	Customer_Gender	Customer_Country	Customer_Group
37	79	Najma Hicks	F	US	Orion Club members
58	11171	Bill Cuddy	M	CA	Orion Club Gold members
66	46966	Lauren Krasowski	F	CA	Orion Club members
...					
76	70210	Alex Santinello	M	CA	Orion Club members

Obs	Customer_Age_Group	Customer_Type
37	15-30 years	Orion Club members medium activity
58	15-30 years	Orion Club Gold members low activity
66	15-30 years	Orion Club members high activity
...		
76	15-30 years	Orion Club members medium activity

The Obs column helps identify observations that span multiple lines in a report.

49

Report width and wrapping depend on the LINESIZE system option, the ODS destination, or both.

ID Statement

The *ID statement* specifies the variable or variables
to print at the beginning of each row instead of an
observation number.

```
proc print data=orion.customer_dim;
   where Customer_Age=21;
   id Customer_ID;
   var Customer_Name Customer_Gender
       Customer_Country Customer_Group
       Customer_Age_Group Customer_Type;
run;
```

ID *variables*;

⚠ Choose ID variables that uniquely identify observations.

50   p104d07

Notice that the ID variable was removed from the VAR statement. If it were not removed, it would be
displayed twice: once as the leftmost column and again in the position specified by the VAR statement.

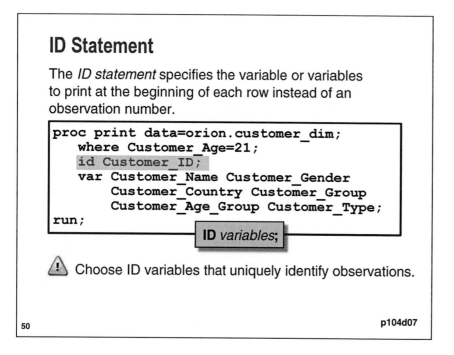

Viewing the Output

PROC PRINT Output

Customer_ID	Customer_Name	Customer_ Gender	Customer_ Country	Customer_Group
79	Najma Hicks	F	US	Orion Club members
11171	Bill Cuddy	M	CA	Orion Club Gold members
46966	Lauren Krasowski	F	CA	Orion Club members
70079	Lera Knott	F	CA	Orion Club members
70187	Soberina Berent	F	CA	Orion Club members
70210	Alex Santinello	M	CA	Orion Club members

Customer_ID	Customer_ Age_Group	Customer_Type
79	15-30 years	Orion Club members medium activity
11171	15-30 years	Orion Club Gold members low activity
46966	15-30 years	Orion Club members high activity
70079	15-30 years	Orion Club members medium activity
70187	15-30 years	Orion Club members medium activity
70210	15-30 years	Orion Club members medium activity

51

Exercises

If you restarted your SAS session since the last exercise, open and submit the **libname.sas** program
that can be found in the data folder.

Level 1

1. **Displaying orion.order_fact with the PRINT Procedure**

    a. Retrieve the starter program **p104e01**. Run the program and view the output. Observe that there are 617 observations. Observations might be displayed over two lines, depending on output settings.

    b. Add a SUM statement to display the sum of **Total_Retail_Price**. The last several lines of the report are shown below.

    ```
         Order_                             Total_Retail_    CostPrice_
    Obs   Type    Product_ID    Quantity       Price          Per_Unit      Discount

    610    1      240700100007     2           $45.70          $9.30           .
    611    1      240700100017     2           $19.98         $11.40          40%
    612    1      240700400003     2           $24.80          $5.60           .
    613    1      240800100042     3          $760.80        $105.30           .
    614    1      240500200016     3           $95.10         $14.50           .
    615    1      240500200122     2           $48.20         $11.50           .
    616    1      240700200018     4           $75.20         $10.30           .
    617    1      220101400130     2           $33.80          $5.70           .
                                          =============
                                            $100,077.46
    ```

    c. Add a WHERE statement to select only the observations with **Total_Retail_Price** more than 500. Submit the program. Verify that 35 observations are displayed.

        What do you notice about the Obs column? _____

        Did the sum of **Total_Retail_Price** change to reflect only the subset? _____

    d. Add an option to suppress the Obs column. Verify that there are 35 observations in the results.

        How can you verify the number of observations in the results? _____

    e. Add an ID statement to use **Customer_ID** as the identifying variable. Submit the program. The results contain 35 observations.

        How did the output change? _____

    f. Add a VAR statement to display **Customer_ID, Order_ID, Order_Type, Quantity**, and **Total_Retail_Price**.

        What do you notice about **Customer_ID**? _____

    g. Modify the VAR statement to address the issue with **Customer_ID**.

Level 2

2. **Displaying orion.customer_dim with the PRINT Procedure**

    a. Write a PRINT step to display **orion.customer_dim**.

    b. Modify the program to display a subset of **orion.customer_dim** by selecting only the observations for customers between the ages of 30 and 40. Also, suppress the Obs column. The resulting report should contain 17 observations.

   c. Add a statement to use **Customer_ID** instead of Obs as the identifying column. Submit the program and verify the results.

   d. Add a statement to limit the variables to those shown in the report below.

```
                          Customer_
Customer_ID    Customer_Name        Age      Customer_Type

          4    James Kvarniq         33      Orion Club members low activity
          9    Cornelia Krahl        33      Orion Club Gold members medium activity
         11    Elke Wallstab         33      Orion  Club members high activity
        ...    ...                  ...       ...
      54655    Lauren Marx           38      Internet/Catalog Customers
      70201    Angel Borwick         38      Orion Club Gold members low activity
```

Challenge

3. Producing a Default Listing Report of orion.order_fact

   ✎   This exercise assumes that you are creating LISTING output in the SAS windowing environment.

   a. Produce a default listing report of **orion.order_fact**. The output might wrap onto a second line.

   b. Investigate the use of the LINESIZE= SAS system option to adjust the width of the lines. What are the minimum and maximum values for the LINESIZE= option? _____

   Submit an OPTIONS statement with LINESIZE= set to the highest allowed value. Resubmit the step, and observe the horizontal scroll bar, if it is displayed.

   Reset the line size to 96 when you are finished.

   c. Another way to create compact output is to request vertical headings. Investigate the HEADING= option in the PROC PRINT statement, and then experiment with it to generate vertical headings and then horizontal headings.

   How do you specify vertical headings? _____

   How do you specify horizontal headings? _____

4. Producing a Default Listing Report of orion.product_dim

   ✎   This exercise assumes that you are creating LISTING output in the SAS windowing environment.

   a. Produce a default listing report to display **orion.product_dim**. Notice that the column width varies from one page to the next, depending on the width of the values that are displayed on each page.

   b. Investigate the WIDTH= option of the PROC PRINT statement, and modify the program to use this option with a value of UNIFORM.

   How are the results different when you use the WIDTH=UNIFORM option? _____

   _____

c. Why might the procedure run more slowly with this option? _____

_____

d. How can you save computer resources and still display columns consistently across pages? _____

_____

4.2 Sorting and Grouping Report Data

Objectives

- Sort the observations in a SAS data set based on the values of one or more variables.
- Display the sorted observations.
- Display a data set with report totals and subtotals for each BY group.

55

Business Scenario

Display observations from **orion.sales** in ascending order by the variable **Salary**.

Employee_ID	Last_Name	Salary
999999	XXXXXXXXXX	99999
999999	XXXXXXXXXX	99999
999999	XXXXXXXXXX	99999

56

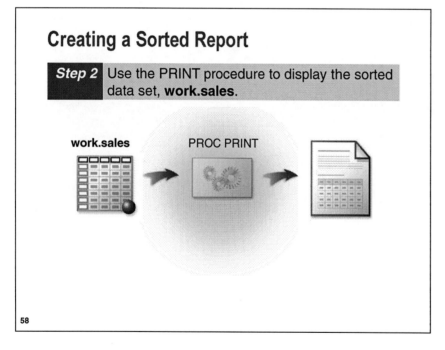

Step 1: SORT Procedure

The *SORT procedure* rearranges the observations in the input data set based on the values of the variable or variables listed in the BY statement.

```
proc sort data=orion.sales
          out=work.sales;
  by Salary;
run;
```

PROC SORT DATA=*input-SAS-data-set*
  <**OUT=***output-SAS-data-set*>;
BY <DESCENDING> *variables*;
RUN;

The BY statement in a PROC SORT step specifies the sort variables, and if you indicate it, the sort order.

p104d08

59

Viewing the Log

The SORT procedure does not produce a report. Check the log for errors or warnings.

Partial SAS Log

```
34    proc sort data=orion.sales
35            out=work.sales;
36       by Salary;
37    run;

NOTE: There were 165 observations read from the data set
ORION.SALES.
NOTE: The data set WORK.SALES has 165 observations and 9
variables.
```

60

Step 2: Viewing the Output

```
proc print data=work.sales noobs;
   var Employee_ID Last_Name Salary;
run;
```

Partial PROC PRINT Output

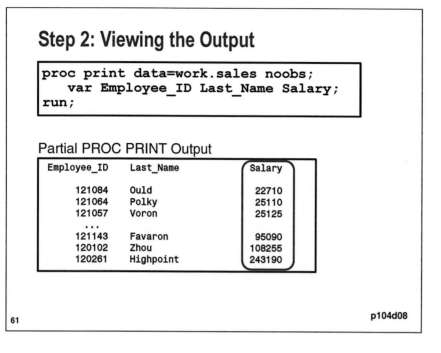

Employee_ID	Last_Name	Salary
121084	Ould	22710
121064	Polky	25110
121057	Voron	25125
...		
121143	Favaron	95090
120102	Zhou	108255
120261	Highpoint	243190

61

p104d08

SORT Procedure

The SORT procedure
- replaces the original data set or creates a new one
- can sort on multiple variables
- sorts in ascending (default) or descending order
- does not generate printed output.

⚠ The input data set is overwritten unless the
   OUT= option is used to specify an output data set.

62

4.05 Short Answer Poll

Which step sorts the observations in a SAS data set and overwrites the same data set?

a.
```
proc sort data=work.EmpsAU
          out=work.sorted;
   by First;
run;
```

b.
```
proc sort data=orion.EmpsAU
          out=EmpsAU;
   by First;
run;
```

c.
```
proc sort data=work.EmpsAU;
   by First;
run;
```

63

Business Scenario

Produce a report that lists sales employees grouped by **Country**, in descending **Salary** order within country.

```
---------------------------------Country=AU---------------------------------

                First_  Last_                            Birth_  Hire_
Employee_ID     Name    Name    Gender  Salary  Job_Title  Date   Date

    9999        xxxx    xxxxx     x      99999   xxxxxx    9999   9999
    9999        xxxx    xxxxx     x      99999   xxxxxx    9999   9999


---------------------------------Country=US---------------------------------

                First_  Last_                            Birth_  Hire_
Employee_ID     Name    Name    Gender  Salary  Job_Title  Date   Date

    9999        xxxx    xxxxx     x      99999   xxxxxx    9999   9999
    9999        xxxx    xxxxx     x      99999   xxxxxx    9999   9999
    9999        xxxx    xxxxx     x      99999   xxxxxx    9999   9999
```

66

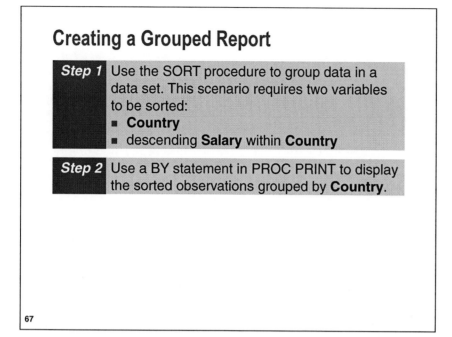

Creating a Grouped Report

Step 1	Use the SORT procedure to group data in a data set. This scenario requires two variables to be sorted: ■ **Country** ■ descending **Salary** within **Country**
Step 2	Use a BY statement in PROC PRINT to display the sorted observations grouped by **Country**.

67

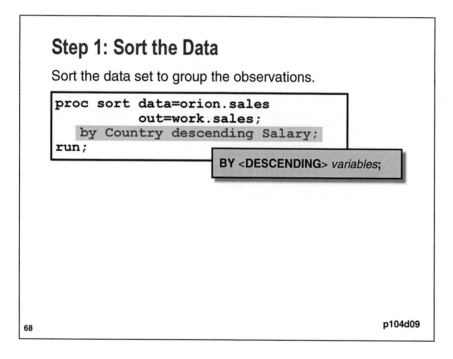

Step 1: Sort the Data

Sort the data set to group the observations.

```
proc sort data=orion.sales
          out=work.sales;
   by Country descending Salary;
run;
```

BY <DESCENDING> *variables*;

68   p104d09

Specifying Sort Order

The *DESCENDING option* reverses the sort order for the variable that immediately follows it. The observations are sorted from the largest value to the smallest value.

Examples:

```
by descending Last First;
```

```
by Last descending First;
```

```
by descending Last descending First;
```

69

Specifying Multiple BY Variables

- PROC SORT first arranges the data set by the values of the first BY variable.

- PROC SORT then arranges any observations that have the same value as the first BY variable by the values of the second BY variable.

- This sorting continues for every specified BY variable.

70

Step 2: Specify Report Groupings

The BY statement in a PROC PRINT step specifies
the variable or variables to use to form *BY groups*.

```
proc print data=work.sales noobs;
   by Country;
run;
```

BY <DESCENDING> *variables*;

- The variables in the BY statement are called
  BY variables.
- The observations in the data set **must** be in order
  according to the order of the BY variable (or
  variables).

71   p104d09

Viewing the Output

Partial PROC PRINT Output

```
---------------------------- Country=AU ----------------------------

                                                       Hire_
Employee_ID   First_Name   Last_Name   Gender   Salary   Date

    120102    Tom          Zhou          M      108255   12205
    120103    Wilson       Dawes         M       87975  ... 6575
    120168    Selina       Barcoe        M       36605   18567

---------------------------- Country=US ----------------------------

                                                       Hire_
Employee_ID   First_Name   Last_Name   Gender   Salary   Date

    120261    Harry        Highpoint     M      243190   11535
    121143    Louis        Favaron       M       95090  ... 15157
    121064    Asishana     Polky         M       84260   13027
```

72

4.06 Short Answer Poll

Open and submit **p104a02**. View the log. Why did the program fail?

73

Business Scenario

Modify the previous report to display selected variables, the salary subtotal for each country, and the salary grand total.

```
-------------------- Country=AU --------------------

First_Name    Last_Name      Gender       Salary

XXXX          XXXXXXX          X           99999
XXXX          XXXXXXX          X           99999
--------                                 ---------
Country                                    999999

-------------------- Country=US --------------------

First_Name    Last_Name      Gender       Salary

XXXXXXX       XXXXXXX          X           99999
XXXXXXX       XXXXXXX          X           99999
--------                                 ---------
Country                                    999999
                                         =========
                                          9999999
```

subtotals

grand total

75

Generating Subtotals

Use a BY statement and a SUM statement
in a PROC PRINT step.

```
proc sort data=orion.sales
          out=work.sales;
   by Country descending Salary;
run;

proc print data=work.sales noobs;
   by Country;
   sum Salary;
   var First_Name Last_Name Gender Salary;
run;
```

76   p104d10

Viewing the Output

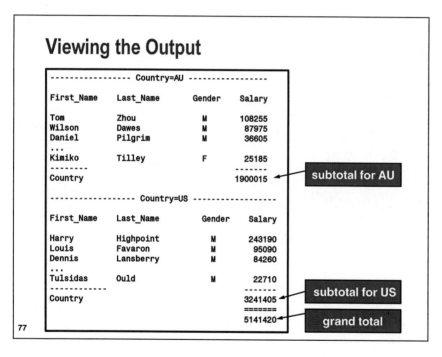

77

Setup for the Poll

Modify the previous report to display only employees earning less than 25,500. Which WHERE statement (or statements) results in the most efficient processing?

```
proc sort data=orion.sales
          out=work.sales;
   /* where Salary<25500; */
   by Country descending Salary;
run;
proc print data=work.sales noobs;
   by Country;
   sum Salary;
   /* where Salary<25500; */
   var First_Name Last_Name Gender Salary;
run;
```

78   p104a03

4.07 Multiple Choice Poll

Which WHERE statement (or statements) results in the most efficient processing?

a. The WHERE statement in the PROC SORT step.

b. The WHERE statement in the PROC PRINT step.

c. Both WHERE statements are needed.

d. The WHERE statements are equally efficient.

79

 Exercises

If you restarted your SAS session since the last exercise, open and submit the **libname.sas** program that can be found in the data folder.

Level 1

5. **Sorting orion.employee_payroll and Displaying the New Data Set**

   a. Open **p104e05**. Add a PROC SORT step before the PROC PRINT step to sort
   orion.employee_payroll by **Salary**. Place the sorted observations into a temporary data set
   named **sort_salary**.

   b. Modify the PROC PRINT step to display the new data set. Verify that your output matches the
   report below.

Obs	Employee_ID	Employee_ Gender	Salary	Birth_ Date	Employee_ Hire_Date	Employee_ Term_Date	Marital_ Status	Dependents
1	121084	M	22710	3150	12784	.	M	3
2	120191	F	24015	1112	17167	17347	S	0
...								
422	120261	M	243190	4800	11535	.	O	1
423	120262	M	268455	5042	11932	.	M	2
424	120259	M	433800	2946	12297	.	M	1

6. **Sorting orion.employee_payroll and Displaying Grouped Observations**

   a. Open **p104e06**. Add a PROC SORT step before the PROC PRINT step to sort
   orion.employee_payroll by **Employee_Gender**, and within gender, by **Salary** in descending
   order. Place the sorted observations into a temporary data set named **sort_salary2**.

   b. Modify the PROC PRINT step to display the new data set with the observations grouped by
   Employee_Gender.

```
-------------------------------- Employee_Gender=F --------------------------------
```

Obs	Employee_ID	Salary	Birth_ Date	Employee_ Hire_Date	Employee_ Term_Date	Marital_ Status	Dependents
1	120260	207885	3258	10532	.	M	2
2	120719	87420	4770	14641	.	M	1
3	120661	85495	-400	10227	17347	M	3
...							
190	120196	24025	10257	17167	17347	S	0
191	120191	24015	1112	17167	17347	S	0

```
-------------------------------- Employee_Gender=M --------------------------------
```

Obs	Employee_ID	Salary	Birth_ Date	Employee_ Hire_Date	Employee_ Term_Date	Marital_ Status	Dependents
192	120259	433800	2946	12297	.	M	1
193	120262	268455	5042	11932	.	M	2
...							
423	120190	24100	10566	17837	18017	M	2
424	121084	22710	3150	12784	.	M	3

Level 2

7. **Sorting orion.employee_payroll and Displaying a Subset of the New Data Set**

   a. Sort **orion.employee_payroll** by **Employee_Gender**, and by descending **Salary** within gender. Place the sorted observations into a temporary data set named **sort_sal**.

   b. Print a subset of the **sort_sal** data set. Select only the observations for active employees (those without a value for **Employee_Term_Date**) who earn more than $65,000. Group the report by **Employee_Gender**, and include a total and subtotals for **Salary**. Suppress the Obs column. Display only **Employee_ID**, **Salary**, and **Marital_Status**. The results contain 18 observations.

```
-------------------------------- Employee_Gender=F --------------------------------

                                              Marital_
                   Employee_ID     Salary      Status

                      120260       207885        M
                      120719        87420        M
                       ...
                      120677        65555        M
                   ---------------  ------
                   Employee_Gender  605190


-------------------------------- Employee_Gender=M --------------------------------

                                              Marital_
                   Employee_ID     Salary      Status

                      120259       433800        M
                      120262       268455        M
                       ...
                      120268        76105        S
                   ---------------  -------
                   Employee_Gender  2072410
                                    =======
                                    2677600
```

Challenge

8. **Retaining the First Observation of Each BY Group**

   a. Sort **orion.orders** by **Customer_ID**. Place the sorted observations in a temporary data set.

   b. Display the sorted data set. The resulting report should contain 490 observations. **Customer_ID** is listed multiple times for customers that placed more than one order.

   c. Investigate an option that causes PROC SORT to retain only the first observation in each BY group.

   d. Add the appropriate option to the PROC SORT step to retain only the first observation in each BY group. The results contain 75 observations with no duplicate values for **Customer_ID**.

   e. Explore the DUPOUT= option to write duplicate observations to a separate output data set.

4.3 Enhancing Reports

Objectives

- Include titles and footnotes in a report.
- Use the LABEL statement to define descriptive column headings.
- Control the use of column headings with the LABEL and SPLIT= options.

84

Business Scenario

Enhance the payroll report by adding titles, footnotes, and descriptive column headings.

85

Displaying Titles and Footnotes

Use TITLE and FOOTNOTE statements to enhance the report.

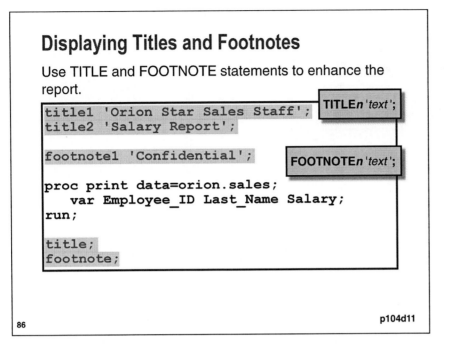

```
title1 'Orion Star Sales Staff';
title2 'Salary Report';

footnote1 'Confidential';

proc print data=orion.sales;
   var Employee_ID Last_Name Salary;
run;

title;
footnote;
```

TITLEn '*text*';

FOOTNOTEn '*text*';

86   p104d11

Viewing the Output

Partial PROC PRINT Output

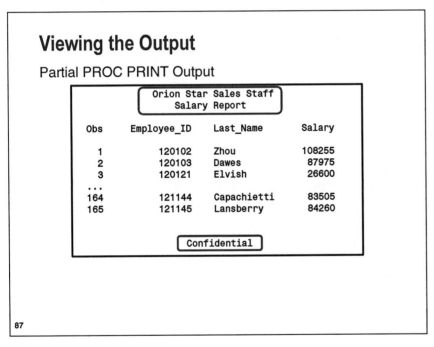

```
              Orion Star Sales Staff
                   Salary Report

   Obs    Employee_ID    Last_Name       Salary

    1        120102       Zhou           108255
    2        120103       Dawes           87975
    3        120121       Elvish          26600
   ...
   164       121144       Capachietti     83505
   165       121145       Lansberry       84260


                    Confidential
```

87

TITLE Statement

The global *TITLE statement* specifies title lines
for SAS output.

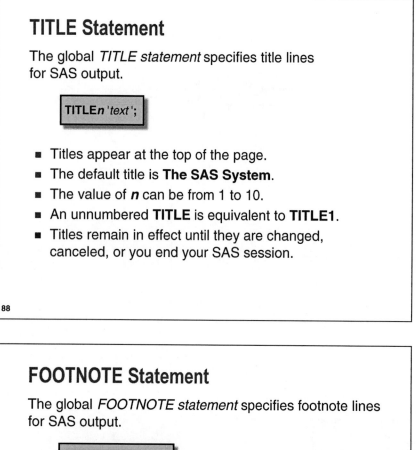

TITLE*n* '*text*';

- Titles appear at the top of the page.
- The default title is **The SAS System**.
- The value of *n* can be from 1 to 10.
- An unnumbered **TITLE** is equivalent to **TITLE1**.
- Titles remain in effect until they are changed,
  canceled, or you end your SAS session.

88

FOOTNOTE Statement

The global *FOOTNOTE statement* specifies footnote lines
for SAS output.

FOOTNOTE*n* '*text*';

- Footnotes appear at the bottom of the page.
- No footnote is printed unless one is specified.
- The value of *n* can be from 1 to 10.
- An unnumbered **FOOTNOTE** is equivalent
  to **FOOTNOTE1**.
- Footnotes remain in effect until they are changed,
  canceled, or you end your SAS session.

89

Changing Titles and Footnotes

To change a title line, submit a TITLE statement with the same number but different text.

- This replaces a previous title with the same number.
- It cancels all titles with higher numbers.

```
title1 'ABC Company';
title2 'Sales Division';
title3 'Salary Report';

title1 'Salary Report';
```

This statement changes title 1 and cancels titles 2 and 3.

Footnotes are changed the same way.

90

Canceling All Titles and Footnotes

- The null TITLE statement cancels all titles.
```
title;
```

- The null FOOTNOTE statement cancels all footnotes.
```
footnote;
```

91

Changing and Canceling Titles and Footnotes

PROC PRINT Code	Resultant Title(s)

```title1 'The First Line';```
 ```title2 'The Second Line';```
 ```proc print data=orion.sales;```
 ```run;```
	The First Line
	 The Second Line

```title2 'The Next Line';```
 ```proc print data=orion.sales;```
 ```run;```
	The First Line
	 The Next Line

```title 'The Top Line';```
 ```proc print data=orion.sales;```
 ```run;```
	The Top Line

```title3 'The Third Line';```
 ```proc print data=orion.sales;```
 ```run;```
	The Top Line
	
	 The Third Line

```title;```
 ```proc print data=orion.sales;```
 ```run;```	

102

4.08 Short Answer Poll

Which footnote or footnotes appear in the second procedure output?

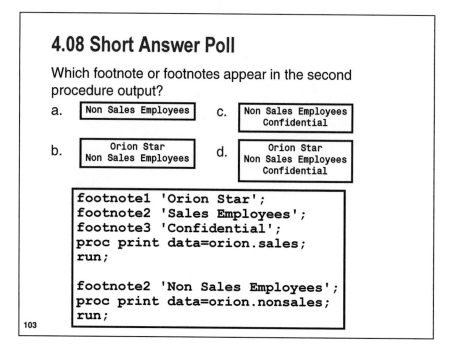

a. Non Sales Employees

c. Non Sales Employees
 Confidential

b. Orion Star
 Non Sales Employees

d. Orion Star
 Non Sales Employees
 Confidential

```
footnote1 'Orion Star';
footnote2 'Sales Employees';
footnote3 'Confidential';
proc print data=orion.sales;
run;

footnote2 'Non Sales Employees';
proc print data=orion.nonsales;
run;
```

103

Idea Exchange

Which of the following programs do you prefer and why?

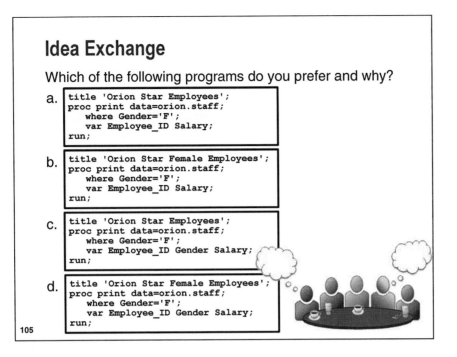

a.
```
title 'Orion Star Employees';
proc print data=orion.staff;
   where Gender='F';
   var Employee_ID Salary;
run;
```

b.
```
title 'Orion Star Female Employees';
proc print data=orion.staff;
   where Gender='F';
   var Employee_ID Salary;
run;
```

c.
```
title 'Orion Star Employees';
proc print data=orion.staff;
   where Gender='F';
   var Employee_ID Gender Salary;
run;
```

d.
```
title 'Orion Star Female Employees';
proc print data=orion.staff;
   where Gender='F';
   var Employee_ID Gender Salary;
run;
```

105

LABEL Statement and Option

Use a LABEL statement and the LABEL option to display descriptive column headings instead of variable names.

```
title1 'Orion Star Sales Staff';
title2 'Salary Report';
footnote1 'Confidential';

proc print data=orion.sales label;
   var Employee_ID Last_Name Salary;
   label Employee_ID='Sales ID'
         Last_Name='Last Name'
         Salary='Annual Salary';
run;

title;
footnote;
```

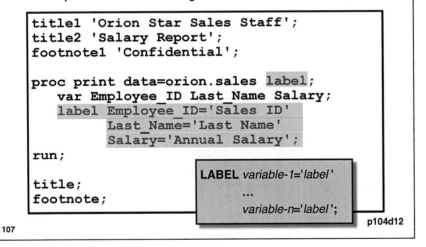

LABEL *variable-1='label'*
    ...
    variable-n='label';

p104d12

107

LABEL Statement

The LABEL statement assigns descriptive labels
to variables.

- A label can be up to 256 characters and include
  any characters, including blanks.
- Labels are used automatically by many procedures.
- The PRINT procedure uses labels only
  when the LABEL or SPLIT= option is specified.

108

Viewing the Output

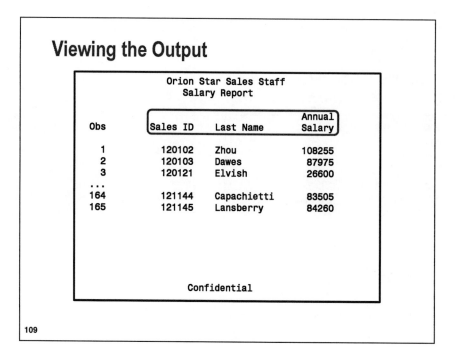

109

SPLIT= Option

The SPLIT= option in PROC PRINT specifies a split character to control line breaks in column headings.

```
proc print data=orion.sales split='*';
   var Employee_ID Last_Name Salary;
   label Employee_ID='Sales ID'
         Last_Name='Last*Name'
         Salary='Annual*Salary';
run;
```

SPLIT='*split-character*'*

The SPLIT= option can be used instead of the LABEL option in a PROC PRINT step.

110   p104d13

Viewing the Output

Partial PROC PRINT Output

```
              Orion Star Sales Staff
                  Salary Report

                           Last        Annual
   Obs     Sales ID        Name        Salary

    1       120102      Zhou          108255
    2       120103      Dawes          87975
    3       120121      Elvish         26600
   ...
   164      121144      Capachietti    83505
   165      121145      Lansberry      84260




                   Confidential
```

111

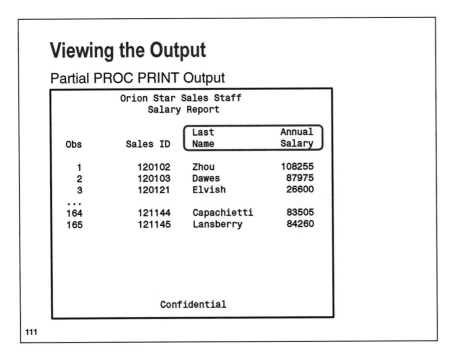

Exercises

If you restarted your SAS session since the last exercise, open and submit the **libname.sas** program that can be found in the data folder.

Level 1

9. Displaying Titles and Footnotes in a Detail Report

    a. Open and submit **p104e09** to display all observations for Australian Sales Rep IVs

    b. Add a VAR statement to display only the variables shown in the report below.

    c. Add TITLE and FOOTNOTE statements to include the titles and footnotes shown in the report below.

    d. Submit the program and verify the output. The results contain five observations as shown below.

    e. Submit a null TITLE and null FOOTNOTE statement to clear all titles and footnotes.

```
                    Australian Sales Employees
                  Senior Sales Representatives


                          First_
         Obs    Employee_ID    Name      Last_Name     Gender     Salary

          7        120125     Fong       Hofmeister       M        32040
         10        120128     Monica     Kletschkus       F        30890
         17        120135     Alexei     Platts           M        32490
         41        120159     Lynelle    Phoumirath       F        30765
         48        120166     Fadi       Nowd             M        30660


                       Job_Title: Sales Rep. IV
```

10. Displaying Column Headings in a Detail Report

    a. Open and submit **p104e10**. Modify the program to define and use the following labels:

Variable	Label
Employee_ID	Employee ID
First_Name	First Name
Last_Name	Last Name
Salary	Annual Salary

Submit the program and verify the output.

```
              Entry-level Sales Representatives


                                             Annual
       Employee ID    First Name   Last Name   Gender    Salary

           121023     Shawn        Fuller        M        26010
           121028     William      Smades        M        26585
           121029     Kuo-Chung    Mcelwee       M        27225
      ...
           121138     Hershell     Tolley        M        27265
           121140     Saunders     Briggi        M        26335


                    Job_Title: Sales Rep. I
```

b. Modify the program to use a blank space as the SPLIT= character to generate two-line column headings. Submit the modified program and verify that two-line column labels are displayed.

```
                    Entry-level Sales Representatives

        Employee    First        Last                     Annual
              ID    Name         Name        Gender       Salary

          121023    Shawn        Fuller         M          26010
          121028    William      Smades         M          26585
          121029    Kuo-Chung    Mcelwee        M          27225
          ...
          121138    Hershell     Tolley         M          27265
          121140    Saunders     Briggi         M          26335

                        Job_Title: Sales Rep. I
```

Level 2

11. Writing an Enhanced Detail Report

a. Write a program to display a subset of **orion.employee_addresses** as shown below. The program should sort the observations by **State**, **City**, and **Employee_Name** and then display the sorted observations grouped by **State**. The resulting report should contain 311 observations.

```
                        US Employees by State

        -------------------------- State=CA --------------------------

        Employee                                          Zip
              ID    Name                        City      Code

          120656    Amos, Salley             San Diego    92116
          120759    Apr, Nishan              San Diego    92071
          121017    Arizmendi, Gilbert       San Diego    91950
          121062    Armant, Debra            San Diego    92025
          121049    Bataineh, Perrior        San Diego    92126
          ...
```

4.4 Solutions

Solutions to Exercises

1. Displaying orion.order_fact with the PRINT Procedure

```
proc print data=orion.order_fact noobs;
   where Total_Retail_Price>500;
   id Customer_ID;
   var Order_ID Order_Type Quantity Total_Retail_Price;
   sum Total_Retail_Price;
run;
```

a. Run the program and view the output.

b. Add a SUM statement and verify the resulting sum.

c. What do you notice about the Obs column? **The numbers are not sequential. The original observation numbers are displayed.**

Did the sum of **Total_Retail Price** change to reflect only the subset? **Yes**

d. If the Obs column is suppressed, how can you verify the number of observations in the results? **Check the log.**

e. When the ID statement was added, how did the output change? **Customer_ID is the leftmost column and is displayed on each line for an observation.**

f. When the VAR statement is added, what do you notice about **Customer_ID**? **There are two Customer_ID columns. The first column is the ID field, and a second one is included because Customer_ID is listed in the VAR statement.**

g. Remove the duplicate column by removing **Customer_ID** from the VAR statement.

2. **Displaying orion.customer_dim with the PRINT Procedure**

```
proc print data=orion.customer_dim noobs;
   where Customer_Age between 30 and 40;
   id Customer_ID;
   var Customer_Name Customer_Age Customer_Type;
run;
```

3. **Producing a Default Listing Report of orion.order_fact (SAS Windowing Environment)**

```
options ls=max;

proc print data=orion.order_fact;
run;

options ls=96;

proc print data=orion.order_fact headings=v;
run;
```

a. Submit a simple PROC PRINT step to produce a default listing report.

b. What are the minimum and maximum values for the LINESIZE= option? **The minimum value for LINESIZE= is 64 and the maximum size is MAX.**

When you are finished, use the following statement to reset the line size to 96:
```
options ls=96;
```

c. How do you specify vertical headings? **HEADINGS=V forces all column headings to be displayed vertically.**

How do you specify horizontal headings? **HEADINGS=H forces all column headings to be displayed horizontally.**

4. **Producing a Default Listing Report of orion.product_dim (SAS Windowing Environment)**

```
proc print data=orion.product_dim width=uniform;
run;
```

a. Submit a simple PROC PRINT step.

b. Add the WIDTH=UNIFORM option. How are the results different? **Each column has the same column width on each page.**

c. Why might the procedure run more slowly with this option? **With this option, PROC PRINT must read through the entire data set twice.**

d. How can you save computer resources and still display columns consistently across pages? **Use a format on every column to explicitly specify a field width so that PROC PRINT reads the data only once.**

5. **Sorting orion.employee_payroll and Displaying the New Data Set**

```
proc sort data=orion.employee_payroll out=work.sort_salary;
   by Salary;
run;

proc print data=work.sort_salary;
run;
```

6. **Sorting orion.employee_payroll and Displaying Grouped Observations**

```
proc sort data=orion.employee_payroll out=work.sort_salary2;
   by Employee_Gender descending Salary;
run;

proc print data=work.sort_salary2;
   by Employee_Gender;
run;
```

7. **Sorting orion.employee_payroll and Displaying a Subset of the New Data Set**

```
proc sort data=orion.employee_payroll out=work.sort_sal;
   by Employee_Gender descending Salary;
run;

proc print data=work.sort_sal noobs;
   by Employee_Gender;
   sum Salary;
   where Employee_Term_Date is missing and Salary>65000;
   var Employee_ID Salary Marital_Status;
run;
```

8. **Retaining the First Observation of Each BY Group**

```
proc sort data=orion.orders out=work.custorders nodupkey
          dupout=work.duplicates;
   by Customer_ID;
run;

title 'Unique Customers';
proc print data=work.custorders;
run;

title 'Duplicate Customer Observations';
proc print data=work.duplicates;
run;
title;
```

9. Displaying Titles and Footnotes in a Detail Report

```
title1 'Australian Sales Employees';
title2 'Senior Sales Representatives';
footnote1 'Job_Title: Sales Rep. IV';

proc print data=orion.sales;
   where Country='AU' and Job_Title contains 'Rep. IV';
   var Employee_ID First_Name Last_Name Gender Salary;
run;
title;
footnote;
```

10. Displaying Column Headings in a Detail Report

a.

```
title 'Entry-level Sales Representatives';
footnote 'Job_Title: Sales Rep. I';

proc print data=orion.sales noobs label;
   where Country='US' and Job_Title='Sales Rep. I';
   var Employee_ID First_Name Last_Name Gender Salary;
   label Employee_ID="Employee ID"
         First_Name="First Name"
         Last_Name="Last Name"
         Salary="Annual Salary";
run;

title;
footnote;
```

b.

```
title 'Entry-level Sales Representatives';
footnote 'Job_Title: Sales Rep. I';

proc print data=orion.sales noobs split=' ';
   where Country='US' and Job_Title='Sales Rep. I';
   var Employee_ID First_Name Last_Name Gender Salary;
   label Employee_ID="Employee ID"
         First_Name="First Name"
         Last_Name="Last Name"
         Salary="Annual Salary";
run;

title;
footnote;
```

11. Writing an Enhanced Detail Report

```
proc sort data=orion.employee_addresses out=work.address;
   where Country='US';
   by State City Employee_Name;
run;

title "US Employees by State";
proc print data=work.address noobs split=' ';
   var Employee_ID Employee_Name City Postal_Code;
   label Employee_ID='Employee ID'
         Employee_Name='Name'
         Postal_Code='Zip Code';
   by State;
run;
```

Solutions to Student Activities (Polls/Quizzes)

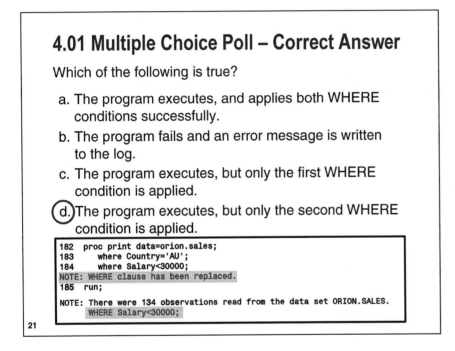

4.01 Multiple Choice Poll – Correct Answer

Which of the following is true?

a. The program executes, and applies both WHERE conditions successfully.

b. The program fails and an error message is written to the log.

c. The program executes, but only the first WHERE condition is applied.

d. The program executes, but only the second WHERE condition is applied.

```
182  proc print data=orion.sales;
183     where Country='AU';
184     where Salary<30000;
NOTE: WHERE clause has been replaced.
185  run;

NOTE: There were 134 observations read from the data set ORION.SALES.
      WHERE Salary<30000;
```

21

4.02 Short Answer Poll – Correct Answer

Which WHERE statement correctly subsets the numeric values for May, June, or July and missing character names?

a.
```
where Month in (5-7)
      and Names=.;
```

(b.)
```
where Month in (5,6,7)
      and Names=' ';
```

c.
```
where Month in ('5','6','7')
      and Names='.';
```

27

4.03 Short Answer Poll – Correct Answer

Open **p104a01b**. Change WHERE SAME AND to WHERE ALSO. Submit the program and view the log.

What message is written to the log?

```
27    proc print data=orion.sales;
28        where Country='AU'  and Salary<30000;
29        where also Gender='F';
NOTE: WHERE clause has been augmented.
30        var First_Name Last_Name Gender Salary Country;
31    run;

NOTE: There were 23 observations read from the data set ORION.SALES.
      WHERE (Country='AU') and (Gender='F') and (Salary<30000);
```

WHERE ALSO results in the same message:
   WHERE clause has been augmented.

40

4.04 Short Answer Poll – Correct Answer

Which WHERE statement returns all the observations that have a first name starting with the letter M for the given values?

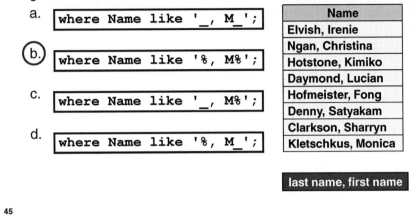

a.
```
where Name like '_, M_';
```

b. (circled)
```
where Name like '%, M%';
```

c.
```
where Name like '_, M%';
```

d.
```
where Name like '%, M_';
```

Name
Elvish, Irenie
Ngan, Christina
Hotstone, Kimiko
Daymond, Lucian
Hofmeister, Fong
Denny, Satyakam
Clarkson, Sharryn
Kletschkus, Monica

last name, first name

45

4.05 Short Answer Poll – Correct Answer

Which step sorts the observations in a SAS data set and overwrites the same data set?

a.
```
proc sort data=work.EmpsAU
          out=work.sorted;
   by First;
run;
```

b.
```
proc sort data=orion.EmpsAU
          out=EmpsAU;
   by First;
run;
```

c. (circled)
```
proc sort data=work.EmpsAU;
   by First;
run;
```

64

4.06 Short Answer Poll – Correct Answer

Open and submit **p104a02**. View the log. Why did the program fail?

The input data set was not sorted by Gender.

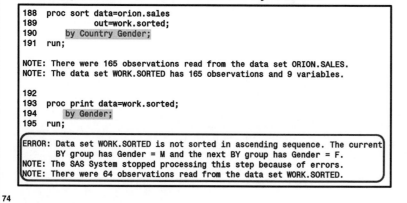

```
188   proc sort data=orion.sales
189         out=work.sorted;
190      by Country Gender;
191   run;

NOTE: There were 165 observations read from the data set ORION.SALES.
NOTE: The data set WORK.SORTED has 165 observations and 9 variables.

192
193   proc print data=work.sorted;
194      by Gender;
195   run;

ERROR: Data set WORK.SORTED is not sorted in ascending sequence. The current
       BY group has Gender = M and the next BY group has Gender = F.
NOTE: The SAS System stopped processing this step because of errors.
NOTE: There were 64 observations read from the data set WORK.SORTED.
```

74

4.07 Multiple Choice Poll – Correct Answer

Which WHERE statement (or statements) results in the most efficient processing?

a. The WHERE statement in the PROC SORT step.
b. The WHERE statement in the PROC PRINT step.
c. Both WHERE statements are needed.
d. The WHERE statements are equally efficient.

Subsetting in PROC SORT is more efficient. It selects and sorts only the required observations.

⚠ **Be sure to use the OUT= option when you subset in PROC SORT or you will overwrite your original data set with the subset.**

80   p104a03s

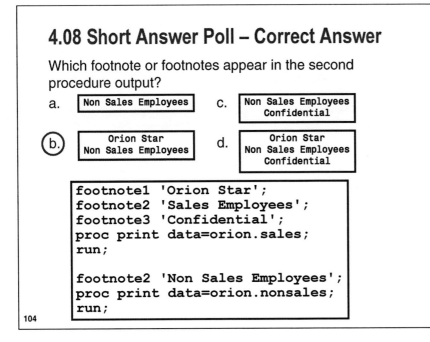

4.08 Short Answer Poll – Correct Answer

Which footnote or footnotes appear in the second procedure output?

a. Non Sales Employees

c. Non Sales Employees / Confidential

b. Orion Star / Non Sales Employees ✓

d. Orion Star / Non Sales Employees / Confidential

```
footnote1 'Orion Star';
footnote2 'Sales Employees';
footnote3 'Confidential';
proc print data=orion.sales;
run;

footnote2 'Non Sales Employees';
proc print data=orion.nonsales;
run;
```

104

Chapter 5   Formatting Data Values

5.1 Using SAS Formats

Objectives

- Describe SAS formats.
- Apply SAS formats with the FORMAT statement.

3

Business Scenario

Enhance the appearance of variable values in reports.

Last_Name	First_Name	Country	Job_Title	Salary	Hire_Date
Zhou	Tom	AU	Sales Manager	108255	12205
Dawes	Wilson	AU	Sales Manager	87975	6575
Elvish	Irenie	AU	Sales Rep. II	26600	6575

Last_Name	First_Name	Country	Job_Title	Salary	Hire_Date
Zhou	Tom	AU	Sales Manager	$108,255	06/01/1993
Dawes	Wilson	AU	Sales Manager	$87,975	01/01/1978
Elvish	Irenie	AU	Sales Rep. II	$26,600	01/01/1978

4

SAS Formats

SAS formats can be used in a PROC step to change how values are displayed in a report.

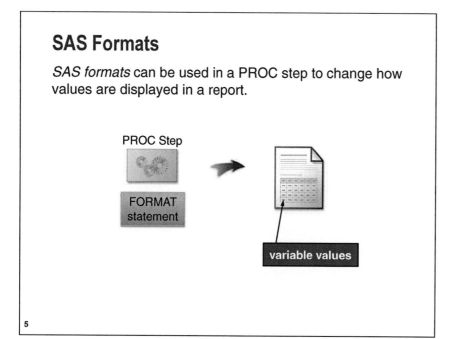

5

FORMAT Statement

The *FORMAT statement* associates a format with a variable.

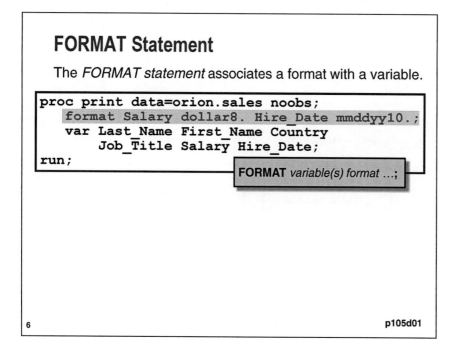

```
proc print data=orion.sales noobs;
   format Salary dollar8. Hire_Date mmddyy10.;
   var Last_Name First_Name Country
       Job_Title Salary Hire_Date;
run;
```

FORMAT *variable(s) format ...;*

6   **p105d01**

Viewing the Output

Partial PROC PRINT Output

```
            First_
Last_Name   Name       Country  Job_Title        Salary    Hire_Date

Zhou        Tom        AU       Sales Manager   $108,255   06/01/1993
Dawes       Wilson     AU       Sales Manager    $87,975   01/01/1978
Elvish      Irenie     AU       Sales Rep. II    $26,600   01/01/1978
Ngan        Christina  AU       Sales Rep. II    $27,475   07/01/1982
Hotstone    Kimiko     AU       Sales Rep. I     $26,190   10/01/1989
```

DOLLAR8.   **MMDDYY10.**

7

What Is a Format?

A *format* is an instruction to write data values.

- A format changes the appearance of a variable's value in a report.
- The values stored in the data set are **not** changed.

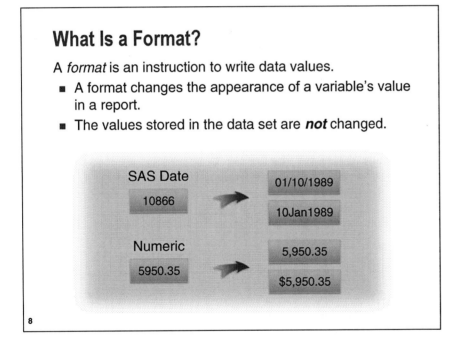

8

SAS Formats

SAS formats have the following form:

> <$>format<w>.<d>

$	Indicates a character format.
format	Names the SAS format.
w	Specifies the total format width, including decimal places and special characters.
.	Is required syntax. Formats always contain a period (.) as part of the name.
d	Specifies the number of decimal places to display in numeric formats.

9

SAS Formats

Selected SAS formats:

Format	Definition
$w.	Writes standard character data.
w.D	Writes standard numeric data.
COMMAw.d	Writes numeric values with a comma that separates every three digits and a period that separates the decimal fraction.
DOLLARw.d	Writes numeric values with a leading dollar sign, a comma that separates every three digits, and a period that separates the decimal fraction.
COMMAXw.d	Writes numeric values with a period that separates every three digits and a comma that separates the decimal fraction.
EUROXw.d	Writes numeric values with a leading euro symbol (€), a period that separates every three digits, and a comma that separates the decimal fraction.

10

SAS Format Examples

Selected SAS formats:

Format	Stored Value	Displayed Value
$4.	Programming	Prog
12.	27134.5864	27135
12.2	27134.5864	27134.59
COMMA12.2	27134.5864	27,134.59
DOLLAR12.2	27134.5864	$27,134.59
COMMAX12.2	27134.5864	27.134,59
EUROX12.2	27134.5864	€27.134,59

11

SAS Format Examples

If the format width is not large enough to accommodate a numeric value, the displayed value is automatically adjusted to fit the width.

Format	Stored Value	Displayed Value
DOLLAR12.2	27134.5864	$27,134.59
DOLLAR9.2	27134.5864	$27134.59
DOLLAR8.2	27134.5864	27134.59
DOLLAR5.2	27134.5864	27135
DOLLAR4.2	27134.5864	27E3

12

One aspect of the adjustment is rounding.

5.01 Short Answer Poll

Use SAS documentation or the SAS Help Facility
to explore the Z$w.d$ numeric format. What is it used for?

Hint: Search for Z$w.d$ or explore "Formats by Category."

13

SAS Date Format Examples

SAS date formats display SAS date values in standard
date forms.

Format	Stored Value	Displayed Value
MMDDYY10.	0	01/01/1960
MMDDYY8.	0	01/01/60
MMDDYY6.	0	010160
DDMMYY10.	365	31/12/1960
DDMMYY8.	365	31/12/60
DDMMYY6.	365	311260

15

SAS Date Format Examples

Additional date formats:

Format	Stored Value	Displayed Value
DATE7.	-1	31DEC59
DATE9.	-1	31DEC1959
WORDDATE.	0	January 1, 1960
WEEKDATE.	0	Friday, January 1, 1960
MONYY7.	0	JAN1960
YEAR4.	0	1960

16

5.02 Short Answer Poll

Which FORMAT statement creates the output shown below?

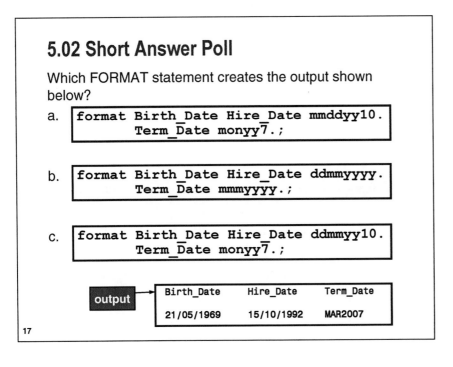

a.
```
format Birth_Date Hire_Date mmddyy10.
       Term_Date monyy7.;
```

b.
```
format Birth_Date Hire_Date ddmmyyyy.
       Term_Date mmmyyyy.;
```

c.
```
format Birth_Date Hire_Date ddmmyy10.
       Term_Date monyy7.;
```

```
output →   Birth_Date   Hire_Date   Term_Date

           21/05/1969   15/10/1992  MAR2007
```

17

Format	Locale	Example
NLDATEw.	English_UnitedStates	January 01, 1960
	German_Germany	01. Januar 1960
NLDATEMNw.	English_UnitedStates	January
	German_Germany	Januar
NLDATEWw.	English_UnitedStates	Fri, Jan 01, 60
	German_Germany	Fr, 01. Jan 60
NLDATEWNw.	English_UnitedStates	Friday
	German_Germany	Freitag

National Language Support (NLS) enables a software product to function properly in every global market for which the product is targeted. SAS contains NLS features to ensure that SAS applications conform to local language conventions.

NLS date formats convert SAS date values to a locale-sensitive date string. The LOCALE= system option is used to specify the locale, which reflects the local conventions, language, and culture of a geographical region. For example, a locale value of *English_Canada* represents the country of Canada with a language of English. A locale value of *French_Canada* represents the country of Canada with a language of French.

The LOCALE= system option can be specified in a configuration file, at SAS invocation, or in the OPTIONS statement. For more information, refer to *SAS® 9.3 National Language Support Reference Guide* in the SAS documentation.

 Exercises

If you restarted your SAS session since the last exercise, open and submit the **libname.sas** program, which can be found in the data folder.

Level 1

1. **Displaying Formatted Values in a Detail Report**

   a. Open **p105e01** and submit it. Review the output.

   b. Modify the PROC PRINT step to display only **Employee_ID**, **Salary**, **Birth_Date**, and **Employee_Hire_Date**.

   c. Add a FORMAT statement to display **Salary** in a DOLLAR format, **Birth_Date** in the 01/31/2012 date style, and **Employee_Hire_Date** in the 01JAN2012 date style, as shown in the report below.

```
                                        Employee_
     Obs     Employee_ID     Salary     Birth_Date     Hire_Date

       1        120101    $163,040.00   08/18/1980    01JUL2007
       2        120102    $108,255.00   08/11/1973    01JUN1993
       3        120103     $87,975.00   01/22/1953    01JAN1978
     ...
     423        121147     $29,145.00   05/28/1973    01SEP1991
     424        121148     $52,930.00   01/01/1973    01JAN2002
```

Level 2

2. Displaying Formatted Values in a Detail Report

Write a PROC PRINT step to display the report below using **orion.sales** as input. Subset the observations and variables to produce the report. Include titles, labels, and formats. The results contain 13 observations.

```
                              US Sales Employees
                             Earning Under $26,000

                       First                                         Date
     Employee_ID       Name       Last Name      Title      Salary    Hired

          121036      Teresa      Mesley      Sales Rep. I   $25,965   OCT2007
          121038      David       Anstey      Sales Rep. I   $25,285   AUG2010
          121044      Ray         Abbott      Sales Rep. I   $25,660   AUG1979
          ...
          121106      James       Hilburger   Sales Rep. I   $25,880   FEB2000
          121108      Libby       Levi        Sales Rep. I   $25,930   NOV2010
```

Challenge

3. Exploring Formats by Category

Display **orion.sales** as shown in the report below. Refer to SAS Help or product documentation to explore the **Dictionary of Formats** and investigate **Formats by Category**. Identify and use the character format that displays values in uppercase and a format that displays a character value in quotation marks. The results contain 165 observations.

```
                   First_
     Employee_ID   Name        Last_Name      Job_Title

          120102   TOM         ZHOU          "Sales Manager"
          120103   WILSON      DAWES         "Sales Manager"
          120121   IRENIE      ELVISH        "Sales Rep. II"
          ...
          121144   RENEE       CAPACHIETTI   "Sales Manager"
          121145   DENNIS      LANSBERRY     "Sales Manager"
```

5.2 User-Defined Formats

Objectives

- Use the FORMAT procedure to create user-defined formats.
- Use a FORMAT statement to apply user-defined formats in a report.
- Use formats to recode data values.
- Use formats to collapse or aggregate data.

22

Business Scenario

Display country names instead of country codes in a report.

Current Report (partial output)

Obs	Employee_ID	Salary	Country	Birth_ Date	Hire_ Date
1	120102	$108,255	AU	AUG1973	JUN1993
2	120103	$87,975	AU	JAN1953	JAN1978
3	120121	$26,600	AU	AUG1948	JAN1978

Desired Report (partial output)

Obs	Employee_ID	Salary	Country	Birth_ Date	Hire_ Date
1	120102	$108,255	Australia	AUG1973	JUN1993
2	120103	$87,975	Australia	JAN1953	JAN1978
3	120121	$26,600	Australia	AUG1948	JAN1978

23   p105d02

User-Defined Formats: Part 1

Use PROC FORMAT to create a user-defined format.

```
proc format;
   value $ctryfmt   'AU'='Australia'
                    'US'='United States'
                    other='Miscoded';
run;
```

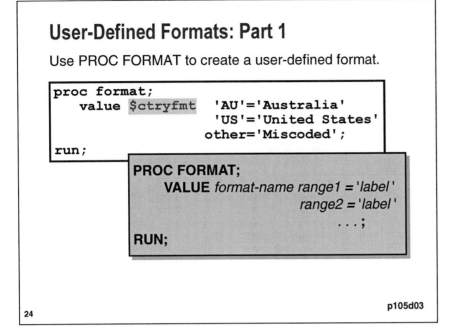

```
PROC FORMAT;
   VALUE format-name range1 = 'label'
                     range2 = 'label'
                              . . . ;
RUN;
```

24   p105d03

User-Defined Formats: Part 2

Use a FORMAT statement in the PROC PRINT step
to apply the format to a specific variable.

```
proc print data=orion.sales;
   var Employee_ID Salary Country
       Birth_Date Hire_Date;
   format Salary dollar10.
          Birth_Date Hire_Date monyy7.
          Country $ctryfmt.;
run;
```

25   p105d03

Viewing the Output

Partial PROC PRINT Output

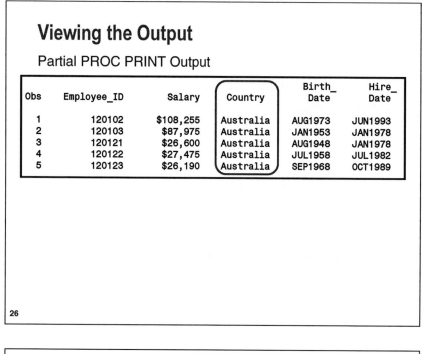

Obs	Employee_ID	Salary	Country	Birth_Date	Hire_Date
1	120102	$108,255	Australia	AUG1973	JUN1993
2	120103	$87,975	Australia	JAN1953	JAN1978
3	120121	$26,600	Australia	AUG1948	JAN1978
4	120122	$27,475	Australia	JUL1958	JUL1982
5	120123	$26,190	Australia	SEP1968	OCT1989

26

VALUE Statement

```
VALUE format-name range1='label'
                   range2='label'
                   . . . ;
```

A format name

- can be up to 32 characters in length
- for character formats, must begin with a dollar sign ($), followed by a letter or underscore
- for numeric formats, must begin with a letter or underscore
- cannot end in a number
- cannot be given the name of a SAS format
- cannot include a period in the VALUE statement.

27

VALUE Statement

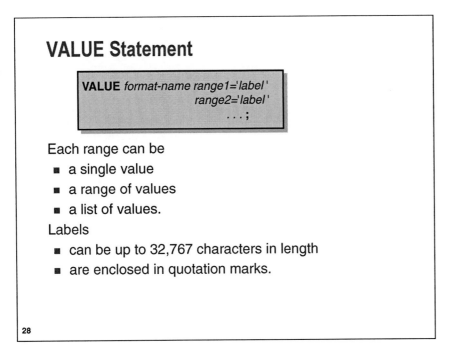

Each range can be
- a single value
- a range of values
- a list of values.

Labels
- can be up to 32,767 characters in length
- are enclosed in quotation marks.

28

Enclosing labels in quotation marks is a best practice, and it is required if a label contains internal blanks.

5.03 Multiple Answer Poll

Which names are invalid for user-defined formats?

a. $stfmt
b. $3levels
c. _4years
d. salranges
e. dollar

29

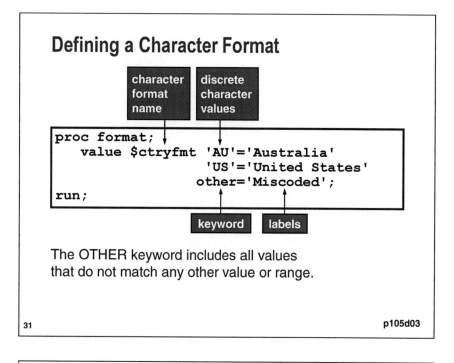

Defining a Character Format

```
proc format;
    value $ctryfmt 'AU'='Australia'
                   'US'='United States'
                   other='Miscoded';
run;
```

The OTHER keyword includes all values
that do not match any other value or range.

p105d03

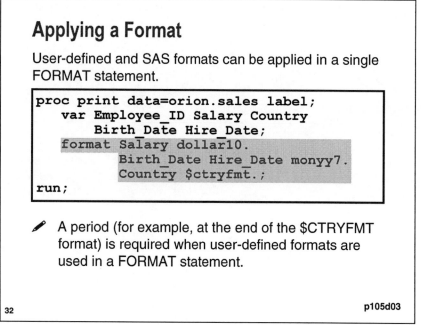

Applying a Format

User-defined and SAS formats can be applied in a single
FORMAT statement.

```
proc print data=orion.sales label;
    var Employee_ID Salary Country
        Birth_Date Hire_Date;
    format Salary dollar10.
           Birth_Date Hire_Date monyy7.
           Country $ctryfmt.;
run;
```

✎   A period (for example, at the end of the $CTRYFMT
    format) is required when user-defined formats are
    used in a FORMAT statement.

p105d03

Idea Exchange

The formatting examples shown in this section are sometimes referred to as *translating values*.

Can you give an example of where this type of application might be useful?

33

Business Scenario

An Orion Star manager wants a report that shows employee salaries collapsed into three user-defined groups or tiers.

Current Report

Obs	Employee_ID	Last_Name	Salary
1	120102	Zhou	108255
2	120103	Dawes	87975
3	120121	Elvish	26600
4	120122	Ngan	27475

Desired Report

Obs	Employee_ID	Last_Name	Salary
1	120102	Zhou	Tier 3
2	120103	Dawes	Tier 2
3	120121	Elvish	Tier 1
4	120122	Ngan	Tier 1

35

Specifying Ranges of Values

Use PROC FORMAT to specify the salary range
for each tier.

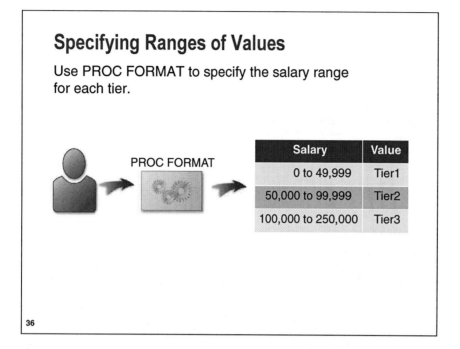

Salary	Value
0 to 49,999	Tier1
50,000 to 99,999	Tier2
100,000 to 250,000	Tier3

36

Defining a Numeric Format

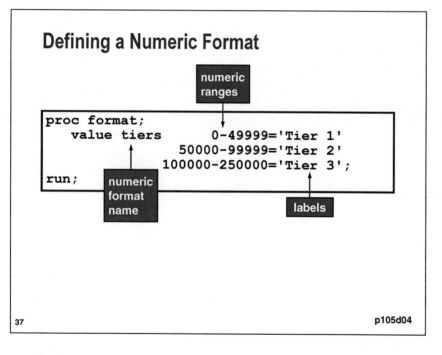

```
proc format;
    value tiers       0-49999='Tier 1'
               50000-99999='Tier 2'
             100000-250000='Tier 3';
run;
```

numeric
ranges

numeric
format
name

labels

37   p105d04

Defining and Using a Numeric Format

p105d04

This demonstration illustrates the use of a user-defined numeric format.

```
proc format;
   value tiers      0-49999 ='Tier 1'
                50000-99999 ='Tier 2'
                100000-250000='Tier 3';
run;

data work.salaries;
   input Name $ Salary;
   Original_Salary=Salary;
   datalines;
Abi 50000
Mike 65000
Jose 50000.00
Joe 37000.50
Ursula 142000
Lu 49999.99
;

proc print data=work.salaries;
   format Salary tiers.;
run;
```

1. Program **p105d04** includes a PROC FORMAT step to create the TIERS format. The DATA step reads data lines within the program to create a data set that contains names and salaries. The PROC PRINT step displays the new data set, and applies the TIERS format. In the program, notice that **Salary** is assigned to **Original_Salary** so that both can be included in the report. (The assignment statement is discussed in a later chapter.)

2. Look at the data values and predict what label should be displayed when the TIERS format is applied to **Salary**. Lu's salary falls within a "gap."

Name	Salary	Coded Salary
Abi	50000	
Mike	65000	
Jose	50000.00	
Joe	37000.50	
Ursula	142000	
Lu	49999.99	

3. Submit the program. What **Salary** value is displayed for Lu? _____

When a value does not match any of the ranges, PROC PRINT attempts to display the actual value. In this case, the column width was determined by the width of the formatted values, which is 6. As mentioned earlier, if the format width is not large enough to accommodate a numeric value, the displayed value is automatically adjusted to fit in the width. What can you do to correct this?

4. Specify a width of 8 in the TIERS format in the FORMAT statement and resubmit the program.

```
proc print data=work.salaries;
   format Salary tiers8.;
run;
```

Now what **Salary** value is displayed for Lu? _____

Defining a Continuous Range

The less than (<) symbol excludes the endpoint
from a range, which enables a continuous range.

- Put < after the starting value in a range to exclude it.
- Put < before the ending value in a range to exclude it.

Range	Starting Value	Ending Value
50000 - 100000	Includes 50000	Includes 100000
50000 - < 100000	Includes 50000	Excludes 100000
50000 < - 100000	Excludes 50000	Includes 100000
50000 < - < 100000	Excludes 50000	Excludes 100000

39

The < symbol is used to define an exclusive range. The > symbol is not permitted in a VALUE statement.

5.04 Short Answer Poll

How is a value of *50000* displayed if the TIERS format
below is applied to the value?

a. Tier 1
b. Tier 2
c. 50000
d. a missing value

```
proc format;
   value tiers   20000-<50000 ='Tier 1'
                 50000-<100000='Tier 2'
                 100000-250000='Tier 3';
run;
```

40   p105d05

LOW and HIGH Keywords

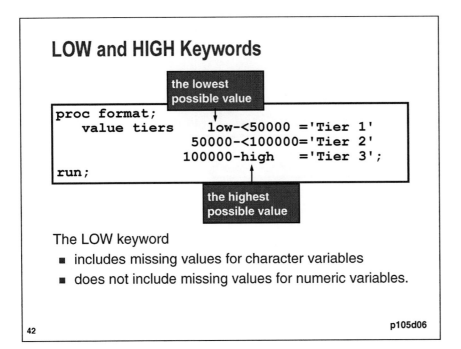

The LOW keyword

- includes missing values for character variables
- does not include missing values for numeric variables.

42   p105d06

Applying a Numeric Format

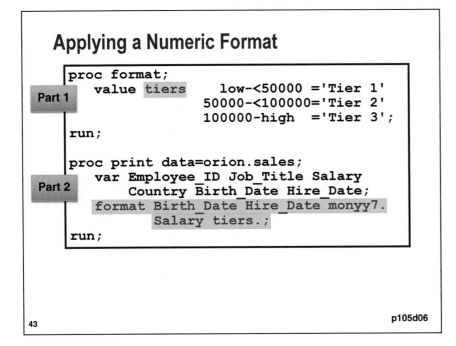

43   p105d06

Viewing the Output

Partial PROC PRINT Output

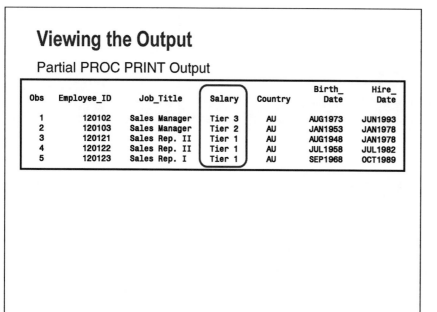

Obs	Employee_ID	Job_Title	Salary	Country	Birth_Date	Hire_Date
1	120102	Sales Manager	Tier 3	AU	AUG1973	JUN1993
2	120103	Sales Manager	Tier 2	AU	JAN1953	JAN1978
3	120121	Sales Rep. II	Tier 1	AU	AUG1948	JAN1978
4	120122	Sales Rep. II	Tier 1	AU	JUL1958	JUL1982
5	120123	Sales Rep. I	Tier 1	AU	SEP1968	OCT1989

44

User-Defined Format Example

Ranges can be specified using lists, ranges, discrete values, and keywords.

```
proc format;
   value mnthfmt 1,2,3='Qtr 1'
                 4-6='Qtr 2'
                 7-9='Qtr 3'
                 10-12='Qtr 4'
                    .='missing'
                 other='unknown';
run;
```

45

Multiple User-Defined Formats

Multiple VALUE statements can be included in a single PROC FORMAT step.

```
proc format;
   value $ctryfmt   'AU'='Australia'
                    'US'='United States'
                    other='Miscoded';

   value tiers      low-<50000  ='Tier 1'
                    50000-<100000='Tier 2'
                    100000-high  ='Tier 3';
run;
```

46   p105d07

Viewing the Output

```
proc print data=orion.sales;
   var Employee_ID Job_Title Salary
       Country Birth_Date Hire_Date;
   format Birth_Date Hire_Date monyy7.
          Country $ctryfmt.
          Salary tiers.;
run;
```

Partial PROC PRINT Output

Obs	Employee_ID	Job_Title	Salary	Country	Birth_ Date	Hire_ Date
1	120102	Sales Manager	Tier 3	Australia	AUG1973	JUN1993
2	120103	Sales Manager	Tier 2	Australia	JAN1953	JAN1978
3	120121	Sales Rep. II	Tier 1	Australia	AUG1948	JAN1978
4	120122	Sales Rep. II	Tier 1	Australia	JUL1958	JUL1982
5	120123	Sales Rep. I	Tier 1	Australia	SEP1968	OCT1989

47   p105d07

Exercises

If you restarted your SAS session since the last exercise, open and submit the **libname.sas** program, which can be found in the data folder.

Level 1

4. **Creating User-Defined Formats**

    a. Retrieve the starter program **p105e04**.

    b. Add a PROC FORMAT step following the DATA step to create a character format named
        $GENDER that displays gender codes as follows:

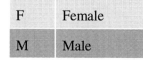

    c. In the same PROC FORMAT step, create a numeric format named MNAME that displays month
        numbers as follows:

    d. Add a PROC PRINT step following the PROC FORMAT step to display the **Q1Birthdays** data
        set. Apply the two user-defined formats to the **Employee_Gender** and **BirthMonth** variables,
        respectively. Include the title *Employees with Birthdays in Q1*, and clear the title at the end
        of the program.

    e. Submit the program to produce the following report. The results contain 113 observations.

```
                        Employees with Birthdays in Q1


                                     Employee_      Birth
                Obs      Employee_ID    Gender       Month

                 1          120103      Male       January
                 2          120107      Female     January
                 3          120108      Female     February
               ...
                112         121142      Male       February
                113         121148      Male       January
```

Level 2

5. **Defining Ranges in User-Defined Formats**

    a. Retrieve the starter program **p105e05**.

    b. Create a character format named $GENDER that displays gender codes as follows:

F	Female
M	Male
Any other value	Invalid code

c. Create a numeric format named SALRANGE that displays salary ranges as follows:

At least 20,000 but less than 100,000	Below $100,000
At least 100,000 and up to 500,000	$100,000 or more
missing	Missing salary
Any other value	Invalid salary

d. In the PROC PRINT step, apply these two user-defined formats to the **Gender** and **Salary** variables, respectively. Submit the program to produce the following report:

Partial PROC PRINT Output

```
                    Salary and Gender Values
                    for Non-Sales Employees

  Obs    Employee_ID    Job_Title                Salary           Gender

   1        120101      Director            $100,000 or more    Male
   2        120104      Administration Manager  Below $100,000   Female
   3        120105      Secretary I            Below $100,000    Female
   4        120106      Office Assistant II    Missing salary    Male
   5        120107      Office Assistant III   Below $100,000    Female
   6        120108      Warehouse Assistant II Below $100,000    Female
   7        120108      Warehouse Assistant I  Below $100,000    Female
   8        120110      Warehouse Assistant III Below $100,000   Male
   9        120111      Security Guard II      Below $100,000    Male
  10        120112                             Below $100,000    Female
  11        120113      Security Guard II      Below $100,000    Female
  12        120114      Security Manager       Below $100,000    Invalid code
  13        120115      Service Assistant I    Invalid salary    Male
```

Challenge

6. **Exploring Format Storage Options**

   User-defined formats are stored in the **formats** catalog in the **Work** library, **work.formats**. Use the SAS Help Facility or product documentation to explore permanent format catalogs in PROC FORMAT.

   What option enables you to store the formats in a permanent library? _____

   What option causes SAS to look for formats in permanent libraries? _____

5.3 Solutions

Solutions to Exercises

1. **Displaying Formatted Values in a Detail Report**

```
proc print data=orion.employee_payroll;
   var Employee_ID Salary Birth_Date Employee_Hire_Date;
   format Salary dollar11.2 Birth_Date mmddyy10.
          Employee_Hire_Date date9.;
run;
```

2. **Displaying Formatted Values in a Detail Report**

```
title1 'US Sales Employees';
title2 'Earning Under $26,000';

proc print data=orion.sales label noobs;
   where Country='US' and Salary<26000;
   var Employee_ID First_Name Last_Name Job_Title Salary Hire_Date;
   label First_Name='First Name'
         Last_Name='Last Name'
         Job_Title='Title'
         Hire_Date='Date Hired';
   format Salary dollar10. Hire_Date monyy7.;
run;
title;
footnote;
```

3. **Exploring Formats by Category**

```
proc print data=orion.sales noobs;
   var Employee_ID First_Name Last_Name Job_Title;
   format First_Name Last_Name $upcase. Job_Title $quote.;
run;
```

4. **Creating User-Defined Formats**

```
data Q1Birthdays;
   set orion.employee_payroll;
   BirthMonth=month(Birth_Date);
   if BirthMonth le 3;
run;

proc format;
   value $gender
      'F'='Female'
      'M'='Male';
   value mname
       1='January'
       2='February'
       3='March';
run;

title 'Employees with Birthdays in Q1';
proc print data=Q1Birthdays;
   var Employee_ID Employee_Gender BirthMonth;
   format Employee_Gender $gender.
          BirthMonth mname.;
run;
title;
```

5. **Defining Ranges in User-Defined Formats**

```
proc format;
   value $gender
         'F'='Female'
         'M'='Male'
      other='Invalid code';

   value salrange  .='Missing salary'
        20000-<100000='Below $100,000'
        100000-500000='$100,000 or more'
                 other='Invalid salary';
run;

title1 'Salary and Gender Values';
title2 'for Non-Sales Employees';

proc print data=orion.nonsales;
   var Employee_ID Job_Title Salary Gender;
   format Salary salrange. Gender $gender.;
run;
title;
```

6. **Exploring Format Storage Options**

What option enables you to store the formats in a permanent library? **LIBRARY=**

What option causes SAS to look for formats in permanent libraries? **FMTSEARCH=**

Solutions to Student Activities (Polls/Quizzes)

5.01 Short Answer Poll – Correct Answer

Use SAS documentation or the SAS Help Facility
to explore the *Zw.d* numeric format. What is it used for?

Hint: Search for *Zw.d* or explore "Formats by Category."

**The *Zw.d* format writes standard numeric data with
leading zeros. It is similar to the *w.d* format except
that *Zw.d* pads right-aligned output with zeros instead
of blanks.**

14

5.04 Short Answer Poll – Correct Answer

How is a value of *50000* displayed if the TIERS format below is applied to the value?

a. Tier 1
b. Tier 2
c. 50000
d. a missing value

```
proc format;
   value tiers  20000-<50000 ='Tier 1'
                50000-<100000='Tier 2'
                100000-250000='Tier 3';
run;
```

p105d05

41

Chapter 6   Reading SAS® Data Sets

6.1 Reading a SAS Data Set

Objectives

- Define the business scenario that is used when you read from a data source to create a SAS data set.
- Use a DATA step to create a SAS data set from an existing SAS data set.
- Subset observations with a WHERE statement.
- Create a new variable with an assignment statement.

3

Business Scenario

Information about Orion Star sales employees resides in several input sources.

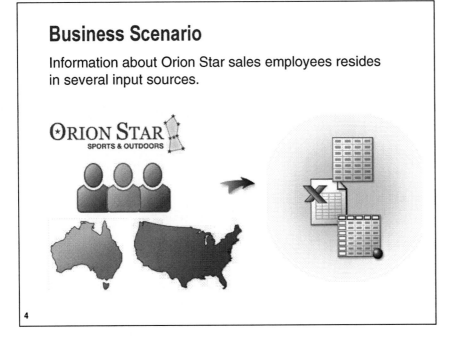

4

Considerations

Management wants a series of reports for Australian sales employees. You read data from various input sources to create a SAS data set that can be analyzed and presented.

SAS data set

5

6.01 Multiple Answer Poll

Which types of files will you read into SAS?

a. SAS data sets
b. Excel worksheets
c. database tables
d. raw data files
e. other
f. not sure

6

Business Scenario: Part 1

Read an existing SAS data set to create a new data set.
The new data set should include only the observations
for the Australian sales representatives.

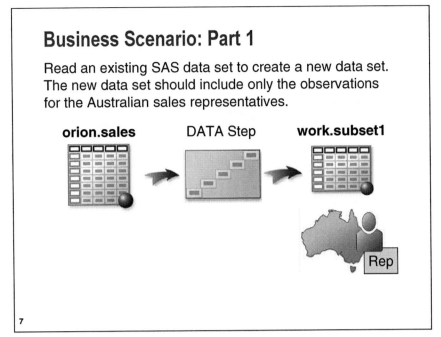

7

Using a SAS Data Set as Input

```
data work.subset1;
   set orion.sales;
   where Country='AU' and
         Job_Title contains 'Rep';
run;
```

DATA *output-SAS-data-set*;
   SET *input-SAS-data-set*;
      WHERE *WHERE-expression*;
RUN;

p106d01

8

DATA Statement

The *DATA statement* begins a DATA step and provides the name of the SAS data set to create.

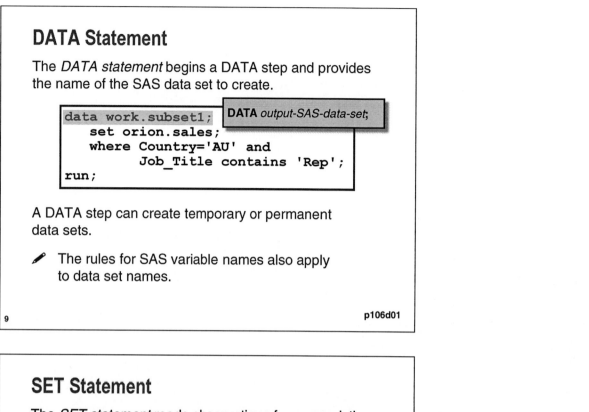

```
data work.subset1;         DATA output-SAS-data-set;
    set orion.sales;
    where Country='AU' and
          Job_Title contains 'Rep';
run;
```

A DATA step can create temporary or permanent data sets.

✐ The rules for SAS variable names also apply to data set names.

9   p106d01

SET Statement

The *SET statement* reads observations from an existing SAS data set for further processing in the DATA step.

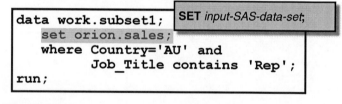

```
data work.subset1;         SET input-SAS-data-set;
    set orion.sales;
    where Country='AU' and
          Job_Title contains 'Rep';
run;
```

- The SET statement reads all observations and all variables from the input data set.
- Observations are read sequentially, one at a time.
- The SET statement can read temporary or permanent data sets.

10   p106d01

WHERE Statement

The *WHERE statement* selects observations from a SAS data set that meet a particular condition.

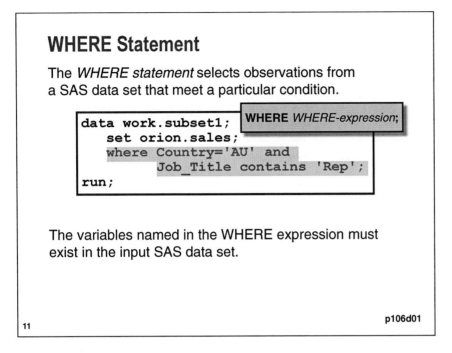

```
data work.subset1;        WHERE WHERE-expression;
   set orion.sales;
   where Country='AU' and
         Job_Title contains 'Rep';
run;
```

The variables named in the WHERE expression must exist in the input SAS data set.

p106d01

11

Using a WHERE statement might improve the efficiency of your SAS programs because SAS processes only the observations that meet the condition or conditions in the WHERE expression.

Viewing the Log

Partial SAS Log

```
42   data work.subset1;
43      set orion.sales;
44      where Country='AU' and
45            Job_Title contains 'Rep';
46   run;

NOTE: There were 61 observations read from the data set ORION.SALES.
      WHERE (Country='AU') and Job_Title contains 'Rep';
NOTE: The data set WORK.SUBSET1 has 61 observations and 9 variables.
```

SAS read 61 of the 165 observations.

12

Viewing the Output

```
proc print data=work.subset1 noobs;
run;
```

Partial PROC PRINT Output

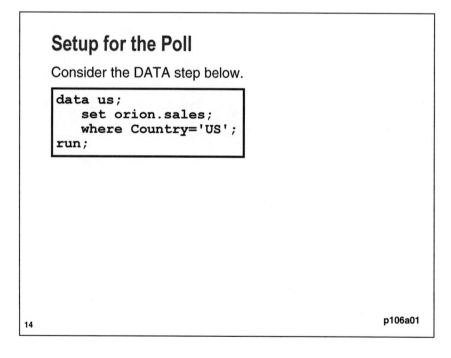

Employee_ID	First_Name	Last_Name	Gender	Salary	Job_Title	Country	Birth_Date	Hire_Date
120121	Irenie	Elvish	F	26600	Sales Rep. II	AU	-4169	6575
120122	Christina	Ngan	F	27475	Sales Rep. II	AU	-523	8217
120123	Kimiko	Hotstone	F	26190	Sales Rep. I	AU	3193	10866
120124	Lucian	Daymond	M	26480	Sales Rep. I	AU	1228	8460
120125	Fong	Hofmeister	M	32040	Sales Rep. IV	AU	-391	8460

13   p106d01

Setup for the Poll

Consider the DATA step below.

```
data us;
   set orion.sales;
   where Country='US';
run;
```

14   p106a01

6.02 Multiple Choice Poll

Considering this DATA step, which statement is true?

a. It reads a temporary data set and creates a permanent data set.

b. It reads a permanent data set and creates a temporary data set.

c. It contains a syntax error and does not execute.

d. It does not execute because you cannot work with permanent and temporary data sets in the same step.

15

Business Scenario: Part 2

Orion Star management wants to give a 10% bonus to each Australian Sales representative hired before January 1, 2000.

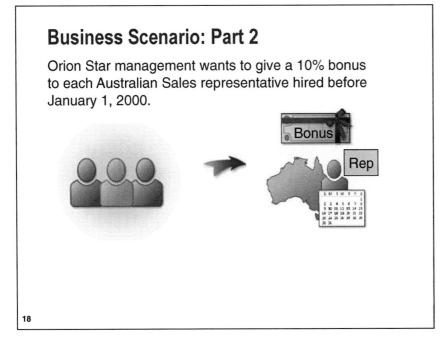

18

Considerations

Subsetting is based on **Hire_Date**, which contains
a SAS date value. How can you compare a SAS date
value to a calendar date?

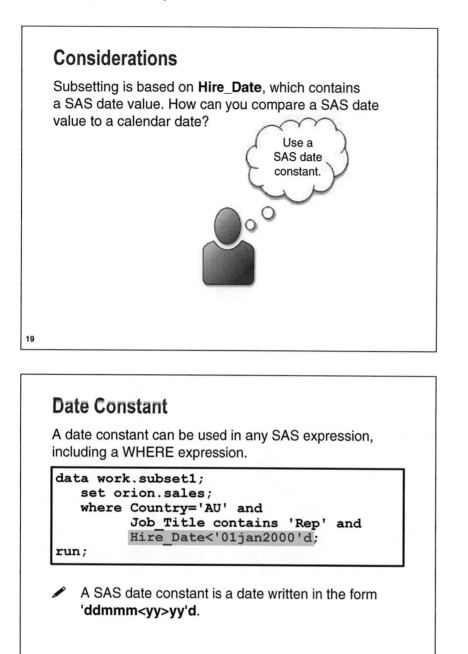

Use a
SAS date
constant.

19

Date Constant

A date constant can be used in any SAS expression,
including a WHERE expression.

```
data work.subset1;
   set orion.sales;
   where Country='AU' and
         Job_Title contains 'Rep' and
         Hire_Date<'01jan2000'd;
run;
```

✐   A SAS date constant is a date written in the form
'ddmmm<yy>yy'd.

20   p106d02

Considerations

Create a data set that includes the new variable, **Bonus**,
which represents a 10% bonus.

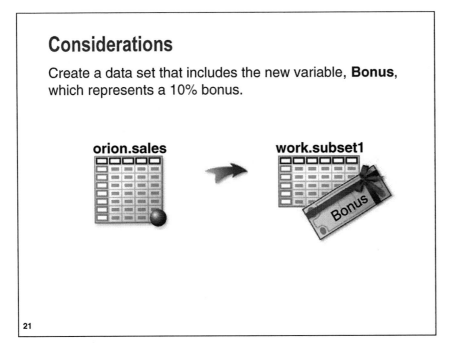

21

Assignment Statement

The *assignment statement* evaluates an expression
and assigns the result to a new or existing variable.

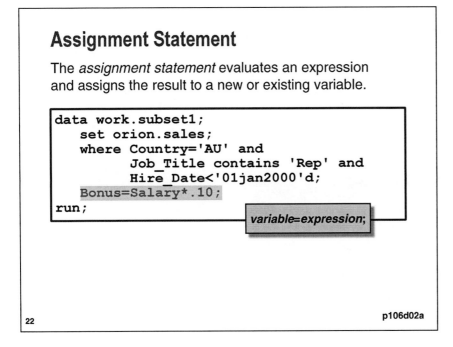

```
data work.subset1;
   set orion.sales;
   where Country='AU' and
         Job_Title contains 'Rep' and
         Hire_Date<'01jan2000'd;
   Bonus=Salary*.10;
run;
```

variable=expression;

22   p106d02a

The operators can be character or arithmetic operators or SAS functions. A *function* is a routine that accepts arguments, performs a calculation or manipulation using the arguments, and returns a single value.

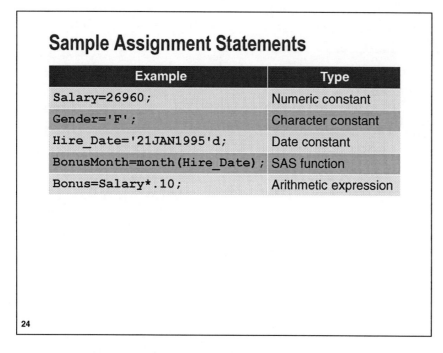

The MONTH function accepts a SAS date and returns the month portion of the date as an integer between 1 and 12. (You investigate this and other SAS functions in a later chapter.)

Arithmetic Operators

If any operand in an arithmetic expression has a missing value, the result is a missing value.

Symbol	Definition	Priority
**	Exponentiation	I
*	Multiplication	II
/	Division	II
+	Addition	III
-	Subtraction	III

Parentheses can be used to clarify or alter the order of operations in an arithmetic expression.

25

Viewing the Log

Partial SAS Log

```
214   data work.subset1;
215      set orion.sales;
216      where Country='AU' and
217            Job_Title contains 'Rep' and
218            Hire_Date<'01jan2000'd;
219      Bonus=Salary*.10;
220   run;

NOTE: There were 29 observations read from the data set ORION.SALES.
      WHERE (Country='AU') and Job_Title contains 'Rep' and
      (Hire_Date<'01JAN2000'D);
NOTE: The data set WORK.SUBSET1 has 29 observations and 10 variables.
```

The input data set has 9 variables, and the new data set has 10 variables.

26

Viewing the Output

```
proc print data=work.subset1 noobs;
   var First_Name Last_Name Salary
       Job_Title Bonus Hire_Date;
   format Hire_Date date9.;
run;
```

Partial PROC PRINT Output

First_Name	Last_Name	Salary	Job_Title	Bonus	Hire_Date
Irenie	Elvish	26600	Sales Rep. II	2660.0	01JAN1978
Christina	Ngan	27475	Sales Rep. II	2747.5	01JUL1982
Kimiko	Hotstone	26190	Sales Rep. I	2619.0	01OCT1989
Lucian	Daymond	26480	Sales Rep. I	2648.0	01MAR1983
Fong	Hofmeister	32040	Sales Rep. IV	3204.0	01MAR1983

27   p106d02a

No format was specified for **Bonus**, so PROC PRINT uses a BEST*w.d* format. One decimal position is sufficient to display the values on this page.

6.03 Short Answer Poll

What are the values of **n1** and **n2** given the following variables and values?

x	y	z
.	4	10

a. `n1=y+z/2;`

_____

b. `n2=x+z/2;`

28

Exercises

If you restarted your SAS session since the last exercise, open and submit the **libname.sas** program that can be found in the data folder.

Level 1

1. **Creating a SAS Data Set**

    a. Retrieve and submit the starter program **p106e01**.

      What is the name of the variable that contains gender values? _____

      What are the two observed gender values? _____

    b. Add a DATA step before the PROC PRINT step to create a new data set named **work.youngadult**. Use the data set **orion.customer_dim** as input. Include a WHERE statement to select only female customers.

      Submit the program and confirm that **work.youngadult** was created with 30 observations and 11 variables.

    c. Modify the program to select female customers whose ages are between 18 and 36. Submit the program and confirm that **work.youngadult** was created with 15 observations and 11 variables.

    d. Modify the program to select 18- to 36-year-old female customers who have the word *Gold* in their **Customer_Group** values. Submit the program and confirm that **work.youngadult** was created with five observations and 11 variables.

    e. Add an assignment statement to the DATA step to create a new variable, **Discount**, and assign it a value of *.25*.

    f. Modify the PROC PRINT step to print the new data set as shown below. Use an ID statement to display **Customer_ID** instead of the Obs column. Results should contain five observations.

Customer_ID	Customer_Name	Customer_Age	Customer_Gender	Customer_Group	Discount
5	Sandrina Stephano	28	F	Orion Club Gold members	0.25
9	Cornelia Krahl	33	F	Orion Club Gold members	0.25
45	Dianne Patchin	28	F	Orion Club Gold members	0.25
49	Annmarie Leveille	23	F	Orion Club Gold members	0.25
2550	Sanelisiwe Collier	19	F	Orion Club Gold members	0.25

Level 2

2. **Creating a SAS Data Set**

    a. Write a DATA step to create a new data set named **work.assistant**. Use the data set **orion.staff** as input.

    b. The **work.assistant** data set should contain only the observations where **Job_Title** contains *Assistant* and **Salary** is less than *$26,000*.

   c. Create two new variables, **Increase** and **New_Salary**.

   - **Increase** is **Salary** multiplied by 0.10.

   - **New_Salary** is **Salary** added to **Increase**.

   d. Generate a detail listing report as shown below. Display **Employee_ID** as the identifier in place of the Obs column. The results should contain five observations.

```
Employee_ID         Job_Title          Salary      Increase    New_Salary

     120685     Warehouse Assistant I   $25,130.00   $2,513.00   $27,643.00
     120688     Warehouse Assistant I   $25,905.00   $2,590.50   $28,495.50
     120690     Warehouse Assistant I   $25,185.00   $2,518.50   $27,703.50
     121010     Service Assistant I     $25,195.00   $2,519.50   $27,714.50
     121011     Service Assistant I     $25,735.00   $2,573.50   $28,308.50
```

Challenge

3. **Using the SOUNDS-LIKE Operator to Select Observations**

   a. Write a DATA step to create a new data set named **work.tony**. Use **orion.customer_dim** as input.

   b. Include a WHERE statement in the DATA step to select observations in which the **Customer_FirstName** value sounds like *Tony*.

    Documentation about the SOUNDS-LIKE operator can be found in the SAS Help Facility or product documentation by searching for "sounds-like operator."

   c. Write a PROC PRINT step to create the following report:

```
              Customer_    Customer_
       Obs    FirstName    LastName

        1      Tonie       Asmussen
        2      Tommy       Mcdonald
```

6.2 Customizing a SAS Data Set

Objectives

- Subset variables by using the DROP and KEEP statements.
- Explore the compilation and execution phases of the DATA step.
- Store labels and formats in the descriptor portion of a SAS data set.

33

Business Scenario: Part 3

All Australian sales representatives receive a bonus, regardless of hire date. The new data set should contain a subset of the variables from the input data set.

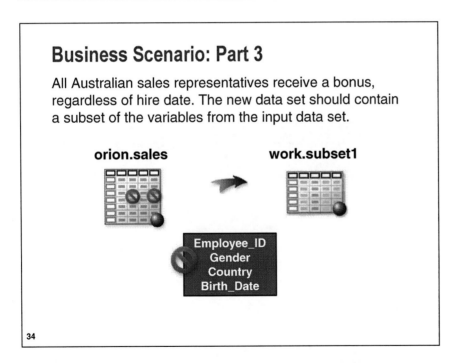

orion.sales   **work.subset1**

Employee_ID
Gender
Country
Birth_Date

34

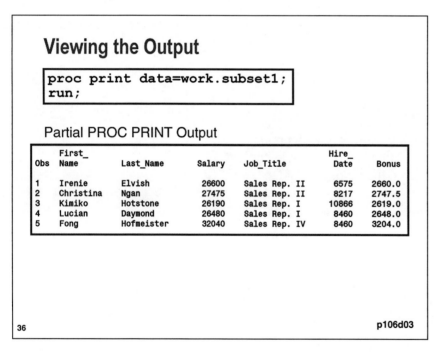

KEEP Statement

The KEEP statement specifies all variables to *include* in
the output data set.

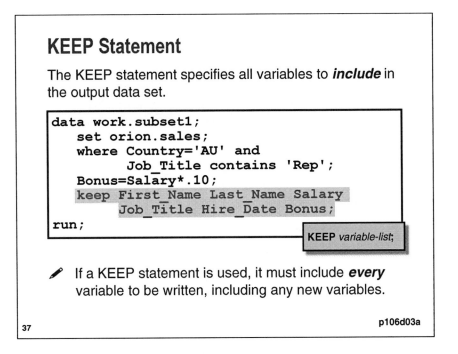

```
data work.subset1;
   set orion.sales;
   where Country='AU' and
         Job_Title contains 'Rep';
   Bonus=Salary*.10;
   keep First_Name Last_Name Salary
        Job_Title Hire_Date Bonus;
run;
```

KEEP *variable-list*;

🖋 If a KEEP statement is used, it must include *every*
variable to be written, including any new variables.

37   p106d03a

When you use a KEEP statement, be sure to name every variable to be written to the new SAS data set.
Include any variables that are created within the step, such as **Bonus**.

Viewing the Log

Partial SAS Log

```
NOTE: There were 61 observations read from the data set ORION.SALES.
      WHERE (Country='AU') and Job_Title contains 'Rep';
NOTE: The data set WORK.SUBSET1 has 61 observations and 6 variables.
```

38

Viewing the Output

```
proc print data=work.subset1;
run;
```

Partial PROC PRINT Output

Obs	First_Name	Last_Name	Salary	Job_Title	Hire_Date	Bonus
1	Irenie	Elvish	26600	Sales Rep. II	6575	2660.0
2	Christina	Ngan	27475	Sales Rep. II	8217	2747.5
3	Kimiko	Hotstone	26190	Sales Rep. I	10866	2619.0
4	Lucian	Daymond	26480	Sales Rep. I	8460	2648.0
5	Fong	Hofmeister	32040	Sales Rep. IV	8460	3204.0

39   p106d03a

Business Scenario: Behind the Scenes

Orion Star programmers need to understand the internal processing that occurs when a DATA step is submitted.

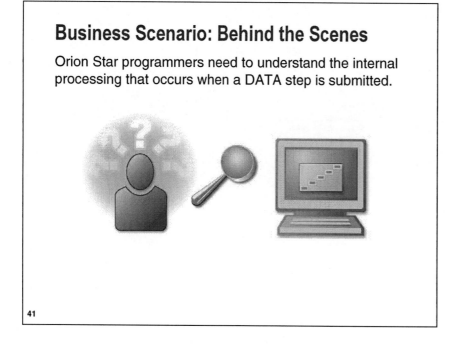

41

DATA Step Processing

SAS processes the DATA step in two phases.

Compilation Phase

Scans the program for syntax errors; translates the program into machine language.

PDV

Creates the *program data vector* (*PDV*) to hold one observation.

Creates the descriptor portion of the output data set.

Compilation

```
data work.subset1;
   set orion.sales;
   where Country='AU' and
        Job_Title contains 'Rep';
   Bonus=Salary*.10;
   drop Employee_ID Gender Country
        Birth_Date;
run;
```

44   p106d03
                                                           ...

Compilation

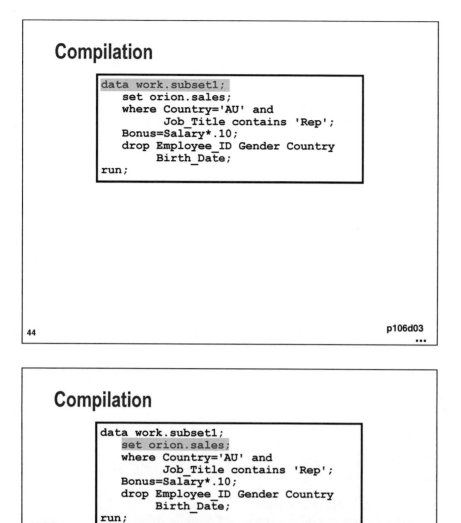

PDV

Employee_ID	First_Name	Last_Name	Gender	Salary	Job_Title
N 8	$ 12	$ 18	$ 1	N 8	$ 25

Country	Birth_Date	Hire_Date
$ 2	N 8	N 8

45   ...

Compilation

```
data work.subset1;
   set orion.sales;
   where Country='AU' and
         Job_Title contains 'Rep';
   Bonus=Salary*.10;
   drop Employee_ID Gender Country
        Birth_Date;
run;
```

PDV

Employee_ID	First_Name	Last_Name	Gender	Salary	Job_Title
N 8	$ 12	$ 18	$ 1	N 8	$ 25

Country	Birth_Date	Hire_Date	Bonus
$ 2	N 8	N 8	N 8

↑

46   ...

Compilation

```
data work.subset1;
   set orion.sales;
   where Country='AU' and
         Job_Title contains 'Rep';
   Bonus=Salary*.10;
   drop Employee_ID Gender Country
        Birth_Date;
run;
```

PDV

Employee_ID	First_Name	Last_Name	Gender	Salary	Job_Title
▷ N 8	$ 12	$ 18	▷ $ 1	N 8	$ 25

Country	Birth_Date	Hire_Date	Bonus
▷ $ 2	▷ N 8	N 8	N 8

47   ...

Compilation

```
data work.subset1;
    set orion.sales;
    where Country='AU' and
            Job_Title contains 'Rep';
    Bonus=Salary*.10;
    drop Employee_ID Gender Country
            Birth_Date;
run;
```

PDV

Employee_ID	First_Name	Last_Name	Gender	Salary	Job_Title
D N 8	$ 12	$ 18	D $ 1	N 8	$ 25

Country	Birth_Date	Hire_Date	Bonus
D $ 2	D N 8	N 8	N 8

Descriptor Portion of **work.subset1**

First_Name	Last_Name	Salary	Job_Title	Hire_Date	Bonus

48

Execution Phase

49

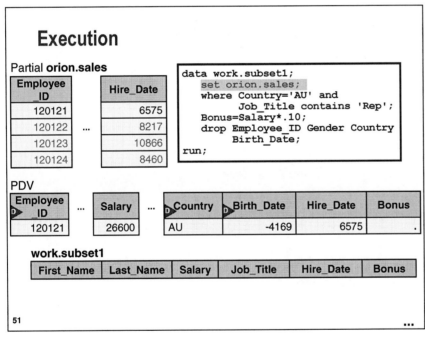

The WHERE statement is executed before the other executable statements.

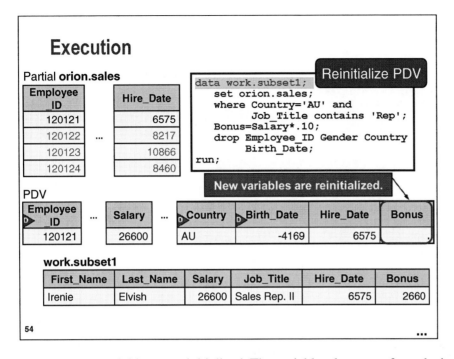

Only the new variables are reinitialized. The variables that come from the input data set are *not* reinitialized because they are overwritten when the next observation is read into the PDV. Values in the PDV are overwritten even if values in the next observation are missing.

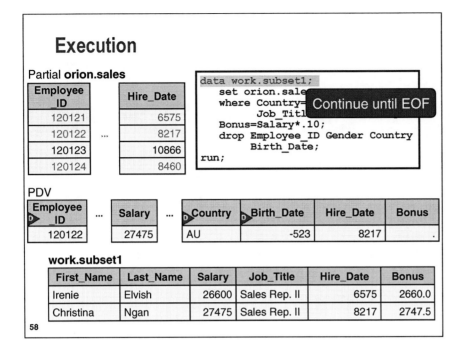

Execution

Partial **orion.sales**

Employee_ID		Hire_Date
120121		6575
120122	...	8217
120123		10866
120124		8460

```
data work.subset1;
   set orion.sale
   where Country=        Continue until EOF
        Job_Titl
Bonus=Salary*.10;
drop Employee_ID Gender Country
        Birth_Date;
run;
```

PDV

Employee_ID	...	Salary	...	Country	Birth_Date	Hire_Date	Bonus
120122		27475		AU	-523	8217	.

work.subset1

First_Name	Last_Name	Salary	Job_Title	Hire_Date	Bonus
Irenie	Elvish	26600	Sales Rep. II	6575	2660.0
Christina	Ngan	27475	Sales Rep. II	8217	2747.5

58

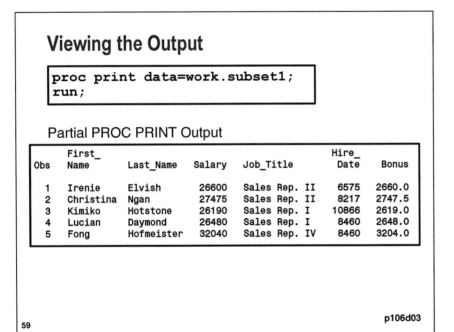

Viewing the Output

```
proc print data=work.subset1;
run;
```

Partial PROC PRINT Output

```
     First_                                    Hire_
Obs  Name       Last_Name    Salary  Job_Title    Date   Bonus

 1   Irenie     Elvish       26600   Sales Rep. II  6575   2660.0
 2   Christina  Ngan         27475   Sales Rep. II  8217   2747.5
 3   Kimiko     Hotstone     26190   Sales Rep. I  10866   2619.0
 4   Lucian     Daymond      26480   Sales Rep. I   8460   2648.0
 5   Fong       Hofmeister   32040   Sales Rep. IV  8460   3204.0
```

59

p106d03

Business Scenario: Part 4

Create a data set that contains all Australian employees whose bonus is at least $3000.

orion.sales

work.auemps

Bonus

61

Selecting Observations

Subsetting is based on the new variable, **Bonus**, that is created with an assignment statement.

```
data work.auemps;
   set orion.sales;
   where Country='AU';
   Bonus=Salary*.10;
   drop Employee_ID Gender Country
        Birth_Date;
run;
```

A WHERE statement is used to subset observations when the selected variables exist in the *input* data set.

62

p106d04

6.04 Short Answer Poll

Open and submit **p106a03**. Is the output data set created successfully?

```
data work.usemps;
   set orion.sales;
   Bonus=Salary*.10;
   where Country='US' and Bonus>=3000;
run;
```

63   p106a03

Subsetting IF

The *subsetting IF* statement tests a condition to determine whether the DATA step should continue processing the current observation.

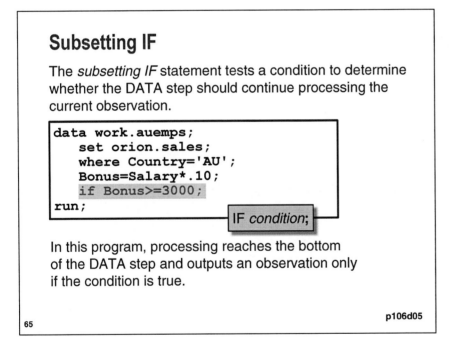

```
data work.auemps;
   set orion.sales;
   where Country='AU';
   Bonus=Salary*.10;
   if Bonus>=3000;
run;
```

IF *condition*;

In this program, processing reaches the bottom of the DATA step and outputs an observation only if the condition is true.

65   p106d05

Viewing the Log

Partial SAS Log

```
11   data work.auemps;
12      set orion.sales;
13      where Country='AU';
14      Bonus=Salary*.10;
15      if Bonus>=3000;
16   run;

NOTE: There were 63 observations read from the data set ORION.SALES.
      WHERE Country='AU';
NOTE: The data set WORK.AUEMPS has 12 observations and 10 variables.
```

Of the 165 observations in **orion.sales**, 63 were read
into the PDV for processing, and only 12 were written
to the new data set.

66

Viewing the Output

```
proc print data=work.auemps;
    var First_Name Last_Name Salary Bonus;
run;
```

PROC PRINT Output

Obs	First_Name	Last_Name	Salary	Bonus
1	Tom	Zhou	108255	10825.5
2	Wilson	Dawes	87975	8797.5
3	Fong	Hofmeister	32040	3204.0
4	Monica	Kletschkus	30890	3089.0
5	Alvin	Roebuck	30070	3007.0
6	Alexei	Platts	32490	3249.0
7	Viney	Barbis	30265	3026.5
8	Caterina	Hayawardhana	30490	3049.0
9	Daniel	Pilgrim	36605	3660.5
10	Lynelle	Phoumirath	30765	3076.5
11	Rosette	Martines	30785	3078.5
12	Fadi	Nowd	30660	3066.0

67

Processing the Subsetting IF Statement

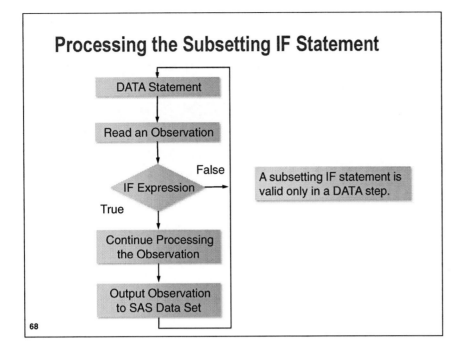

A subsetting IF statement is valid only in a DATA step.

68

Idea Exchange

File **p106a04** contains two versions of the previous program. Submit both programs and compare the output and number of observations read. What do you notice about the results?

```
data work.auemps;
   set orion.sales;
   Bonus=Salary*.10;
   if Country='AU' and Bonus>=3000;
run;
```

69

WHERE versus Subsetting IF Statement

Step and Usage	WHERE	IF
PROC step	Yes	No
DATA step (source of variable)		
SET statement	Yes	Yes
assignment statement	No	Yes

70

Business Scenario: Part 5

Define permanent labels and formats for some
of the variables in the new data set.

labels

formats

work.subset1

72

LABEL Statement

The LABEL statement assigns descriptive labels to variables.

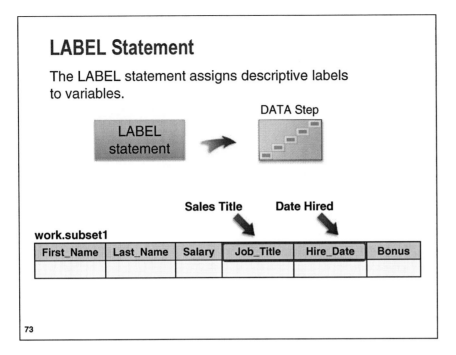

73

Defining Permanent Labels

Use a LABEL statement in a DATA step to permanently assign labels to variables. The labels are stored in the descriptor portion of the data set.

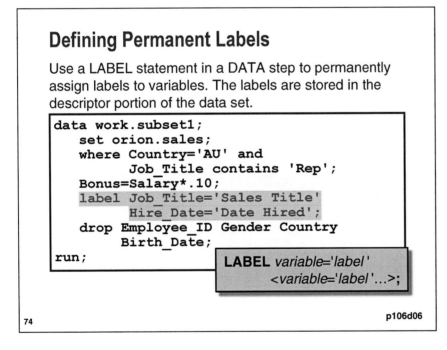

74

p106d06

Viewing the Output

```
proc contents data=work.subset1;
run;
```

Partial PROC CONTENTS Output

```
Alphabetic List of Variables and Attributes

#    Variable      Type    Len    Label

6    Bonus         Num      8
1    First_Name    Char    12
5    Hire_Date     Num      8     Date Hired
4    Job_Title     Char    25     Sales Title
2    Last_Name     Char    18
3    Salary        Num      8
```

75   p106d06

Viewing the Output: Displaying Labels

To use labels in the PRINT procedure, use the LABEL option in the PROC PRINT statement.

```
proc print data=work.subset1 label;
run;
```

Partial PROC PRINT Output

Obs	First_Name	Last_Name	Salary	Sales Title	Date Hired	Bonus
1	Irenie	Elvish	26600	Sales Rep. II	6575	2660.0
2	Christina	Ngan	27475	Sales Rep. II	8217	2747.5
3	Kimiko	Hotstone	26190	Sales Rep. I	10866	2619.0
4	Lucian	Daymond	26480	Sales Rep. I	8460	2648.0
5	Fong	Hofmeister	32040	Sales Rep. IV	8460	3204.0

76   p106d06

Viewing the Output: Splitting Labels

Use the PROC PRINT SPLIT= option to split labels across lines based on a split character.

```
proc print data=work.subset1 split=' ';
run;
```

Partial PROC PRINT Output

Obs	First_Name	Last_Name	Salary	Sales Title	Date Hired	Bonus
1	Irenie	Elvish	26600	Sales Rep. II	6575	2660.0
2	Christina	Ngan	27475	Sales Rep. II	8217	2747.5
3	Kimiko	Hotstone	26190	Sales Rep. I	10866	2619.0
4	Lucian	Daymond	26480	Sales Rep. I	8460	2648.0
5	Fong	Hofmeister	32040	Sales Rep. IV	8460	3204.0

77   p106d06

PROC PRINT is the only SAS procedure that requires either the LABEL option or the SPLIT= option to use custom labels.

6.05 Short Answer Poll

What column heading is displayed for **Job_Title** in the program below?

```
data work.us;
   set orion.sales;
   where Country='US';
   Bonus=Salary*.10;
   label Job_Title='Sales Title';
   drop Employee_ID Gender Country
        Birth_Date;
run;
proc print data=work.us label;
   label Job_Title='Title';
run;
```

78   p106a05

FORMAT Statement

The FORMAT statement associates formats with variables.

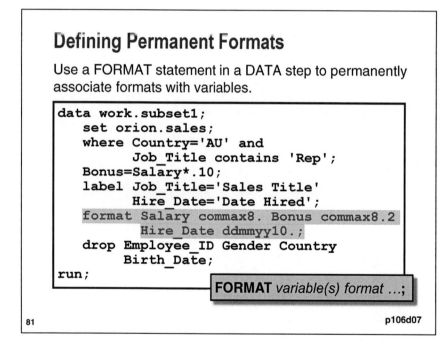

work.subset1

First_Name	Last_Name	Salary	Job_Title	Hire_Date	Bonus
Irenie	Elvish	26600	Sales Rep. II	6575	2660.0

80

Defining Permanent Formats

Use a FORMAT statement in a DATA step to permanently associate formats with variables.

```
data work.subset1;
   set orion.sales;
   where Country='AU' and
         Job_Title contains 'Rep';
   Bonus=Salary*.10;
   label Job_Title='Sales Title'
         Hire_Date='Date Hired';
   format Salary commax8. Bonus commax8.2
          Hire_Date ddmmyy10.;
   drop Employee_ID Gender Country
        Birth_Date;
run;
```

FORMAT *variable(s) format ...;*

81   p106d07

Viewing the Output

```
proc contents data=work.subset1;
run;
```

Partial PROC CONTENTS Output

```
Alphabetic List of Variables and Attributes

#    Variable      Type     Len    Format         Label

6    Bonus         Num      8      COMMAX8.2
1    First_Name    Char     12
5    Hire_Date     Num      8      DDMMYY10.      Date Hired
4    Job_Title     Char     25                    Sales Title
2    Last_Name     Char     18
3    Salary        Num      8      COMMAX8.
```

82   p106d07

Viewing the Output

```
proc print data=work.subset1 label;
run;
```

Partial PROC PRINT Output

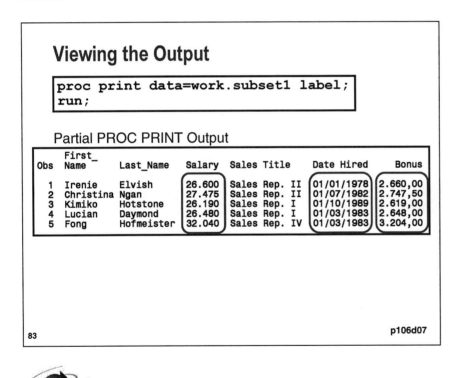

```
       First_
Obs    Name        Last_Name    Salary    Sales Title    Date Hired    Bonus

 1     Irenie      Elvish       26.600    Sales Rep. II  01/01/1978    2.660,00
 2     Christina   Ngan         27.475    Sales Rep. II  01/07/1982    2.747,50
 3     Kimiko      Hotstone     26.190    Sales Rep. I   01/10/1989    2.619,00
 4     Lucian      Daymond      26.480    Sales Rep. I   01/03/1983    2.648,00
 5     Fong        Hofmeister   32.040    Sales Rep. IV  01/03/1983    3.204,00
```

83   p106d07

Exercises

If you restarted your SAS session since the last exercise, open and submit the **libname.sas** program that can be found in the data folder.

Level 1

4. **Subsetting Observations Based on Two Conditions**

   a. Retrieve the starter program **p106e04**.

   b. Modify the DATA step to select only the observations with **Emp_Hire_Date** values on or after July 1, 2010. Subset the observations as they are being read into the program data vector.

   c. In the DATA step, write another statement to select only the observations that have an increase greater than 3000.

   d. The new data set should contain only the following variables: **Employee_ID**, **Emp_Hire_Date**, **Salary**, **Increase**, and **NewSalary**.

   e. Add permanent labels for **Employee_ID**, **Emp_Hire_Date**, and **NewSalary** as shown in the report below.

   f. Add permanent formats to display **Salary** and **NewSalary** with dollar signs, commas, and two decimal places, and **Increase** with commas and no decimal places.

   g. Submit a PROC CONTENTS step to verify that the labels and formats are stored in the descriptor portion of the new data set, **work.increase**.

   Partial PROC CONTENTS Output

   ```
              Alphabetic List of Variables and Attributes

    #    Variable        Type   Len   Format      Informat   Label

    3    Emp_Hire_Date   Num     8    DATE9.      DATE9.     Hire Date
    1    Employee_ID     Num     8    12.                    Employee ID
    4    Increase        Num     8    COMMA5.
    5    NewSalary       Num     8    DOLLAR10.2             New Annual Salary
    2    Salary          Num     8    DOLLAR10.2             Employee Annual Salary
   ```

   h. Some variables have labels and formats that were not defined in this program. How were these created? _____

   i. Submit the program to create the PROC PRINT report below. Split the labels over multiple lines. Results should contain 10 observations.

   ```
                     Employee                                   New
           Employee    Annual      Hire                       Annual
    Obs        ID      Salary      Date       Increase        Salary

     1      120128   $30,890.00   01NOV2010     3,089      $33,979.00
     2      120144   $30,265.00   01OCT2010     3,027      $33,291.50
     3      120161   $30,785.00   01OCT2010     3,079      $33,863.50
    ...
     9      121085   $32,235.00   01JAN2011     3,224      $35,458.50
    10      121107   $31,380.00   01JUL2010     3,138      $34,518.00
   ```

Level 2

5. **Subsetting Observations Based on Three Conditions**

   a. Write a DATA step to create **work.delays**. Use **orion.orders** as input.

b. Create a new variable, **Order_Month**, and set it to the month of **Order_Date**.

Hint: Use the MONTH function.

c. Use a WHERE statement and a subsetting IF statement to select only the observations that meet all of the following conditions:

- **Delivery_Date** values that are more than four days beyond **Order_Date**
- **Employee_ID** values that are equal to *99999999*
- **Order_Month** values occurring in *August*

d. The new data set should include only **Employee_ID**, **Customer_ID**, **Order_Date**, **Delivery_Date**, and **Order_Month**.

e. Add permanent labels for **Order_Date**, **Delivery_Date**, and **Order_Month** as shown below.

f. Add permanent formats to display **Order_Date** and **Delivery_Date** as MM/DD/YYYY.

g. Add a PROC CONTENTS step to verify that the labels and formats were stored permanently.

```
            Alphabetic List of Variables and Attributes

   #    Variable        Type   Len   Format      Label

   2    Customer_ID     Num     8    12.         Customer ID
   4    Delivery_Date   Num     8    MMDDYY10.   Date Delivered
   1    Employee_ID     Num     8    12.         Employee ID
   3    Order_Date      Num     8    MMDDYY10.   Date Ordered
   5    Order_Month     Num     8                Month Ordered
```

h. Write a PROC PRINT step to create the report below. Results should contain nine observations.

```
                                                      Delivery_    Order_
   Obs    Employee_ID    Customer_ID    Order_Date      Date        Month

    1      99999999         70187       08/13/2007    08/18/2007      8
    2      99999999            52       08/20/2007    08/26/2007      8
    3      99999999            16       08/27/2007    09/04/2007      8
    4      99999999            61       08/29/2007    09/03/2007      8
    5      99999999          2550       08/10/2008    08/15/2008      8
    6      99999999         70201       08/15/2008    08/20/2008      8
    7      99999999             9       08/10/2009    08/15/2009      8
    8      99999999            71       08/30/2010    09/05/2010      8
    9      99999999         70201       08/24/2011    08/29/2011      8
```

Challenge

6. Using an IF-THEN/DELETE Statement to Subset Observations

a. Write a DATA step to create **work.bigdonations**. Use **orion.employee_donations** as input.

b. Use the SUM function to create a new variable, **Total**, which holds the sum of the four quarterly donations.

c. Use the N function to create a new variable, **NumQtrs**, which holds the count of nonmissing values in **Qtr1**, **Qtr2**, **Qtr3**, and **Qtr4**. Explore the N function in the SAS Help Facility or online documentation.

d. The new data set should *not* include the charities or method of payment.

e. The final data set should contain only observations that meet the following two conditions:

- **Total** values greater than or equal to 50
- **NumQtrs** value equal to 4

Use an IF-THEN/DELETE statement to eliminate the observations where the conditions are not met. Explore the use of IF-THEN/DELETE in the SAS Help Facility or online documentation.

f. Store permanent labels in the new data set as shown in the report below.

g. Create the following report to verify that the labels were stored:

```
        Alphabetic List of Variables and Attributes

   #    Variable     Type   Len   Format   Label

   1    Employee_ID  Num    8     12.      Employee ID
   7    NumQtrs      Num    8
   2    Qtr1         Num    8              First Quarter
   3    Qtr2         Num    8              Second Quarter
   4    Qtr3         Num    8              Third Quarter
   5    Qtr4         Num    8              Fourth Quarter
   6    Total        Num    8
```

h. Create the report below. The results should contain 50 observations.

Employee ID	First Quarter	Second Quarter	Third Quarter	Fourth Quarter	Total	Num Qtrs
120267	15	15	15	15	60	4
120269	20	20	20	20	80	4
120271	20	20	20	20	80	4
120275	15	15	15	15	60	4
120660	25	25	25	25	100	4

6.3 Solutions

Solutions to Exercises

1. Creating a SAS Data Set

What is the name of the variable that contains gender values? **Customer_Gender**

What are the possible values of this variable? *M or F*

```
data work.youngadult;
   set orion.customer_dim;
   where Customer_Gender='F' and
         Customer_Age between 18 and 36 and
         Customer_Group contains 'Gold';
   Discount=.25;
run;
```

```
proc print data=work.youngadult;
   var Customer_Name Customer_Age
       Customer_Gender Customer_Group Discount;
   id Customer_ID;
run;
```

2. **Creating a SAS Data Set**

```
data work.assistant;
   set orion.staff;
   where Job_Title contains 'Assistant' and
         Salary<26000;
   Increase=Salary*.10;
   New_Salary=Salary+Increase;
run;

proc print data=work.assistant;
   id Employee_ID;
   var Job_Title Salary Increase New_Salary;
   format Salary Increase New_Salary dollar10.2;
run;
```

3. **Using the SOUNDS-LIKE Operator to Select Observations**

```
data work.tony;
   set orion.customer_dim;
   where Customer_FirstName=* 'Tony';
run;

proc print data=work.tony;
   var Customer_FirstName Customer_LastName;
run;
```

4. **Subsetting Observations Based on Two Conditions**

```
data work.increase;
   set orion.staff;
   where Emp_Hire_Date>='01JUL2010'd;
   Increase=Salary*0.10;
   if Increase>3000;
   NewSalary=Salary+Increase;
   label Employee_ID='Employee ID'
         Salary='Annual Salary'
         Emp_Hire_Date='Hire Date'
         NewSalary='New Annual Salary';
   format Salary NewSalary dollar10.2 Increase comma5.;
   keep Employee_ID Emp_Hire_Date Salary Increase NewSalary;
run;

proc print data=work.increase split=' ';
run;
```

The existing labels and formats were inherited from the input data set.

5. Subsetting Observations Based on Three Conditions

```
data work.delays;
   set orion.orders;
   where Order_Date+4<Delivery_Date
         and Employee_ID=99999999;
   Order_Month=month(Order_Date);
   if Order_Month=8;
   label Order_Date='Date Ordered'
         Delivery_Date='Date Delivered'
         Order_Month='Month Ordered';
         format Order_Date Delivery_Date mmddyy10.;
   keep Employee_ID Customer_ID Order_Date Delivery_Date
        Order_Month;
run;

proc contents data=work.delays;
run;

proc print data=work.delays;
run;
```

6. Using an IF-THEN/DELETE Statement to Subset Observations

```
data work.bigdonations;
   set orion.employee_donations;
   Total=sum(Qtr1,Qtr2,Qtr3,Qtr4);
   NumQtrs=n(Qtr1,Qtr2,Qtr3,Qtr4);
   if Total<50 or NumQtrs<4 then delete;
   label Qtr1='First Quarter'
         Qtr2='Second Quarter'
         Qtr3='Third Quarter'
         Qtr4='Fourth Quarter';
   drop Recipients Paid_By;
run;

proc contents data=work.bigdonations;
run;

proc print data=work.bigdonations label noobs;
run;
```

Solutions to Student Activities (Polls/Quizzes)

6.02 Multiple Choice Poll – Correct Answer

Considering this DATA step, which statement is true?

a. It reads a temporary data set and creates a permanent data set.

(b.) It reads a permanent data set and creates a temporary data set.

c. It contains a syntax error and does not execute.

d. It does not execute because you cannot work with permanent and temporary data sets in the same step.

```
data us;              /* Create a temporary data set */
   set orion.sales;   /* Read a permanent data set */
   where Country='US';
run;
```

16

6.03 Short Answer Poll – Correct Answer

What are the values of **n1** and **n2** given the following variables and values?

x	y	z
.	4	10

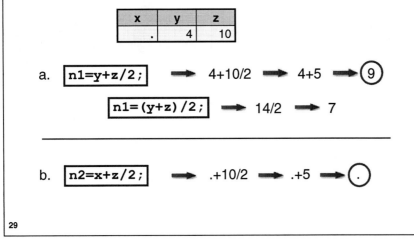

29

6.04 Short Answer Poll – Correct Answer

Open and submit **p106a03**. Is the output data set created successfully?

```
260   data work.usemps;
261      set orion.sales;
262      Bonus=Salary*.10;
263      where Country='US' and Bonus>=3000;
ERROR: Variable Bonus is not on file ORION.SALES.
264   run;

NOTE: The SAS System stopped processing this step because of
errors.
WARNING: The data set WORK.USEMPS may be incomplete.  When
this step was stopped there were 0 observations and 10
variables.
```

No. Bonus cannot be used in a WHERE statement because it is not in the input data set. It is a new variable that is created in this DATA step.

64   p106a03

6.05 Short Answer Poll – Correct Answer

What column heading is displayed for **Job_Title** in the program below?

```
data work.us;
   set orion.sales;
   where Country='US';
   Bonus=Salary*.10;
   label Job_Title='Sales Title';
   drop Employee_ID Gender Country
        Birth_Date;
run;
proc print data=work.us label;
   label Job_Title='Title';
run;
```

The column heading is Title. Labels and formats in PROC steps override permanent labels and formats.

79   p106a05

Chapter 7   Reading Spreadsheet and Database Data

7.1 Reading Spreadsheet Data

Objectives

- Use the VALIDVARNAME option to control special characters in column headings.
- Use SAS/ACCESS engines to access Microsoft Excel workbooks.
- Use the CONTENTS procedure to explore an Excel library.
- Use the PRINT procedure to display a worksheet.
- Create a SAS data set. Use a worksheet as input.

3

Business Scenario

The Sales Manager requested a report about Orion Star sales employees from Australia. The input data is in an Excel workbook.

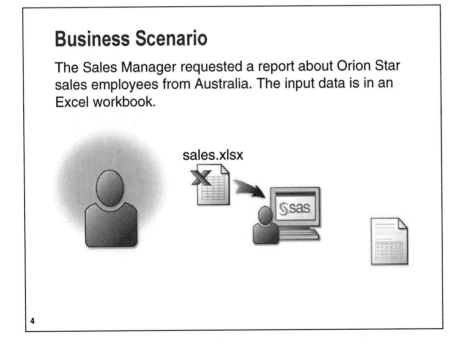

sales.xlsx

4

Business Scenario

Use SAS/ACCESS Interface to PC Files to read the worksheet as if it were a SAS data set.

5

Examining sales.xlsx

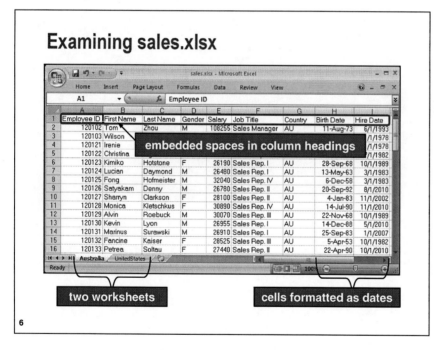

6

7.01 Poll

Based on material already discussed, does SAS allow embedded blanks and special characters in variable names?

○ Yes

○ No

7

SAS Variable Names

Excel column headings are used as variable names.

- The SAS windowing environment replaces blanks and special characters with underscores.
- By default, SAS Studio and SAS Enterprise Guide allow blanks and special characters in variable names.

9

- In the SAS windowing environment, the VALIDVARNAME= option is set to V7 by default. V7 does not allow variable names to contain special characters.

- In SAS Studio and SAS Enterprise Guide, the VALIDVARNAME= option is set to ANY by default. ANY enables variable names to contain special characters. If a variable name contains special characters, the variable name must be expressed as a SAS name literal.

SAS Name Literal

When a variable name contains embedded blanks or special characters, you must use a SAS name literal.

```
'Job Title'n
```

A *SAS name literal* is a string within quotation marks, followed by the upper or lowercase letter *n*.

10

VALIDVARNAME= Option

Set the VALIDVARNAME= option to **V7** to enforce SAS naming rules in SAS Studio and SAS Enterprise Guide.

```
options validvarname=V7;
```

- Up to 32 mixed-case alphanumeric characters are allowed.
- Names must begin with an alphabetic character or an underscore.
- Invalid characters are changed to underscores.
- Any column name that is not unique is made unique by appending a counter to the name.

11

SAS/ACCESS LIBNAME Statement

SAS/ACCESS has multiple LIBNAME engines that access Microsoft Excel workbooks.

```
libname orionx excel "&path\sales.xlsx";
```

```
libname orionx pcfiles path="&path\sales.xlsx";
```

```
libname orionx xlsx "&path\sales.xlsx";
```

✏ The engine that you use depends on the operating environment of SAS and the bitness of SAS and Excel.

12

Both SAS and Microsoft Office offer 32-bit and 64-bit versions. The term *bitness* refers to the 32-bit and 64-bit versions of software. To determine the bitness of SAS and Microsoft Office, see the following usage notes:

- *Installing SAS® 9.3 PC Files Server and using it to convert 32-bit Microsoft Office files to SAS® 64-bit files* (**http://support.sas.com/kb/43/802.html**)
- *Summary of steps to install and use the SAS® 9.4 PC Files Server* (**http://support.sas.com/kb/54/413.html**)

SAS/ACCESS Engines

	EXCEL Engine	PCFILES Engine	XLSX Engine
SAS Operating Environment	Windows	Windows, Linux, and UNIX	Windows, Linux, and UNIX
Bitness	Same	Any combination	Any combination
Additional Software	Yes	Yes	No
Supported Excel File Types	.xls .xlsx	.xls .xlsx	.xlsx
Options	Yes	Yes	Limited

13

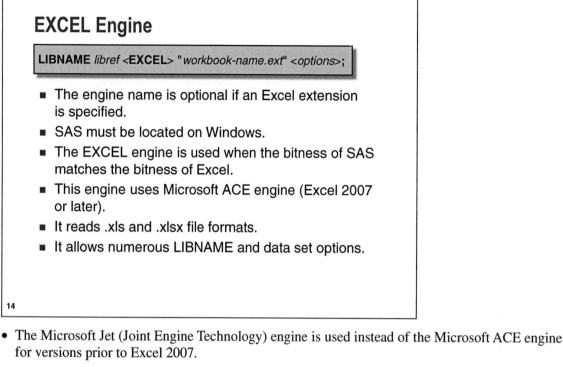

- The Microsoft Jet (Joint Engine Technology) engine is used instead of the Microsoft ACE engine for versions prior to Excel 2007.
- The EXCEL engine can also read .xlsb and .xlsm files.

PCFILES Engine

```
LIBNAME libref PCFILES PATH="workbook-name.ext"
              <SERVER=Windows server> <options>;
```

- SAS can be located on Windows, Linux, or UNIX.
- The PCFILES engine is used with any bitness combination.
- This engine requires SERVER= when Linux or UNIX SAS is used.
- It uses the Microsoft ACE engine (Excel 2007 or later).
- The engine requires the SAS PC Files Server (Windows) in order to connect to the Excel file.
- It reads .xls and .xlsx file formats.
- It allows numerous LIBNAME and data set options.

15

- SERVER= specifies the name of the Windows computer that is running the SAS PC Files Server. This option is required for Linux and UNIX users to connect to the PC Files Server.
- Microsoft Jet (Joint Engine Technology) engine is used instead of Microsoft ACE engine for versions prior to Excel 2007.
- The PCFILES engine can also read .xlsb and .xlsm files.

XLSX Engine

LIBNAME *libref* **XLSX** *"workbook-name.xlsx" <options>*;

- The XLSX engine requires SAS 9.4M2 or later.
- SAS can be located on Windows, Linux, or UNIX.
- This engine is used with any bitness combination.
- It accesses the Excel file directly without using the Microsoft ACE engine.
- The Excel file must be accessible to Linux or UNIX when you use SAS that is not on Windows.
- The engine reads only .xlsx file formats (Excel 2007 or later).
- It can read more than 255 columns.
- It allows limited LIBNAME options.

16

A worksheet in a .xls file can have up to 256 columns and 65,536 rows. Excel 2007 and later files (.xlsx files) were enhanced to support 16,384 columns and 1,048,576 rows in a worksheet. Files that are created with Excel 2007 and later can have an .xlsx, .xlsb, or .xlsm extension. Due to how the Microsoft ACE driver and the Microsoft Jet driver work, the EXCEL and PCFILES engines are limited to 255 columns in an Excel file.

Documentation

For more information about the LIBNAME engines and PC Files Server, refer to the documentation.

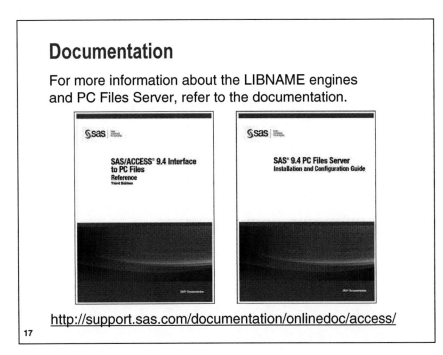

http://support.sas.com/documentation/onlinedoc/access/

17

Exploring the Library

Regardless of the LIBNAME engine that is used, you can use the CONTENTS procedure to explore the library.

```
options validvarname=v7;
libname orionx pcfiles path="&path\sales.xlsx";

proc contents data=orionx._all_;
run;

libname orionx clear;
```

- When SAS has a libref that is assigned to an Excel workbook, the workbook cannot be opened in Excel.
- To disassociate the libref, use a LIBNAME statement with the CLEAR option.

p107d01a
p107d01b

18

Exploring the Library

Partial PROC CONTENTS Output

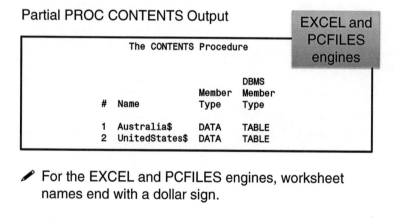

#	Name	Member Type	DBMS Member Type
1	Australia$	DATA	TABLE
2	UnitedStates$	DATA	TABLE

The CONTENTS Procedure

EXCEL and PCFILES engines

✎ For the EXCEL and PCFILES engines, worksheet names end with a dollar sign.

19

p107d01a

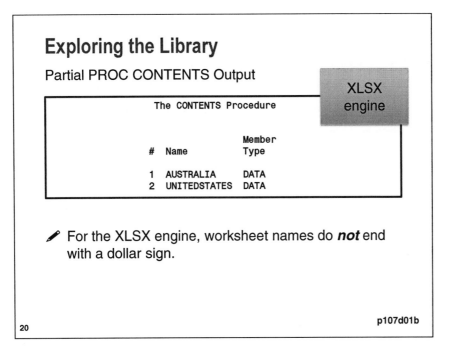

Exploring the Library

Partial PROC CONTENTS Output

#	Name	Member Type
1	AUSTRALIA	DATA
2	UNITEDSTATES	DATA

The CONTENTS Procedure

XLSX engine

✐ For the XLSX engine, worksheet names do **not** end with a dollar sign.

20   p107d01b

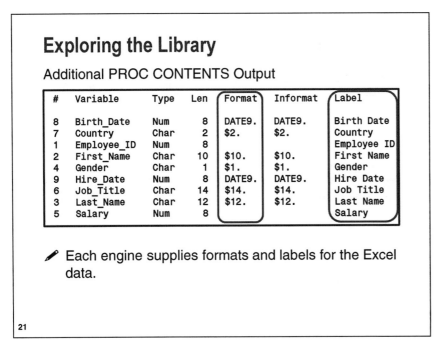

Exploring the Library

Additional PROC CONTENTS Output

#	Variable	Type	Len	Format	Informat	Label
8	Birth_Date	Num	8	DATE9.	DATE9.	Birth Date
7	Country	Char	2	$2.	$2.	Country
1	Employee_ID	Num	8			Employee ID
2	First_Name	Char	10	$10.	$10.	First Name
4	Gender	Char	1	$1.	$1.	Gender
9	Hire_Date	Num	8	DATE9.	DATE9.	Hire Date
6	Job_Title	Char	14	$14.	$14.	Job Title
3	Last_Name	Char	12	$12.	$12.	Last Name
5	Salary	Num	8			Salary

✐ Each engine supplies formats and labels for the Excel data.

21

Named Ranges

The SAS/ACCESS LIBNAME statement with the EXCEL, PCFILES, or XLSX engine is used to access worksheets within an Excel workbook. In addition, the statement can be used to access named ranges within an Excel workbook. A named range refers to a range of cells in a worksheet.

For example, the **sales.xls** file contains two worksheets (**Australia** and **UnitedStates**) and two named ranges (**AU** and **US**).

Given the following program:

```
options validvarname=v7;
libname orionx pcfiles path="&path\sales.xls";


proc contents data=orionx._all_;
run;


libname orionx clear;
```

The results of the CONTENTS procedure show the two worksheets and the two named ranges.

```
                          The CONTENTS Procedure


                                         DBMS
                              Member     Member
              #   Name        Type       Type


              1   AU          DATA       TABLE
              2   Australia$  DATA       TABLE
              3   US          DATA       TABLE
              4   UnitedStates$  DATA     TABLE
```

- For the EXCEL and PCFILES engines, worksheet names end with a dollar sign and named ranges do **not** end with a dollar sign. Both worksheet names and named ranges are visible in PROC CONTENTS output.

- For the XLSX engine, worksheet names and named ranges do **not** end with a dollar sign. Worksheet names are visible in PROC CONTENTS output but named ranges are not.

Regardless of the engine that is used, the named range can be accessed with a two-level name. The following example shows the **AU** named range being used in a PROC step and DATA step:

```
proc print data=orionx.AU;
run;


data work.subset2;
   set orionx.AU;
run;
```

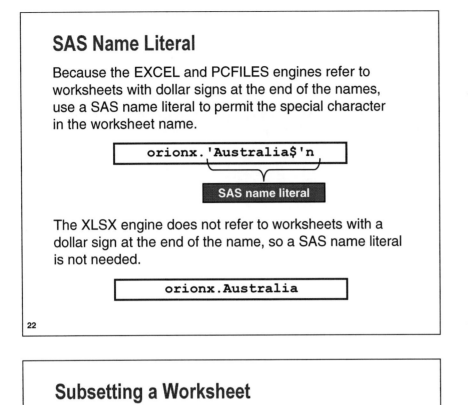

SAS Name Literal

Because the EXCEL and PCFILES engines refer to
worksheets with dollar signs at the end of the names,
use a SAS name literal to permit the special character
in the worksheet name.

```
orionx.'Australia$'n
```

SAS name literal

The XLSX engine does not refer to worksheets with a
dollar sign at the end of the name, so a SAS name literal
is not needed.

```
orionx.Australia
```

22

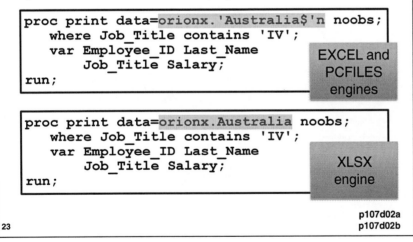

Subsetting a Worksheet

Regardless of the LIBNAME engine used, the PRINT
procedure can be used to display a subset of the worksheet.

```
proc print data=orionx.'Australia$'n noobs;
   where Job_Title contains 'IV';
   var Employee_ID Last_Name
       Job_Title Salary;
run;
```

EXCEL and
PCFILES
engines

```
proc print data=orionx.Australia noobs;
   where Job_Title contains 'IV';
   var Employee_ID Last_Name
       Job_Title Salary;
run;
```

XLSX
engine

p107d02a
p107d02b

23

If the sheet name contains special characters or embedded blanks, a name literal must be used to refer
to the sheet, even when you use the XLSX engine.

Subsetting a Worksheet

PROC PRINT Output

```
Employee_
   ID        Last_Name       Job_Title        Salary

120125       Hofmeister      Sales Rep. IV    32040
120128       Kletschkus      Sales Rep. IV    30890
120135       Platts          Sales Rep. IV    32490
120159       Phoumirath      Sales Rep. IV    30765
120166       Nowd            Sales Rep. IV    30660
```

24

7.02 Short Answer Poll

You submit the statement below. Which step displays the UnitedStates worksheet?

```
libname xl excel 's:\workshop\custusau.xlsx';
```

a.
```
proc print data=xl.UnitedStates;
run;
```

b.
```
proc print data=xl.'UnitedStates';
run;
```

c.
```
proc print data=xl.'UnitedStates'n;
run;
```

d.
```
proc print data=xl.'UnitedStates$'n;
run;
```

25

Business Scenario

Create a SAS data set using a Microsoft Excel workbook as input.

ORION STAR SPORTS & OUTDOORS

sales.xlsx

27

Considerations

Use the SAS/ACCESS LIBNAME engine to read the **Australia** worksheet and create a temporary data set.

Australia DATA Step **work.subset2**

Rep

The new data set should include the following:

- only the employees with **Rep** in their job titles
- a **Bonus** variable that is 10% of **Salary**
- permanent labels and formats

28

Creating a SAS Data Set from an Excel Worksheet

p107d03a

This demonstration uses the SAS/ACCESS EXCEL or PCFILES engine to read an .xlsx file. An alternate version, **p107d03b**, uses the SAS/ACCESS XLSX engine to read the .xlsx file.

```
options validvarname=v7;
*libname xl excel "&path\sales.xlsx";
*libname xl pcfiles path="&path\sales.xlsx";

proc contents data=xl._all_;
run;

data work.subset2;
   set xl.'Australia$'n;
   where Job_Title contains 'Rep';
   Bonus=Salary*.10;
   keep First_Name Last_Name Salary Bonus
        Job_Title Hire_Date;
   label Job_Title='Sales Title'
         Hire_Date='Date Hired';
   format Salary comma10. Hire_Date mmddyy10.
          Bonus comma8.2;
run;

proc contents data=work.subset2;
run;

proc print data=work.subset2 label;
run;

libname xl clear;
```

1. Open **p107d03a** and uncomment the appropriate LIBNAME statement.

2. Submit the OPTIONS and LIBNAME statements, and the first PROC CONTENTS step.

3. Verify that the **xl** library contains the worksheets, **Australia$** and **UnitedStates$**.

4. Submit the DATA step to create a new data set, **work.subset2**.

5. Check the log. Verify that 61 observations were written to **work.subset2**.

6. Submit the second PROC CONTENTS step. Verify that the formats and labels were stored in the descriptor portion of **work.subset2**. Notice that all columns have labels, not only the columns that were assigned labels in the DATA step.

   Partial PROC CONTENTS Output

	Alphabetic List of Variables and Attributes					
#	Variable	Type	Len	Format	Informat	Label
6	Bonus	Num	8	COMMA8.2		
1	First_Name	Char	10	$10.	$10.	First Name
5	Hire_Date	Num	8	MMDDYY10.	DATE9.	Date Hired
4	Job_Title	Char	14	$14.	$14.	Sales Title
2	Last_Name	Char	12	$12.	$12.	Last Name
3	Salary	Num	8	COMMA10.		Salary

7. Submit the PROC PRINT step. Verify that the results contain 61 observations and that the labels were displayed and formats were applied.

Partial PROC PRINT Output

Obs	First Name	Last Name	Salary	Sales Title	Date Hired	Bonus
1	Irenie	Elvish	26,600	Sales Rep. II	01/01/1978	2,660.00
2	Christina	Ngan	27,475	Sales Rep. II	07/01/1982	2,747.50
3	Kimiko	Hotstone	26,190	Sales Rep. I	10/01/1989	2,619.00
4	Lucian	Daymond	26,480	Sales Rep. I	03/01/1983	2,648.00
5	Fong	Hofmeister	32,040	Sales Rep. IV	03/01/1983	3,204.00

8. Submit the LIBNAME statement to clear the resources.

9. Check the log for success.

Exercises

> If you restarted your SAS session since the last exercise, open and submit the **libname** program that can be found in the data folder.

Level 1

1. **Accessing an Excel Worksheet**

   a. Retrieve the starter program **p107e01**.

   b. Add an OPTIONS statement before the PROC CONTENTS step to set VALIDVARNAME to **V7**.

   c. Add a LIBNAME statement after the OPTIONS statement to create a libref named **custfm** that references the Excel workbook, **custfm.xlsx**.

   d. Submit the LIBNAME statement and the PROC CONTENTS step. Verify the output.

   Partial PROC CONTENTS Output

			DBMS
		Member	Member
#	Name	Type	Type
1	Females$	DATA	TABLE
2	Males$	DATA	TABLE

   The CONTENTS Procedure

   e. Add a SET statement in the DATA step to read the worksheet that contains the data for males.

   f. Add a KEEP statement in the DATA step to include only **First_Name**, **Last_Name**, and **Birth_Date** in the new data set.

   g. Add a FORMAT statement in the DATA step to display **Birth_Date** as a four-digit year.

   h. Add a LABEL statement in the DATA step to display **Birth Year** instead of **Birth_Date**.

    i. Add a final LIBNAME statement to the program to clear the libref.

    j. Submit the program to create the report below. Results should contain 47 observations.

Partial PROC PRINT Output

Obs	First Name	Last Name	Birth Year
1	James	Kvarniq	1974
2	David	Black	1969
3	Markus	Sepke	1988
4	Ulrich	Heyde	1939
5	Jimmie	Evans	1954

Level 2

2. Accessing an Excel Worksheet

    a. Open a new program and write an OPTIONS statement to set VALIDVARNAME to **V7**.

    b. Write a LIBNAME statement to create a libref named **prod** that references the Excel workbook **products.xlsx**.

    c. Write a PROC CONTENTS step to view all of the contents of **prod**.

    d. Submit the program to determine the names of the four worksheets in **products.xlsx**.

    e. Write a DATA step that reads the worksheet containing sports data and creates a new data set named **work.golf**.

    f. The data set **work.golf** should have the following characteristics:
- include only the observations where **Category** is equal to *Golf*
- not include the **Category** variable
- include a label of **Golf Products** for the **Name** variable

    f. Write a LIBNAME statement to clear the **prod** libref.

    g. Write a PROC PRINT step to create the report below. Results should contain 56 observations.

Partial PROC PRINT Output

Obs	Golf Products
1	Ball Bag
2	Red/White/Black Staff 9 Bag
3	Tee Holder
4	Bb Softspikes - Xp 22-pack
5	Bretagne Performance Tg Men's Golf Shoes L.

Challenge

3. Creating an Excel Worksheet

     This program fails if the workbook already exists with a **salesemps** worksheet. Delete **employees.xls** from the data folder if it exists.

a. Open **p107e03**. Insert a LIBNAME statement to associate the libref **out** with the Excel workbook **employees.xls** in the default data folder.

b. Modify the program so that it creates a worksheet that is named **salesemps** in the **employees.xls** workbook.

c. Submit the SAS program and verify that it created the data set **out.salesemps** with 71 observations and four variables as shown in the partial SAS log below.

```
NOTE: 71 records were read from the infile "s:\workshop\newemps.csv".
NOTE: The data set OUT.salesemps has 71 observations and 4 variables.
```

d. Verify that the new Excel workbook **employees.xls** was created with one sheet, **salesemps**.

7.2 Reading Database Data

Objectives

- Use a SAS/ACCESS engine to access an Oracle database.
- Use an Oracle table as input and create a SAS data set.

33

Business Scenario

The Northeast Sales Manager requested a report that lists supervisors from New York and New Jersey. The input data is in an Oracle database.

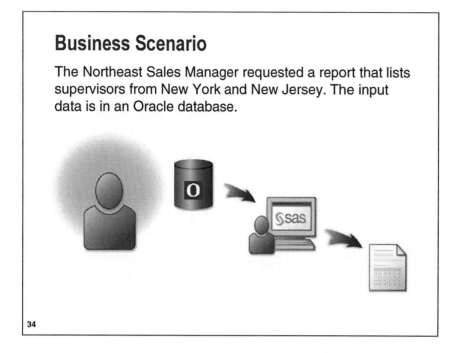

34

SAS/ACCESS LIBNAME Statement

The SAS/ACCESS LIBNAME statement assigns a libref to a relational database.

LIBNAME *libref engine <SAS/ACCESS options>;*

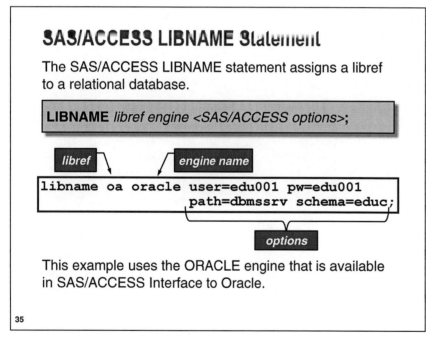

```
libname oa oracle user=edu001 pw=edu001
                   path=dbmssrv schema=educ;
```

This example uses the ORACLE engine that is available in SAS/ACCESS Interface to Oracle.

35

- The engine name, such as Oracle or DB2, is the SAS/ACCESS component that reads and writes to your DBMS. The engine name is required.
- USER= specifies an optional Oracle user name. USER= must be used with PASSWORD=.
- PASSWORD= (or PW=) specifies an optional Oracle password associated with the Oracle user name.
- PATH= specifies the Oracle driver, node, and database. SAS/ACCESS uses the same Oracle path designation that you use to connect to Oracle directly.
- SCHEMA= enables you to read database objects, such as tables and views, in the specified schema. If this option is omitted, you connect to the default schema for your DBMS.

Accessing an Oracle Database

SAS treats the Oracle database as a library, and each
table as a SAS data set. Use the CONTENTS procedure
to explore the library.

```
libname oa oracle user=edu001 pw=edu001
                   path=dbmssrv schema=educ;

proc contents data=oa._all_;
run;

libname oa clear;
```

Submit a LIBNAME statement with the CLEAR option
to release the database and associated resources.

36

Accessing an Oracle Table

Use a two-level name to reference any table in this Oracle
database.

```
libname oa oracle user=edu001 pw=edu001
                   path=dbmssrv schema=educ;

proc print data=oa.supervisors;
   where state in ('NY' 'NJ');
run;

data work.nysup;
   set oa.supervisors;
   where state='NY';
run;

libname oa clear;
```

37

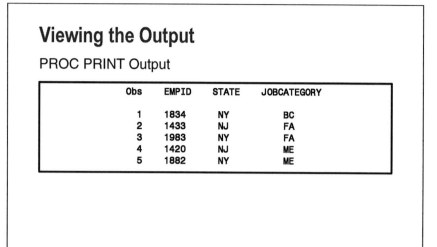

Viewing the Output

PROC PRINT Output

Obs	EMPID	STATE	JOBCATEGORY
1	1834	NY	BC
2	1433	NJ	FA
3	1983	NY	FA
4	1420	NJ	ME
5	1882	NY	ME

38

Documentation

Refer to the documentation for information relating to a specific relational database.

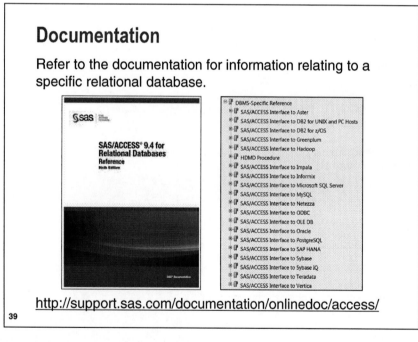

http://support.sas.com/documentation/onlinedoc/access/

39

7.3 Solutions

Solutions to Exercises

1. **Accessing an Excel Worksheet**

```
options validvarname=v7;
*libname custfm excel "&path/custfm.xlsx";
*libname custfm pcfiles path="&path/custfm.xlsx";
```

```
proc contents data=custfm._all_;
run;

data work.males;
   set custfm.'Males$'n;
   keep First_Name Last_Name Birth_Date;
   format Birth_Date year4.;
   label Birth_Date='Birth Year';
run;

proc print data=work.males label;
run;

libname custfm clear;

/* Alternate solution */

options validvarname=v7;
libname custfm xlsx "&path/custfm.xlsx";

proc contents data=custfm._all_;
run;

data work.males;
   set custfm.Males;
   keep First_Name Last_Name Birth_Date;
   format Birth_Date year4.;
   label Birth_Date='Birth Year';
run;

proc print data=work.males label;
run;

libname custfm clear;
```

2. **Accessing an Excel Worksheet**

```
options validvarname=v7;
*libname prod excel "&path\products.xlsx";
*libname prod pcfiles path="&path\products.xlsx";

proc contents data=prod._all_;
run;

data work.golf;
   set prod.'sports$'n;
   where Category='Golf';
   drop Category;
   label Name='Golf Products';
run;

libname prod clear;
```

```
proc print data=work.golf label;
run;

/* Alternate solution */

options validvarname=v7;
libname prod xlsx "&path\products.xlsx";

proc contents data=prod._all_;
run;

data work.golf;
   set prod.sports;
   where Category='Golf';
   drop Category;
   label Name='Golf Products';
run;

libname prod clear;

proc print data=work.golf label;
run;
```

3. **Creating an Excel Worksheet**

```
options validvarname=v7;
*libname out excel "&path\employees.xls";
*libname out pcfiles path="&path\employees.xls";

data out.salesemps;
   length First_Name $ 12 Last_Name $ 18
          Job_Title $ 25;
   infile "&path\newemps.csv" dlm=',';
   input First_Name $ Last_Name $
         Job_Title $ Salary;
run;

libname out clear;
```

Solutions to Student Activities (Polls/Quizzes)

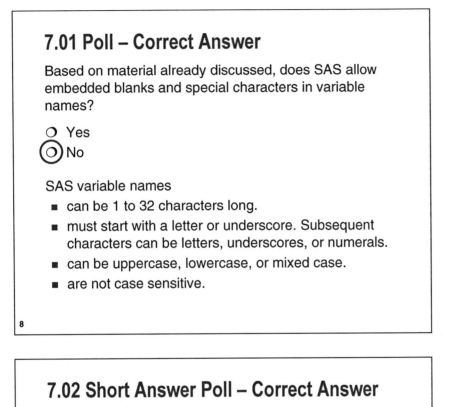

7.01 Poll – Correct Answer

Based on material already discussed, does SAS allow embedded blanks and special characters in variable names?

○ Yes
◉ No

SAS variable names
- can be 1 to 32 characters long.
- must start with a letter or underscore. Subsequent characters can be letters, underscores, or numerals.
- can be uppercase, lowercase, or mixed case.
- are not case sensitive.

8

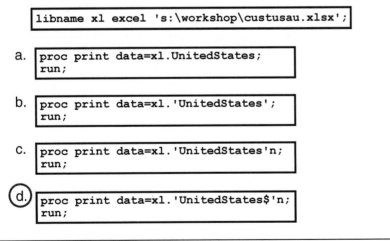

7.02 Short Answer Poll – Correct Answer

You submit the statement below. Which step displays the UnitedStates worksheet?

```
libname xl excel 's:\workshop\custusau.xlsx';
```

a.
```
proc print data=xl.UnitedStates;
run;
```

b.
```
proc print data=xl.'UnitedStates';
run;
```

c.
```
proc print data=xl.'UnitedStates'n;
run;
```

d.
```
proc print data=xl.'UnitedStates$'n;
run;
```

26

Chapter 8   Reading Raw Data Files

8.1 Introduction to Reading Raw Data Files

Objectives

- Identify the types of raw data files and input styles.
- Define the terms *standard* and *nonstandard* data.

3

Business Scenario

Information about Orion Star sales employees from Australia and the United States is stored in a raw data file.

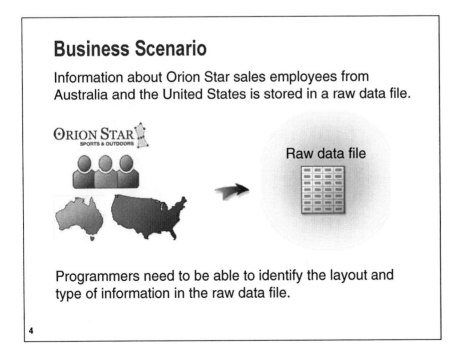

Programmers need to be able to identify the layout and type of information in the raw data file.

4

Raw Data Files

A raw data file is also known as a *flat file*.

- They are text files that contain one record per line.
- A record typically contains multiple fields.
- Flat files do not have internal metadata.
- External documentation, known as a *record layout*, should exist.
- A record layout describes the fields and locations within each record.

5

Raw Data Files

Fields in a raw data file can be delimited or arranged in fixed columns.

Delimited File

```
120102,Tom,Zhou,M,108255,Sales Manager,AU,11AUG1973,06/01/1993
120103,Wilson,Dawes,M,87975,Sales Manager,AU,22JAN1953,01/01/1978
120121,Irenie,Elvish,F,26600,Sales Rep. II,AU,02AUG1948,01/01/1978
120122,Christina,Ngan,F,27475,Sales Rep. II,AU,27JUL1958,07/01/1982
```

Fixed Column File

```
         1    1    2    2    3    3    4    4    5    5    6
1---5----0----5----0----5----0----5----0----5----0----5----0--
120102Tom       Zhou          Sales Manager      108255AU
120103Wilson    Dawes         Sales Manager       87975AU
120121Irenie    Elvish        Sales Rep. II       26600AU
120122Christina Ngan          Sales Rep. II       27475AU
```

6

Fields in Raw Data Files

In order for SAS to read a raw data file, you must specify the following information about each field:

- the location of the data value in the record
- the name of the SAS variable in which to store the data
- the type of the SAS variable

7

Reading Raw Data Files

There are different techniques, or *input styles*, for reading raw data files in SAS.

Input Style	Used for Reading
Column Input	Standard data in fixed columns
Formatted Input	Standard and nonstandard data in fixed columns
List Input	Standard and nonstandard data separated by blanks or some other delimiter

8

Standard and Nonstandard Data

Standard data is data that SAS can read without any additional instruction.

- Character data is always standard.
- Some numeric values are standard and some are not.

9

8.01 Multiple Answer Poll

What type of raw data files do you read?

a. delimited
b. fixed column
c. both delimited and fixed column
d. I do not read raw data files.

10

8.2 Reading Standard Delimited Data

Objectives

- Use list input to create a SAS data set from a delimited raw data file.
- Examine the compilation and execution phases of the DATA step when you read a raw data file.
- Explicitly define the length of a variable.
- Examine behavior when a data error is encountered.

12

Business Scenario

Information about Orion Star sales employees is stored in a comma-delimited raw data file. The file contains both standard and nonstandard data fields.

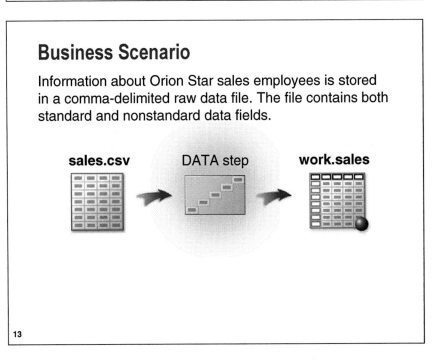

sales.csv   DATA step   work.sales

13

List Input

Use list input to read delimited raw data files.

Partial **sales.csv**

```
120102,Tom,Zhou,M,108255,Sales Manager,AU,11AUG1973,06/01/1993
120103,Wilson,Dawes,M,87975,Sales Manager,AU,22JAN1953,01/01/1978
120121,Irenie,Elvish,F,26600,Sales Rep. II,AU,02AUG1948,01/01/1978
120122,Christina,Ngan,F,27475,Sales Rep. II,AU,27JUL1958,07/01/1982
120123,Kimiko,Hotstone,F,26190,Sales Rep. I,AU,28SEP1968,10/01/1989
```

- SAS considers a space (blank) to be the default delimiter.
- Both standard and nonstandard data can be read.
- Fields must be read sequentially, left to right.

14

8.02 Short Answer Poll

Which fields in this file can be read as standard numeric values?

Partial **sales.csv**

```
120102,Tom,Zhou,M,108255,Sales Manager,AU,11AUG1973,06/01/1993
120103,Wilson,Dawes,M,87975,Sales Manager,AU,22JAN1953,01/01/1978
120121,Irenie,Elvish,F,26600,Sales Rep. II,AU,02AUG1948,01/01/1978
120122,Christina,Ngan,F,27475,Sales Rep. II,AU,27JUL1958,07/01/1982
120123,Kimiko,Hotstone,F,26190,Sales Rep. I,AU,28SEP1968,10/01/1989
```

15

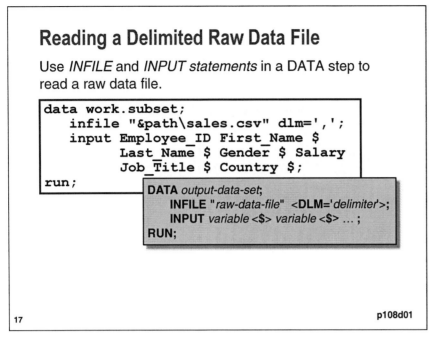

DLM= is an alias for DELIMITER=*delimiter(s)*. It is used to specify an alternate delimiter (other than a blank) to be used for list input. *Delimiter(s)* is one or more characters enclosed in quotation marks. If more than one delimiter is specified, each is treated as a delimiter. The delimiter is case sensitive.

- To specify a tab delimiter on Windows or UNIX, enter **dlm='09'x**.

- To specify a tab delimiter on z/OS (OS/390), enter **dlm='05'x**.

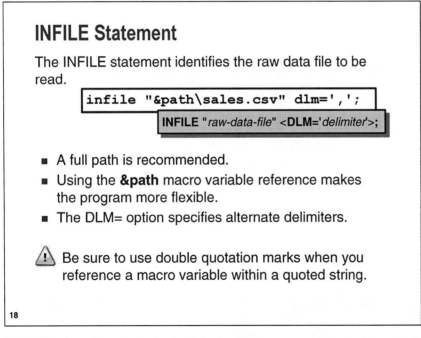

A %LET statement was submitted in the **libname.sas** program to create the user-defined macro variable, **path**. The INFILE statement references the value of the macro variable by placing an ampersand before its name. The macro variable exists for the duration of the SAS session unless it is changed or deleted.

INPUT Statement

The INPUT statement reads the data fields sequentially, left to right. Standard data fields require only a variable name and type.

Partial **sales.csv**

```
120102,Tom,Zhou,M,108255,Sales Manager,AU,11AUG1969,06/01/1989
120103,Wilson,Dawes,M,87975,Sales Manager,AU,22JAN1949,01/01/1974
120121,Irenie,Elvish,F,26600,Sales Rep. II,AU,02AUG1944,01/01/1974
```

```
input Employee_ID First_Name $ Last_Name $
      Gender $ Salary Job_Title $ Country $;
```

INPUT *variable* <$> *variable* <$> ...;

- The dollar sign indicates a character variable.
- Default length for *all* variables is eight bytes, regardless of type.

19

Viewing the Log

Partial SAS Log

```
249  data work.subset;
250     infile "&path\sales.csv" dlm=',';
251     input Employee_ID First_Name $ Last_Name $
252            Gender $ Salary Job_Title $ Country $;
253  run;

NOTE: The infile "s:\workshop\sales.csv" is:
      Filename=s:\workshop\sales.csv,
      RECFM=V,LRECL=256,File Size (bytes)=11340

NOTE: 165 records were read from the infile "s:\workshop\sales.csv".
      The minimum record length was 61.
      The maximum record length was 80.
NOTE: The data set WORK.SUBSET has 165 observations and 7 variables.
```

20   p108d01

Viewing the Output

```
proc print data=work.subset noobs;
run;
```

Partial PROC PRINT Output

Employee_ ID	First_ Name	Last_ Name	Gender	Salary	Job_ Title	Country
120102	Tom	Zhou	M	108255	Sales Ma	AU
120103	Wilson	Dawes	M	87975	Sales Ma	AU
120121	Irenie	Elvish	F	26600	Sales Re	AU
120122	Christin	Ngan	F	27475	Sales Re	AU
120123	Kimiko	Hotstone	F	26190	Sales Re	AU

Some character values are truncated.

21   p108d01

Business Scenario

It is important to understand the processing that occurs
when a DATA step reads a raw data file.

22

Compilation Phase

During compilation, SAS does the following:

- scans the step for syntax errors
- translates each statement into machine language
- creates an *input buffer* to hold one record at a time from the raw data file

Input Buffer   1   2
1 2 3 4 5 6 7 8 9 0 1 2 3 4 5 6   8 9 0
[ ][ ][ ][ ][ ][ ][ ][ ][ ][ ][ ][ ][ ][ ][ ][ ][ ][ ][ ] ...

- creates the program data vector (PDV) to hold one observation
- creates the descriptor portion of the output data set

23

Compilation

```
data work.subset;
   infile "&path\sales.csv" dlm=',';
   input Employee_ID First_Name $ Last_Name $
         Gender $ Salary Job_Title $ Country $;
run;
```

24   p108d01
                                                        ...

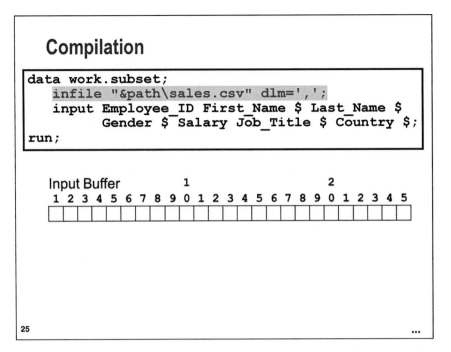

The default length of the input buffer depends on the operating system. You can use the LRECL= option in the INFILE statement to modify it.

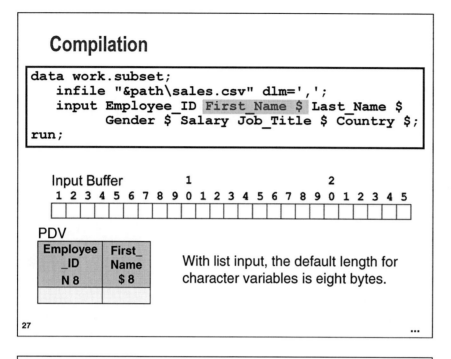

Compilation

```
data work.subset;
   infile "&path\sales.csv" dlm=',';
   input Employee_ID First_Name $ Last_Name $
         Gender $ Salary Job_Title $ Country $;
run;
```

Input Buffer

With list input, the default length for character variables is eight bytes.

27

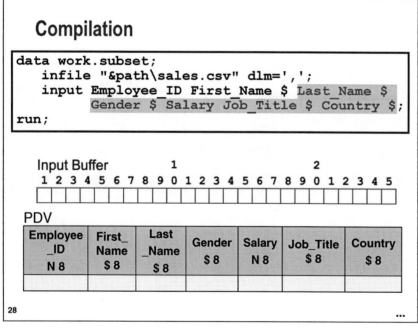

Compilation

```
data work.subset;
   infile "&path\sales.csv" dlm=',';
   input Employee_ID First_Name $ Last_Name $
         Gender $ Salary Job_Title $ Country $;
run;
```

Input Buffer

Employee _ID	First_ Name	Last _Name	Gender	Salary	Job_Title	Country
N 8	$ 8	$ 8	$ 8	N 8	$ 8	$ 8

28

Compilation

```
data work.subset;
   infile "&path\sales.csv" dlm=',';
   input Employee_ID First_Name $ Last_Name $
         Gender $ Salary Job_Title $ Country $;
run;
```

PDV

Employee _ID N 8	First_ Name $ 8	Last _Name $ 8	Gender $ 8	Salary N 8	Job_Title $ 8	Country $ 8

Descriptor Portion of **work.subset**

Employee _ID N 8	First_ Name $ 8	Last _Name $ 8	Gender $ 8	Salary N 8	Job_Title $ 8	Country $ 8

29   ...

8.03 Multiple Choice Poll

Which statement is true?

a. An input buffer is created only if you are reading data from a raw data file.

b. The PDV at compile time holds the variable name, type, byte size, and initial value.

c. The descriptor portion is the first item that is created at compile time.

30

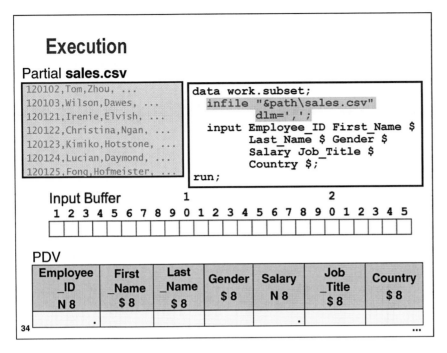

Execution

Partial **sales.csv**

```
120102,Tom,Zhou, ...
120103,Wilson,Dawes, ...
120121,Irenie,Elvish, ...
120122,Christina,Ngan, ...
120123,Kimiko,Hotstone, ...
120124,Lucian,Daymond, ...
120125,Fonq,Hofmeister, ...
```

```
data work.subset;
   infile "&path\sales.csv"
          dlm=',';
   input Employee_ID First_Name $
         Last_Name $ Gender $
         Salary Job_Title $
         Country $;
run;
```

Input Buffer

```
          1                   2
1 2 3 4 5 6 7 8 9 0 1 2 3 4 5 6 7 8 9 0 1 2 3 4 5
☐ ☐ ☐ ☐ ☐ ☐ ☐ ☐ ☐ ☐ ☐ ☐ ☐ ☐ ☐ ☐ ☐ ☐ ☐ ☐ ☐ ☐ ☐ ☐ ☐
```

PDV

Employee _ID N 8	First _Name $ 8	Last _Name $ 8	Gender $ 8	Salary N 8	Job Title $ 8	Country $ 8
.				.		

34

...

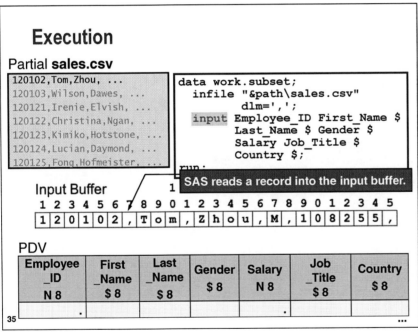

Execution

Partial **sales.csv**

```
120102,Tom,Zhou, ...
120103,Wilson,Dawes, ...
120121,Irenie,Elvish, ...
120122,Christina,Ngan, ...
120123,Kimiko,Hotstone, ...
120124,Lucian,Daymond, ...
120125,Fonq,Hofmeister, ...
```

```
data work.subset;
   infile "&path\sales.csv"
          dlm=',';
   input Employee_ID First_Name $
         Last_Name $ Gender $
         Salary Job_Title $
         Country $;
run;
```

> SAS reads a record into the input buffer.

Input Buffer

```
          1
1 2 3 4 5 6 7 8 9 0 1 2 3 4 5 6 7 8 9 0 1 2 3 4 5
1 2 0 1 0 2 , T o m , Z h o u , M , 1 0 8 2 5 5 ,
```

PDV

Employee _ID N 8	First _Name $ 8	Last _Name $ 8	Gender $ 8	Salary N 8	Job Title $ 8	Country $ 8
.				.		

35

...

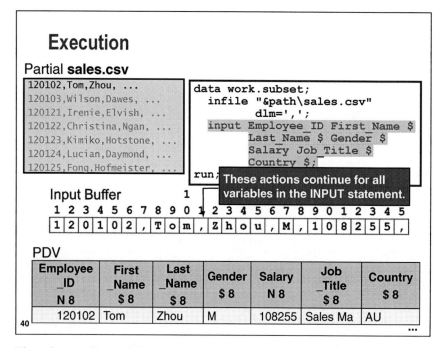

There is usually no delimiter after the last field in a record, so SAS stops reading when it encounters an end-of-record marker.

Execution

Here is the output data set after the first iteration of the DATA step.

work.subset

Employee _ID	First _Name	Last _Name	Gender	Salary	Job _Title	Country
120102	Tom	Zhou	M	108255	Sales Ma	AU

42

...

Execution

Partial **sales.csv**

| 120102,Tom,Zhou, ... |
| 120103,Wilson,Dawes, ... |
| 120121,Irenie,Elvish, ... |
| 120122,Christina,Ngan, ... |
| 120123,Kimiko,Hotstone, ... |
| 120124,Lucian,Daymond, ... |
| 120125,Fong,Hofmeister, ... |

```
data work.subset;
    infile "&path\sales.csv"
           dlm=',';
    input Employee_ID First_Name $
          Last_Name $ Gender $
          Salary Job_Title $
          Country $;
run;
```

Implicit OUTPUT;
Implicit RETURN;

Input Buffer   1

1	2	3	4	5	6	7	8	9	0	1	2	3	4	5	6	7	8	9	0	1	2	3	4	5
1	2	0	1	0	2	,	T	o	m	,	Z	h	o	u	,	M	,	1	0	8	2	5	5	,

PDV

Employee _ID N 8	First _Name $ 8	Last _Name $ 8	Gender $ 8	Salary N 8	Job _Title $ 8	Country $ 8
120102	Tom	Zhou	M	108255	Sales Ma	AU

43

...

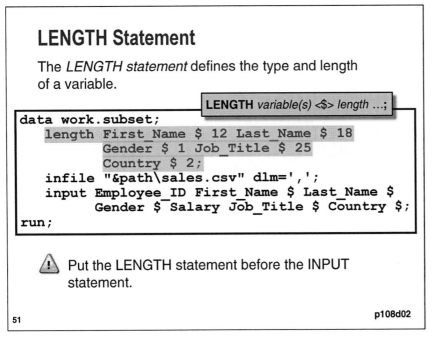

Viewing the Output

```
proc print data=work.subset noobs;
run;
```

Partial PROC PRINT Output

Employee_ID	First_Name	Last_Name	Gender	Salary	Job_Title	Country
120102	Tom	Zhou	M	108255	Sales Ma	AU
120103	Wilson	Dawes	M	87975	Sales Ma	AU
120121	Irenie	Elvish	F	26600	Sales Re	AU
120122	Christin	Ngan	F	27475	Sales Re	AU
120123	Kimiko	Hotstone	F	26190	Sales Re	AU
120124	Lucian	Daymond	M	26480	Sales Re	AU
120125	Fong	Hofmeist	M	32040	Sales Re	AU

Some character values are truncated.

50   p108d01

Some character values contain unnecessary trailing blanks, although this is not obvious in a PROC PRINT report.

LENGTH Statement

The *LENGTH statement* defines the type and length of a variable.

LENGTH *variable(s)* <$> *length* ...;

```
data work.subset;
   length First_Name $ 12 Last_Name $ 18
          Gender $ 1 Job_Title $ 25
          Country $ 2;
   infile "&path\sales.csv" dlm=',';
   input Employee_ID First_Name $ Last_Name $
         Gender $ Salary Job_Title $ Country $;
run;
```

⚠ Put the LENGTH statement before the INPUT statement.

51   p108d02

The LENGTH statement is used primarily for character variables.

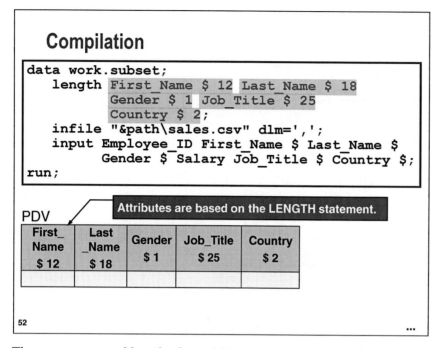

The name, type, and length of a variable are determined at the variable's first use. These specifications can be in a LENGTH statement or the INPUT statement, whichever appears first in the DATA step. The name is used exactly as specified at first use, including the case.

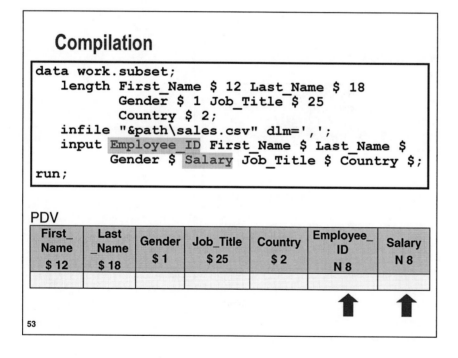

Viewing the Output

```
proc print data=work.subset noobs;
run;
```

Partial PROC PRINT Output

First_Name	Last_Name	Gender	Job_Title	Country	Employee_ID	Salary
Tom	Zhou	M	Sales Manager	AU	120102	108255
Wilson	Dawes	M	Sales Manager	AU	120103	87975
Irenie	Elvish	F	Sales Rep. II	AU	120121	26600
Christina	Ngan	F	Sales Rep. II	AU	120122	27475
Kimiko	Hotstone	F	Sales Rep. I	AU	120123	26190

The character values are no longer truncated, but the order of the variables changed.

54   p108d02

8.04 Short Answer Poll

Suppose you want the order of the variables to match the order of the fields. You can include the numeric variables in the LENGTH statement. Which of the following produces the correct results?

a.
```
length Employee_ID First_Name $ 12
       Last_Name $ 18 Gender $ 1
       Salary Job_Title $ 25
       Country $ 2;
```

b.
```
length Employee_ID 8 First_Name $ 12
       Last_Name $ 18 Gender $ 1
       Salary 8 Job_Title $ 25
       Country $ 2;
```

55

Using a LENGTH Statement

The LENGTH statement identifies the character variables, so dollar signs can be omitted from the INPUT statement.

```
data work.subset;
   length Employee_ID 8 First_Name $ 12
          Last_Name $ 18 Gender $ 1
          Salary 8 Job_Title $ 25
          Country $ 2;
   infile "&path\sales.csv" dlm=',';
   input Employee_ID First_Name Last_Name
         Gender Salary Job_Title Country;
run;
```

57   p108d03

Viewing the Output

Display the variables in creation order.

```
proc contents data=work.subset varnum;
run;
```

Partial PROC CONTENTS Output

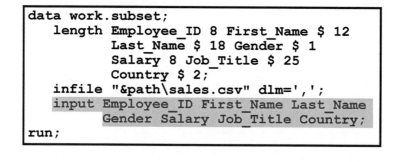

```
Variables in Creation Order

#    Variable      Type    Len

1    Employee_ID   Num       8
2    First_Name    Char     12
3    Last_Name     Char     18
4    Gender        Char      1
5    Salary        Num       8
6    Job_Title     Char     25
7    Country       Char      2
```

58

Viewing the Output

Partial PROC PRINT Output

Employee_ID	First_Name	Last_Name	Gender	Salary	Job_Title	Country
120102	Tom	Zhou	M	108255	Sales Manager	AU
120103	Wilson	Dawes	M	87975	Sales Manager	AU
120121	Irenie	Elvish	F	26600	Sales Rep. II	AU
120122	Christina	Ngan	F	27475	Sales Rep. II	AU
120123	Kimiko	Hotstone	F	26190	Sales Rep. I	AU
120124	Lucian	Daymond	M	26480	Sales Rep. I	AU
120125	Fong	Hofmeister	M	32040	Sales Rep. IV	AU

59

Business Scenario

A raw data file contains information about Orion Star
sales employees. It includes some invalid data values.

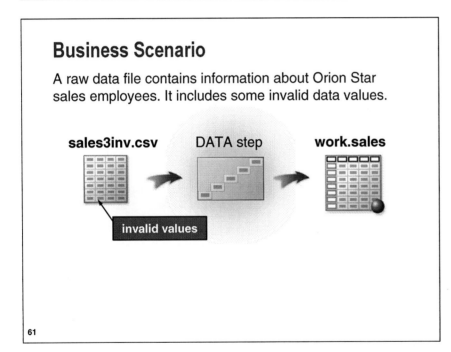

sales3inv.csv   DATA step   work.sales

invalid values

61

8.05 Short Answer Poll

What problems do you see with the data values for the last two data fields, **Salary** and **Country**?

Partial **sales3inv.csv**

```
120102,Tom,Zhou,Manager,108255,AU
120103,Wilson,Dawes,Manager,87975,AU
120121,Irenie,Elvish,Rep. II,26600,AU
120122,Christina,Ngan,Rep. II,n/a,AU
120123,Kimiko,Hotstone,Rep. I,26190,AU
120124,Lucian,Daymond,Rep. I,26480,12
120125,Fong,Hofmeister,Rep. IV,32040,AU
```

62

Reading a Raw Data File with Data Errors

```
data work.sales;
   infile "&path\sales3inv.csv" dlm=',';
   input Employee_ID First $ Last $
         Job_Title $ Salary Country $;
run;

proc print data=work.sales;
run;
```

Salary is defined as numeric and **Country** as character.

64   p108d04

Viewing the Output

Partial PROC PRINT Output

Obs	Employee_ID	First	Last	Job_Title	Salary	Country
1	120102	Tom	Zhou	Manager	108255	AU
2	120103	Wilson	Dawes	Manager	87975	AU
3	120121	Irenie	Elvish	Rep. II	26600	AU
4	120122	Christin	Ngan	Rep. II	.	AU
5	120123	Kimiko	Hotstone	Rep. I	26190	AU
6	120124	Lucian	Daymond	Rep. I	26480	12
7	120125	Fong	Hofmeist	Rep. IV	32040	AU

- A missing value was stored in **Salary** for the input value *n/a*.
- The value *12* was successfully stored in **Country**.
- A data error occurred on observation 4, but not on observation 6.

65

Data Errors

A data error occurs when a data value does not match the field specification. The following information is written to the SAS log:

- a note describing the error
- a column ruler
- the input record
- the contents of the PDV

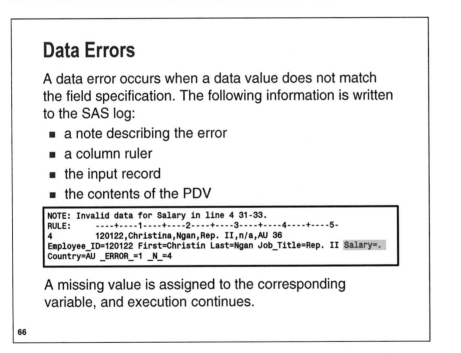

```
NOTE: Invalid data for Salary in line 4 31-33.
RULE:      ----+----1----+----2----+----3----+----4----+----5-
4          120122,Christina,Ngan,Rep. II,n/a,AU 36
Employee_ID=120122 First=Christin Last=Ngan Job_Title=Rep. II Salary=.
Country=AU _ERROR_=1 _N_=4
```

A missing value is assigned to the corresponding variable, and execution continues.

66

Even though these are referred to as *data errors*, they generate notes, not error messages. Syntax errors stop the DATA step, whereas data errors enable processing to continue.

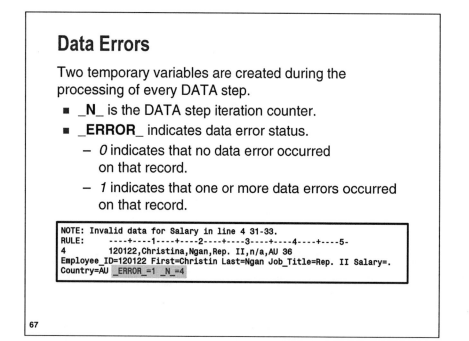

Data Errors

Two temporary variables are created during the processing of every DATA step.

- **_N_** is the DATA step iteration counter.
- **_ERROR_** indicates data error status.
  - *0* indicates that no data error occurred on that record.
  - *1* indicates that one or more data errors occurred on that record.

```
NOTE: Invalid data for Salary in line 4 31-33.
RULE:       ----+----1----+----2----+----3----+----4----+----5-
4          120122,Christina,Ngan,Rep. II,n/a,AU 36
Employee_ID=120122 First=Christin Last=Ngan Job_Title=Rep. II Salary=.
Country=AU _ERROR_=1 _N_=4
```

67

ERROR is reset to *0*, and _N_ is incremented by 1 at the beginning of each iteration.

Examining Data Errors

p108d04

```
data work.sales;
   infile "&path\sales3inv.csv" dlm=',';
   input Employee_ID First $ Last $
         Job_Title $ Salary Country $;
run;


proc print data=work.sales;
run;
```

1. Open the raw data file **sales3inv.csv**.

   In SAS Enterprise Guide, select **File** ⇨ **Open** ⇨ **Data**. Navigate to your data folder.

   In the SAS windowing environment, select **File** ⇨ **Open Program**. Select **All Files (*.*)** from the File of type menu.

File name:	▼ Open
Files of type:	SAS Files (*.sas) ▼ Cancel
	SAS Files (*.sas)
	Log Files (*.log)
Encoding:	List Files (*.lst) □ No BOM
	Data Files (*.dat)
Five Products by F	Web Files (*.htm;*.html;*.xml)
	All Files (*.*)
2011 Orders	

   Select **sales3inv.csv** from the list of files.

2. View the **Salary** values. There are three invalid values and one missing value.

3. Open and submit **p108d04**.

4. Examine the log. The DATA step creates an output data set, **work.sales**, with 50 observations. The three invalid **Salary** values were identified in the log, and the corresponding observations have a missing value for **Salary**. The missing **Salary** value was not reported as a data error because *missing* is a valid value in SAS.

5. Examine the output. Notice that there are four observations with missing **Salary** values.

8.06 Multiple Choice Poll

Submit program **p108a01** and examine the log.

Which statement best describes the reason for the error?

a. The data in the raw data file is invalid.
b. The programmer incorrectly read the data.

69

Use the SAS system option, ERRORS=*n*, to specify the maximum number of observations for which error messages about data input errors are printed.

```
options errors=5;
```

Exercises

If you restarted your SAS session since the last exercise, open and submit the **libname.sas** program that can be found in the data folder.

Level 1

1. **Reading a Comma-Delimited Raw Data File**

   a. Open **p108e01**. Add the appropriate LENGTH, INFILE, and INPUT statements to read the comma-delimited raw data file, which can be named as follows:

Windows	"&path\newemps.csv"
UNIX	"&path/newemps.csv"
z/OS (OS/390)	"&path..rawdata(newemps)"

Partial Raw Data File

```
Satyakam,Denny,Sales Rep. II,26780
Monica,Kletschkus,Sales Rep. IV,30890
Kevin,Lyon,Sales Rep. I,26955
Petrea,Soltau,Sales Rep. II,27440
Marina,Iyengar,Sales Rep. III,29715
```

b. Read the following fields from the raw data file:

Name	Type	Length
First	Character	12
Last	Character	18
Title	Character	25
Salary	Numeric	8

c. Submit the program to create the report below. The results should contain 71 observations.

Partial PROC PRINT Output

```
      Obs    First        Last             Title         Salary

        1    Satyakam     Denny         Sales Rep. II     26780
        2    Monica       Kletschkus    Sales Rep. IV     30890
        3    Kevin        Lyon          Sales Rep. I      26955
        4    Petrea       Soltau        Sales Rep. II     27440
        5    Marina       Iyengar       Sales Rep. III    29715
```

Level 2

2. Reading a Space-Delimited Raw Data File

a. Write a DATA step to create a new data set named **work.qtrdonation**. Read the space-delimited raw data file, which can be named as follows:

Windows	"&path\donation.dat"
UNIX	"&path/donation.dat"
z/OS (OS/390)	"&path..rawdata(donation)"

Partial Raw Data File

```
120265 . . . 25
120267 15 15 15 15
120269 20 20 20 20
120270 20 10 5 .
120271 20 20 20 20
```

b. Read the following fields from the raw data file:

Name	Type	Length
IDNum	Character	6
Qtr1	Numeric	8
Qtr2	Numeric	8
Qtr3	Numeric	8
Qtr4	Numeric	8

c. Write a PROC PRINT step to create the report below. The results contain 124 observations.

Partial PROC PRINT Output

Obs	IDNum	Qtr1	Qtr2	Qtr3	Qtr4
1	120265	.	.	.	25
2	120267	15	15	15	15
3	120269	20	20	20	20
4	120270	20	10	5	.
5	120271	20	20	20	20

Challenge

3. Reading a Tab-Delimited Raw Data File

a. Create a temporary data set, **managers2**. Use the tab-delimited raw data file, which can be named as follows:

Windows	**"&path\managers2.dat"**
UNIX	**"&path/ managers2.dat"**
z/OS (OS/390)	**"&path..rawdata(managers2)"**

Raw Data File

```
120102  Tom     Zhou        M       108255  Sales Manager
120103  Wilson  Dawes       M       87975   Sales Manager
120261  Harry   Highpoint   M       243190  Chief Sales Officer
121143  Louis   Favaron M           95090   Senior Sales Manager
121144  Renee   Capachietti F       83505   Sales Manager
121145  Dennis  Lansberry   M       84260   Sales Manager
```

b. Read the following fields from the raw data file:

Name	Type
ID	Numeric
First	Character
Last	Character

Name	Type
Gender	Character
Salary	Numeric
Title	Character

c. The new data set should contain only **First**, **Last**, and **Title**.

d. Generate the report below. The results should contain six observations.

```
Obs      First      Last            Title

 1       Tom        Zhou            Sales Manager
 2       Wilson     Dawes           Sales Manager
 3       Harry      Highpoint       Chief Sales Officer
 4       Louis      Favaron         Senior Sales Manager
 5       Renee      Capachietti     Sales Manager
 6       Dennis     Lansberry       Sales Manager
```

8.3 Using Informats to Read Delimited Data

Objectives

- Use informats to read character data.
- Use informats to read nonstandard data.
- Subset observations and add permanent attributes.

74

Business Scenario

Create a temporary SAS data set by reading both standard and nonstandard values from a comma-delimited raw data file.

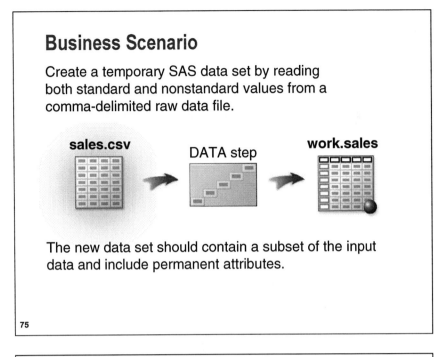

sales.csv → DATA step → work.sales

The new data set should contain a subset of the input data and include permanent attributes.

75

Considerations

Use modified list input to read all the fields from **sales.csv**. Store the date fields as SAS dates.

Partial **sales.csv**

```
120102,Tom,Zhou,M,108255,Sales Manager,AU,11AUG1973,06/01/1993
120103,Wilson,Dawes,M,87975,Sales Manager,AU,22JAN1953,01/01/1978
120121,Irenie,Elvish,F,26600,Sales Rep. II,AU,02AUG1948,01/01/1978
120122,Christina,Ngan,F,27475,Sales Rep. II,AU,27JUL1958,07/01/1982
120123,Kimiko,Hotstone,F,26190,Sales Rep. I,AU,28SEP1968,10/01/1989
```

76

Modified List Input

This DATA step uses *modified list input*. Instead of a
LENGTH statement, an informat specifies the length
for each character variable.

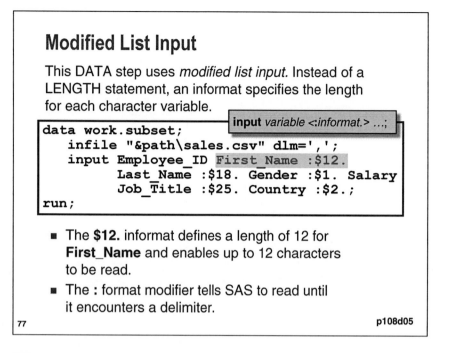

```
data work.subset;
   infile "&path\sales.csv" dlm=',';
   input Employee_ID First_Name :$12.
         Last_Name :$18. Gender :$1. Salary
         Job_Title :$25. Country :$2.;
run;
```

> **input** *variable <:informat.> ...;*

- The **$12.** informat defines a length of 12 for
  First_Name and enables up to 12 characters
  to be read.
- The **:** format modifier tells SAS to read until
  it encounters a delimiter.

77   p108d05

Modified List Input

⚠ Omitting the colon modifier causes unexpected results.

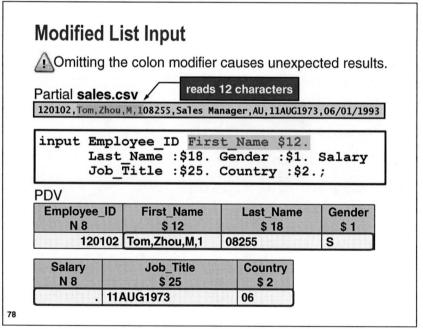

Partial **sales.csv** / reads 12 characters

```
120102,Tom,Zhou,M,108255,Sales Manager,AU,11AUG1973,06/01/1993
```

```
input Employee_ID First_Name $12.
      Last_Name :$18. Gender :$1. Salary
      Job_Title :$25. Country :$2.;
```

PDV

Employee_ID N 8	First_Name $ 12	Last_Name $ 18	Gender $ 1
120102	Tom,Zhou,M,1	08255	S

Salary N 8	Job_Title $ 25	Country $ 2
.	11AUG1973	06

78

Reading Nonstandard Data

An informat is **required** to read nonstandard numeric data.

Partial **sales.csv**

```
120102,Tom,Zhou,M,108255,Sales Manager,AU,11AUG1973,06/01/1993
120103,Wilson,Dawes,M,87975,Sales Manager,AU,22JAN1953,01/01/1978
120121,Irenie,Elvish,F,26600,Sales Rep. II,AU,02AUG1948,01/01/1978
120122,Christina,Ngan,F,27475,Sales Rep. II,AU,27JUL1958,07/01/1982
120123,Kimiko,Hotstone,F,26190,Sales Rep. I,AU,28SEP1968,10/01/1989
```

In this example, informats are needed to specify the style of the date fields so that they can be read and converted to SAS dates.

79

8.07 Short Answer Poll

A *format* is an instruction that tells SAS how to display data values. What formats could you specify to display a SAS date in the styles shown below?

a) 01JAN2000

b) 01/16/2000

80

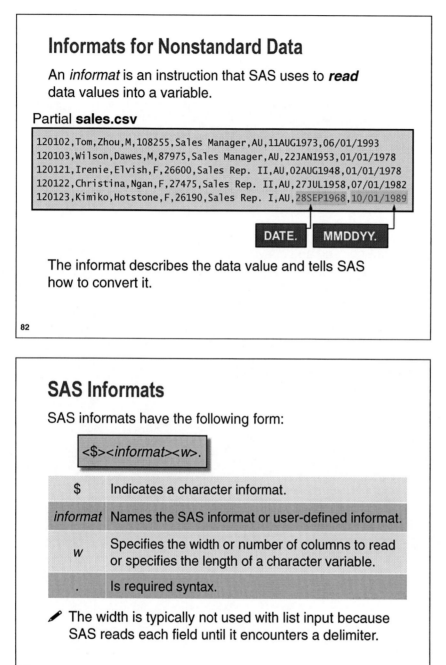

Informats for Nonstandard Data

An *informat* is an instruction that SAS uses to **read** data values into a variable.

Partial **sales.csv**

```
120102,Tom,Zhou,M,108255,Sales Manager,AU,11AUG1973,06/01/1993
120103,Wilson,Dawes,M,87975,Sales Manager,AU,22JAN1953,01/01/1978
120121,Irenie,Elvish,F,26600,Sales Rep. II,AU,02AUG1948,01/01/1978
120122,Christina,Ngan,F,27475,Sales Rep. II,AU,27JUL1958,07/01/1982
120123,Kimiko,Hotstone,F,26190,Sales Rep. I,AU,28SEP1968,10/01/1989
```

DATE.   MMDDYY.

The informat describes the data value and tells SAS how to convert it.

SAS Informats

SAS informats have the following form:

<$><informat><w>.

$	Indicates a character informat.
informat	Names the SAS informat or user-defined informat.
w	Specifies the width or number of columns to read or specifies the length of a character variable.
.	Is required syntax.

The width is typically not used with list input because SAS reads each field until it encounters a delimiter.

SAS Informats

Selected SAS Informats

Informat	Definition
COMMA. DOLLAR.	Reads nonstandard numeric data and removes embedded commas, blanks, dollar signs, percent signs, and dashes.
COMMAX. DOLLARX.	Reads nonstandard numeric data and removes embedded non-numeric characters; reverses the roles of the decimal point and the comma.
EUROX.	Reads nonstandard numeric data and removes embedded non-numeric characters in European currency.
$CHAR.	Reads character values and preserves leading blanks.
$UPCASE.	Reads character values and converts them to uppercase.

84

SAS Informats

Informats are used to read and convert raw data.

Informat	Raw Data Value	SAS Data Value
COMMA. DOLLAR.	$12,345	12345
COMMAX. DOLLARX.	$12.345	12345
EUROX.	€12.345	12345
$CHAR.	##Australia	##Australia
$UPCASE.	au	AU

🖊 The character # represents a blank space.

85

SAS Informats

Use date informats to read and convert dates
to SAS date values.

Informat	Raw Data Value	SAS Data Value
MMDDYY.	010160 01/01/60 01/01/1960 1/1/1960	0
DDMMYY.	311260 31/12/60 31/12/1960	365
DATE.	31DEC59 31DEC1959	-1

86

8.08 Short Answer Poll

Use the SAS Help Facility or documentation to investigate
the **DATE***w.* informat and answer the following questions:

a) What does the *w* represent?

b) What is the default width of this informat?

87

Using Informats to Read Nonstandard Data

```
120102,Tom,Zhou,M,108255,Sales Manager,AU,11AUG1973,6/1/1993
120103,Wilson,Dawes,M,87975,Sales Manager,AU,7JAN1953,1/10/1978
```

DATE.
Default: 7

MMDDYY.
Default: 6

- An informat is needed to read a nonstandard value.
- The width is optional when you use list input.
- If the width and the colon format modifier are omitted, the default width for that informat is used.

89

Modified List Input

The colon format modifier (:) tells SAS to read
until it encounters a delimiter.

```
input Employee_ID First_Name :$12.
      Last_Name :$18. Gender :$1.
      Salary Job_Title :$25. Country :$2.
      Birth_Date :date. Hire_Date :mmddyy.;
```

INPUT *variable <$> variable <:informat> ...;*

colon format modifier

90   p108d06

Viewing the Log

```
37    data work.sales;
38        infile "&path\sales.csv" dlm=',';
39        input Employee_ID First_Name :$12. Last_Name :$18.
40              Gender :$1. Salary Job_Title :$25. Country :$2.
41              Birth_Date :date. Hire_Date :mmddyy.;
42    run;

NOTE: The infile "s:\workshop\sales.csv" is:
      Filename=s:\workshop\sales.csv,
      RECFM=V,LRECL=256,File Size (bytes)=11340,

NOTE: 165 records were read from the infile "s:\workshop\sales.csv".
NOTE: The data set WORK.SALES has 165 observations and 9 variables.
```

91   p108d06

Viewing the Output

```
proc print data=work.sales;
run;
```

Partial PROC PRINT Output

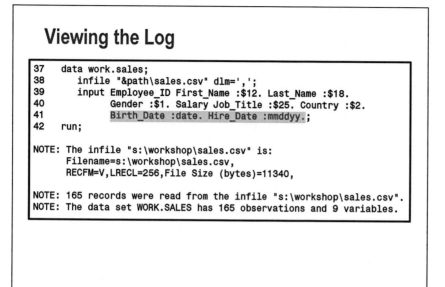

Obs	First_ Name	Last_Name	Gender	Job_Title	Country	Employee_ ID	Salary	Birth_ Date	Hire_ Date
1	Tom	Zhou	M	Sales Manager	AU	120102	108255	4971	12205
2	Wilson	Dawes	M	Sales Manager	AU	120103	87975	-2535	6575
3	Irenie	Elvish	F	Sales Rep. II	AU	120121	26600	-4169	6575
4	Christina	Ngan	F	Sales Rep. II	AU	120122	27475	-523	8217
5	Kimiko	Hotstone	F	Sales Rep. I	AU	120123	26190	3193	10866

92   p108d06

Additional SAS Statements

Additional SAS statements can be added to perform
further processing in the DATA step.

```
data work.sales;
   infile "&path\sales.csv" dlm=',';
   input Employee_ID First_Name :$12. Last_Name :$18.
         Gender :$1. Salary Job_Title :$25. Country :$2.
         Birth_Date :date. Hire_Date :mmddyy.;
   if Country='AU';
   keep First_Name Last_Name Salary
        Job_Title Hire_Date;
   label Job_Title='Sales Title'
         Hire_Date='Date Hired';
   format Salary dollar12. Hire_Date monyy7.;
run;
```

A subsetting IF statement is used to subset observations
when SAS reads from a raw data file.

93   p108d07

Viewing the Output

```
proc print data=work.sales label;
run;
```

Partial PROC PRINT Output

Obs	First_ Name	Last_Name	Sales Title	Salary	Date Hired
1	Tom	Zhou	Sales Manager	$108,255	JUN1993
2	Wilson	Dawes	Sales Manager	$87,975	JAN1978
3	Irenie	Elvish	Sales Rep. II	$26,600	JAN1978
4	Christina	Ngan	Sales Rep. II	$27,475	JUL1982
5	Kimiko	Hotstone	Sales Rep. I	$26,190	OCT1989

94   p108d07

WHERE versus Subsetting IF Statement

Step and Usage	WHERE	IF
PROC step	Yes	No
DATA step (source of variable)		
SET statement	Yes	Yes
assignment statement	No	Yes
➡ INPUT statement	No	Yes

95

Idea Exchange

What factors need to be considered when SAS reads **salary.dat**, which is shown below?

Partial **salary.dat**

```
          1    1    2    2    3    3
1---5----0----5----0----5----0----5
Donny 5MAY2008 25 FL $43,132.50
Margaret 20FEB2008 43 NC $65,150
Dan 1JUN2008 27 FL $40,000.00
Subash 2FEB2008 45 NC $75,750
Antonio 25MAY2008 35 FL $43,500.50
```

p108a02

96

Using List Input: Importance of Colon Format Modifier

p108a02

1. Open **p108a02** and examine the INPUT statement.
    - The INFILE statement does not contain DLM= because the file is space delimited.
    - **HireDate** and **Salary** are nonstandard numeric fields, so an informat is needed.

2. In the SAS windowing environment, select **File** ⇨ **Open Program**, change the value for **Files of type** to **Data Files (*.dat)**, and select **salary.dat**.

 Files with a .dat extension can be imported in SAS Enterprise Guide but not viewed in an editor.

Partial **salary.dat**

```
Donny 5MAY2008 25 FL $43,132.50
Margaret 20FEB2008 43 NC 65,150
Dan 1JUN2008 27 FL $40,000.00
Subash 2FEB2008 45 NC 75,750
Antonio 25MAY2008 35 FL $43,500.50
```

3. Submit Part 1 and view the log and output. The expected output is shown below.

```
    /* Part 1 - using colon format modifiers*/
data work.salaries;
    infile "&path\salary.dat";
    input Name $ HireDate :date. Age State $ Salary :comma.;
run;


proc print data=work.salaries;
run;
```

Partial PROC PRINT Output

Obs	Name	Hire Date	Age	State	Salary
1	Donny	17657	25	FL	43132.5
2	Margaret	17582	43	NC	65150.0
3	Dan	17684	27	FL	40000.0
4	Subash	17564	45	NC	75750.0
5	Antonio	17677	35	FL	43500.5

4. Observe what happens when a colon format modifier is omitted from **Salary**. Submit Part 2.

```
    /* Part 2 - omit the colon format modifier for Salary */
data work.salaries;
    infile "&path\salary.dat";
    input Name $ HireDate :date. Age State $ Salary comma.;
run;


proc print data=work.salaries;
run;
```

5. Examine the log. There are no errors or warnings.

```
923     /* Part 2 ⫪ omit the colon format modifier for Salary */
924   data work.salaries;
925       infile "&path\salary.dat";
926       input Name $ HireDate :date. Age State $ Salary comma.;
927   run;

NOTE: The infile "s:\workshop\salary.dat" is:
      Filename=s:\workshop\salary.dat,
NOTE: 8 records were read from the infile "s:\workshop\salary.dat".
NOTE: The data set WORK.SALARIES has 8 observations and 5 variables.
```

6. Examine the output.

Obs	Name	Date	Age	State	Salary
1	Donny	17657	25	FL	.
2	Margaret	17582	43	NC	6
3	Dan	17684	27	FL	.
4	Subash	17564	45	NC	7
5	Antonio	17677	35	FL	.

The **Salary** values are incorrect. Why are the values either missing or only one digit in length?

- The COMMA. informat has a default width of 1, so SAS reads one column from the input file. This reads the first character of the **Salary** value.

- When the first column contains a dollar sign, a missing value is assigned to the numeric variable. This does not cause a data error because the COMMA. informat removes non-numeric characters, including the dollar sign. When the first column contains a digit, that digit becomes the value of the variable.

  In some cases, omitting a colon results in missing or invalid values. In other cases, it results in data errors.

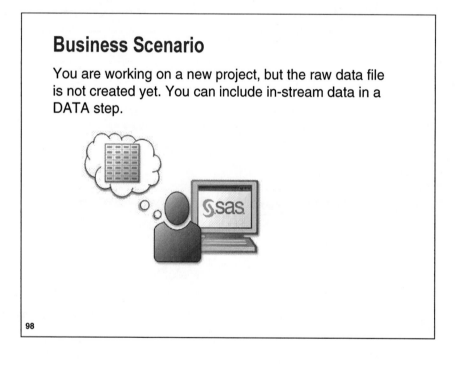

Business Scenario

You are working on a new project, but the raw data file is not created yet. You can include in-stream data in a DATA step.

98

DATALINES Statement

The DATALINES statement supplies data within a program.

```
data work.newemps;
   input First_Name :$12. Last_Name :$18.
         Job_Title :$15. Salary :dollar.;
datalines;
Steven Worton Auditor $40,450
Marta-Lyn Bamberger Manager $32,000
Merle Hieds Trainee $24,025
;
```

```
DATALINES;
...
;
```

- DATALINES is the last statement in the DATA step and immediately precedes the first data line.
- A null statement (a single semicolon) indicates the end of the input data.

99   p108d08

To take advantage of INFILE statement options, you can use an INFILE statement with DATALINES.

```
data work.newemps;
   infile datalines dsd;
   length First_Name Last_Name $ 15 Job_Title $ 25;
   input First_Name $ Last_Name $  Job_Title $ Salary :dollar.;
datalines;
Mary Ann,Worthman,Internal Auditor,"$87,500"
Alena M.,Moody,Sales Trainee,"$20,000"
Edwin,Comber,Sales Rep. III,"$45,500"
;
```

Viewing the Output

```
proc print data=work.newemps;
run;
```

PROC PRINT Output

Obs	First_Name	Last_Name	Job_Title	Salary
1	Steven	Worton	Auditor	40450
2	Marta-Lyn	Bamberger	Manager	32000
3	Merle	Hieds	Trainee	24025

100   p108d08

Exercises

> If you restarted your SAS session since the last exercise, open and submit the **libname.sas** program that can be found in the data folder.

Level 1

4. **Reading Nonstandard Data from a Comma-Delimited Raw Data File**

    a. Open **p108e04**. Add the appropriate LENGTH, INFILE, and INPUT statements to read the comma-delimited raw data file, which can be named as follows:

Windows	**"&path\custca.csv"**
UNIX	**"&path/custca.csv"**
z/OS (OS/390)	**"&path..rawdata(custca)"**

Partial Raw Data File

```
Bill,Cuddy,11171,M,16/10/1986,21,15-30 years
Susan,Krasowski,17023,F,09/07/1959,48,46-60 years
Andreas,Rennie,26148,M,18/07/1934,73,61-75 years
Lauren,Krasowski,46966,F,24/10/1986,21,15-30 years
Lauren,Marx,54655,F,18/08/1969,38,31-45 years
```

Read the following fields:

Name	Type	Length
First	Character	20
Last	Character	20
ID	Numeric	8
Gender	Character	1
BirthDate	Numeric	8
Age	Numeric	8
AgeGroup	Character	12

b. Use FORMAT and DROP statements in the DATA step to create a data set that results in the report below when it is displayed with a PROC PRINT step. Include an appropriate title. The results should contain 15 observations.

Partial PROC PRINT Output

					Birth
Obs	First	Last	Gender	AgeGroup	Date
1	Bill	Cuddy	M	15-30 years	OCT1986
2	Susan	Krasowski	F	46-60 years	JUL1959
3	Andreas	Rennie	M	61-75 years	JUL1934
4	Lauren	Krasowski	F	15-30 years	OCT1986
5	Lauren	Marx	F	31-45 years	AUG1969

Canadian Customers

Level 2

5. Reading a Delimited Raw Data File with Nonstandard Data Values

a. Write a DATA step to create a temporary data set, **prices**. Read the delimited raw data file named as follows:

Windows	"&path\pricing.dat"
UNIX	"&path/ pricing.dat"
z/OS (OS/390)	"&path..rawdata(pricing)"

All data fields are numeric.

Partial Raw Data File

```
210200100009*09JUN2011*31DEC9999*$15.50*$34.70
210200100017*24JAN2011*31DEC9999*$17.80*22.80
210200200023*04JUL2011*31DEC9999*$8.25*$19.80
210200600067*27OCT2011*31DEC9999*$28.90*47.00
210200600085*28AUG2011*31DEC9999*$17.85*$39.40
```

b. Generate the report below. The results should contain 16 observations.

Partial PROC PRINT Output

					Sales
Obs	ProductID	StartDate	EndDate	Cost	Price
1	210200100009	06/09/2011	12/31/9999	15.50	34.70
2	210200100017	01/24/2011	12/31/9999	17.80	22.80
3	210200200023	07/04/2011	12/31/9999	8.25	19.80
4	210200600067	10/27/2011	12/31/9999	28.90	47.00
5	210200600085	08/28/2011	12/31/9999	17.85	39.40

2011 Pricing

Challenge

6. Reading In-Stream Delimited Data

a. Open **p108e06**. Write a DATA step to read the delimited in-stream data shown below.

✏️ An INFILE statement is required. Use SAS Help or online documentation to explore the use of DATALINES as a file specification in an INFILE statement.

```
120102/Tom/Zhou/M/108,255/Sales Manager/01Jun1993
120103/Wilson/Dawes/M/87,975/Sales Manager/01Jan1978
120261/Harry/Highpoint/M/243,190/Chief Sales Officer/01Aug1991
121143/Louis/Favaron/M/95,090/Senior Sales Manager/01Jul2001
121144/Renee/Capachietti/F/83,505/Sales Manager/01Nov1995
121145/Dennis/Lansberry/M/84,260/Sales Manager/01Apr1980
```

b. Generate the report below.

```
                          Orion Star Management Team

First      Last         Title                  ID     Gender    Salary     HireDate

Tom        Zhou         Sales Manager         120102    M       108255    06/01/1993
Wilson     Dawes        Sales Manager         120103    M        87975    01/01/1978
Harry      Highpoint    Chief Sales Officer   120261    M       243190    08/01/1991
Louis      Favaron      Senior Sales Manager  121143    M        95090    07/01/2001
Renee      Capachietti  Sales Manager         121144    F        83505    11/01/1995
Dennis     Lansberry    Sales Manager         121145    M        84260    04/01/1980
```

8.4 Handling Missing Data

Objectives

- Use the DSD option to read consecutive delimiters as missing values.
- Use the MISSOVER option to recognize missing values at the end of a record.

104

Business Scenario

Orion Star programmers discovered that some files have records with missing data in one or more fields.

105

Missing Values in the Middle of the Record

The records in **phone2.csv** have a contact name, phone number, and a mobile number. The phone number is missing from some of the records.

phone2.csv

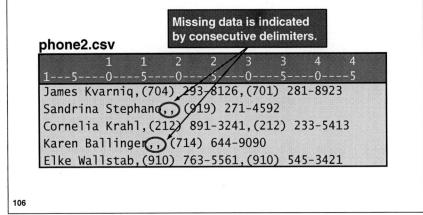

Missing data is indicated by consecutive delimiters.

```
              1    1    2    2    3    3    4    4
1---5----0----5----0----5----0----5----0----5
James Kvarniq,(704) 293-8126,(701) 281-8923
Sandrina Stephano,,(919) 271-4592
Cornelia Krahl,(212) 891-3241,(212) 233-5413
Karen Ballinger,,(714) 644-9090
Elke Wallstab,(910) 763-5561,(910) 545-3421
```

106

Consecutive Delimiters in List Input

List input treats two or more consecutive delimiters
as a single delimiter and not as a missing value.

Partial phone2.csv

```
          1    1    2    2    3    3    4    4
1---5----0----5----0----5----0----5----0----5
Sandrina Stephano,,(919) 271-4592
Cornelia Krahl,(212) 891-3241,(212) 233-5413
```

When there is missing data in a record, SAS does the
following:

- loads the next record to finish the observation
- writes a note to the log

107

8.09 Short Answer Poll

Submit **p108a03 and e**xamine the log and output.

How many input records were read and how many
observations were created?

Does the output look correct?

```
data work.contacts;
   length Name $ 20 Phone Mobile $ 14;
   infile "&path\phone2.csv" dlm=',';
   input Name $ Phone $ Mobile $;
run;

proc print data=work.contacts noobs;
run;
```

108   p108a03

DSD Option

Use the DSD option to correctly read **phone2.csv**.

```
data work.contacts;
   length Name $ 20 Phone Mobile $ 14;
   infile "&path\phone2.csv" dsd;
   input Name $ Phone $ Mobile $;
run;
```
INFILE "*raw-data-file*" <DLM=> DSD;

The DSD option does the following:
- sets the default delimiter to a comma
- treats consecutive delimiters as missing values
- enables SAS to read values with embedded delimiters if the value is enclosed in quotation marks

110   p108d09

The DLM= option can be used with the DSD option, but it is not needed for comma-delimited files.

Viewing the Output

Adding the DSD option gives the correct results.

PROC PRINT Output

Name	Phone	Mobile
James Kvarniq	(704) 293-8126	(701) 281-8923
Sandrina Stephano		(919) 271-4592
Cornelia Krahl	(212) 891-3241	(212) 233-5413
Karen Ballinger		(714) 644-9090
Elke Wallstab	(910) 763-5561	(910) 545-3421

Partial SAS Log

```
NOTE: 5 records were read from the infile "S:\workshop\phone2.csv".
      The minimum record length was 31.
      The maximum record length was 44.
NOTE: The data set WORK.CONTACTS has 5 observations and 3
variables.
```

111

Business Scenario

Orion Star programmers discovered that some files have observations with missing data at the end of the record. As a result, there are fewer fields in the record than specified in the INPUT statement.

113

Missing Values at the End of a Record

The raw data file **phone.csv** contains missing values at the end of some records.

phone.csv

```
              1     1     2    missing values   4     4
1---5----0----5----0----5----0----5----0----5
James Kvarniq,(704) 293-8126,(701) 281-8923
Sandrina Stephano,(919) 871-7830
Cornelia Krahl,(212) 891-3241,(212) 233-5413
Karen Ballinger,(714) 344-4321
Elke Wallstab,(910) 763-5561,(910) 545-3421
```

The DSD option is not appropriate because the missing data is not marked by consecutive delimiters.

114

MISSOVER Option

The *MISSOVER option* prevents SAS from loading a new record when the end of the current record is reached.

```
data contacts;
   length Name $ 20 Phone Mobile $ 14;
   infile "&path\phone.csv" dlm=',' missover;
   input Name $ Phone $ Mobile $;
run;

proc print data=contacts noobs;
run;
```

> **INFILE** "*raw-data-file*" <DLM=> **MISSOVER;**

If SAS reaches the end of a record without finding values for all fields, variables without values are set to missing.

115   p108d10

Viewing the Output

Partial SAS Log

```
NOTE: 5 records were read from the infile "S:\workshop\phone.csv".
      The minimum record length was 31.
      The maximum record length was 44.
NOTE: The data set WORK.CONTACTS has 5 observations and 3
variables.
```

PROC PRINT Output

Name	Phone	Mobile
James Kvarniq	(704) 293-8126	(701) 281-8923
Sandrina Stephano	(919) 871-7830	
Cornelia Krahl	(212) 891-3241	(212) 233-5413
Karen Ballinger	(714) 344-4321	
Elke Wallstab	(910) 763-5561	(910) 545-3421

116

INFILE Options

> INFILE "*raw-data-file*" <DLM=> <DSD> <MISSOVER>;

Option	Description
DLM=	Specifies an alternate delimiter.
DSD	Sets the default delimiter to a comma, treats consecutive delimiters as missing values, and allows embedded delimiters when the data value is enclosed in quotation marks.
MISSOVER	Sets variables to missing if the end of the record is reached before finding values for all fields.

117

Exercises

If you restarted your SAS session since the last exercise, open and submit the **libname.sas** program that can be found in the data folder.

Level 1

7. **Reading a Comma-Delimited File with Missing Values**

    a. Open **p108e07**. Insert INFILE and INPUT statements to read the comma-delimited raw data, which can be named as follows:

Windows	**"&path\donation.csv"**
UNIX	**"&path/donation.csv"**
z/OS (OS/390)	**"&path..rawdata(donation)"**

    Partial Raw Data File

    ```
    120265,,,,25
    120267,15,15,15,15
    120269,20,20,20,20
    120270,20,10,5
    120271,20,20,20,20
    ```

b. There might be missing data in the middle or at the end of a record. Read the following fields from the raw data file:

Name	Type
EmpID	Numeric
Q1	Numeric
Q2	Numeric
Q3	Numeric
Q4	Numeric

c. Submit the PROC PRINT step to generate the report below. The results should include 124 observations.

```
Obs    EmpID    Q1    Q2    Q3    Q4

  1    120265    .     .     .    25
  2    120267   15    15    15    15
  3    120269   20    20    20    20
  4    120270   20    10     5     .
  5    120271   20    20    20    20
```

Level 2

8. Reading a Delimited File with Missing Values

a. Write a DATA step to create a temporary data set, **prices**. Use the asterisk-delimited raw data file, which can be named as follows:

Windows	**"&path\prices.dat"**
UNIX	**"&path/prices.dat"**
z/OS (OS/390)	**"&path..rawdata(prices)"**

Partial Raw Data File

```
210200100009*09JUN2007*31DEC9999*$15.50*$34.70
210200100017*24JAN2007*31DEC9999*$17.80
210200200023*04JUL2007*31DEC9999*$8.25*$19.80
210200600067*27OCT2007*31DEC9999*$28.90
210200600085*28AUG2007*31DEC9999*$17.85*$39.40
```

There might be missing data at the end of some records. Read the following fields from the raw data file:

Name	Type	Length
ProductID	Numeric	8
StartDate	Numeric	8
EndDate	Numeric	8
UnitCostPrice	Numeric	8
UnitSalesPrice	Numeric	8

b. Define labels and formats in the DATA step to create a data set that generates the following output when they are used in the PROC PRINT step. The results should contain 259 observations.

Partial PROC PRINT Output

```
                                2007 Prices

                                                           Sales
                         Start of       End of      Cost Price   Price per
   Obs    Product ID    Date Range    Date Range     per Unit       Unit

     1   210200100009   06/09/2007    12/31/9999       15.50       34.70
     2   210200100017   01/24/2007    12/31/9999       17.80         .
     3   210200200023   07/04/2007    12/31/9999        8.25       19.80
     4   210200600067   10/27/2007    12/31/9999       28.90         .
     5   210200600085   08/28/2007    12/31/9999       17.85       39.40
```

Challenge

9. **Reading a Delimited File with Missing Values and Embedded Delimiters**

a. Write a DATA step to create a temporary data set, **salesmgmt**. Use the raw data file, which can be named as follows:

Windows	"&path\managers.dat"
UNIX	"&path/managers.dat"
z/OS (OS/390)	"&path..rawdata(managers)"

Partial Raw Data File

```
120102/Tom/Zhou/M//Sales Manager/AU/11AUG1969/'06/01/1989'
120103/Wilson/Dawes/M/87975/Sales Manager/AU/22JAN1949/'01/01/1974'
120261/Harry/Highpoint/M/243190//US/21FEB1969/'08/01/1987'
121143/Louis/Favaron/M/95090/Senior Sales Manager/US/26NOV1969/'07/01/1997'
121144/Renee/Capachietti/F/83505/Sales Manager/US/28JUN1964
121145/Dennis/Lansberry/M/84260/Sales Manager/US/22NOV1949/'04/01/1976'
```

b. **ID** is a numeric value. The **salesmgmt** data set should contain only the variables shown in the report below.

c. Write a PROC PRINT step to generate the report below. The results should contain six observations.

PROC PRINT Output

```
                          Orion Star Managers

   Obs     ID      Last         Title                 HireDate    Salary

     1    120102   Zhou         Sales Manager         01JUN1989      .
     2    120103   Dawes        Sales Manager         01JAN1974     87975
     3    120261   Highpoint                          01AUG1987    243190
     4    121143   Favaron      Senior Sales Manager  01JUL1997     95090
     5    121144   Capachietti  Sales Manager              .       83505
     6    121145   Lansberry    Sales Manager         01APR1976     84260
```

8.5 Solutions

Solutions to Exercises

1. **Reading a Comma-Delimited Raw Data File**

```
data work.newemployees;
   length First $ 12 Last $ 18 Title $ 25;
   infile "&path\newemps.csv" dlm=',';
   input First $ Last $ Title $ Salary;
run;

proc print data=work.newemployees;
run;
```

2. **Reading a Space-Delimited Raw Data File**

```
data work.qtrdonation;
   length IDNum $ 6;
   infile "&path\donation.dat";
   input IDNum $ Qtr1 Qtr2 Qtr3 Qtr4;
run;

proc print data=work.qtrdonation;
run;
```

3. **Reading a Tab-Delimited Raw Data File**

```
data work.managers2;
   length First Last $ 12 Title $ 25;
   infile "&path\managers2.dat" dlm='09'x;
   input ID First $ Last $ Gender $ Salary Title $;
   keep First Last Title;
run;

proc print data=work.managers2;
run;
```

4. **Reading Nonstandard Data from a Comma-Delimited Raw Data File**

```
data work.canada_customers;
   length First Last $ 20 Gender $ 1 AgeGroup $ 12;
   infile "&path\custca.csv" dlm=',';
   input First $ Last $ ID Gender $
         BirthDate :ddmmyy. Age AgeGroup $;
   format BirthDate monyy7.;
   drop ID Age;
run;

title 'Canadian Customers';
proc print data=work.canada_customers;
run;
title;
   /* Alternate solution using informats */
```

```
data work.canada_customers;
   infile "&path\custca.csv" dlm=',';
   input First :$20. Last :$20. ID Gender :$1.
         BirthDate :ddmmyy. Age AgeGroup :$12.;
   format BirthDate monyy7.;
   drop ID Age;
run;


title 'Canadian Customers';
proc print data=work.canada_customers;
run;
title;
```

5. **Reading a Delimited Raw Data File with Nonstandard Values**

```
data work.prices;
   infile "&path\pricing.dat" dlm='*';
   input ProductID StartDate :date. EndDate :date.
         Cost :dollar. SalesPrice :dollar.;
   format StartDate EndDate mmddyy10.
          Cost SalesPrice 8.2;
run;


title '2011 Pricing';
proc print data=work.prices;
run;
title;
```

6. **Reading In-Stream Delimited Data**

```
data work.managers;
   infile datalines dlm='/';
   input ID First :$12. Last :$12. Gender $ Salary :comma.
           Title :$25. HireDate :date.;
   datalines;
120102/Tom/Zhou/M/108,255/Sales Manager/01Jun1993
120103/Wilson/Dawes/M/87,975/Sales Manager/01Jan1978
120261/Harry/Highpoint/M/243,190/Chief Sales Officer/01Aug1991
121143/Louis/Favaron/M/95,090/Senior Sales Manager/01Jul2001
121144/Renee/Capachietti/F/83,505/Sales Manager/01Nov1995
121145/Dennis/Lansberry/M/84,260/Sales Manager/01Apr1980
;


title 'Orion Star Management Team';
proc print data=work.managers noobs;
   format HireDate mmddyy10.;
run;
title;
```

7. Reading a Comma-Delimited File with Missing Values

```
data work.donations;
    infile "&path\donation.csv" dsd missover;
    input EmpID Q1 Q2 Q3 Q4;
run;


proc print data=work.donations;
run;
```

8. Reading a Delimited File with Missing Values

```
data work.prices;
    infile "&path\prices.dat" dlm='*' missover;
    input ProductID StartDate :date. EndDate :date.
        UnitCostPrice :dollar. UnitSalesPrice :dollar.;
    label ProductID='Product ID'
        StartDate='Start of Date Range'
        EndDate='End of Date Range'
        UnitCostPrice='Cost Price per Unit'
        UnitSalesPrice='Sales Price per Unit';
    format StartDate EndDate mmddyy10.
        UnitCostPrice UnitSalesPrice 8.2;
run;


title '2007 Prices';
proc print data=work.prices label;
run;
title;
```

9. Reading a Delimited File with Missing Values and Embedded Delimiters

```
data work.salesmgmt;
    length First Last $ 12 Gender $ 1 Title $ 25 Country $ 2;
    format BirthDate HireDate date9.;
    infile "&path\managers.dat" dsd dlm='/' missover;
    input ID First Last Gender Salary Title Country
        BirthDate :date. HireDate :mmddyy.;
run;


title 'Orion Star Managers';
proc print data=work.salesmgmt;
    var ID Last Title HireDate Salary;
run;
title;

  /* Alternate solution using informats */
data work.salesmgmt;
    format BirthDate HireDate date9.;
    infile "&path\managers.dat" dsd dlm='/' missover;
    input ID First :$12. Last :$12. Gender :$1. Salary Title :$25.
        Country :$2. BirthDate :date. HireDate :mmddyy.;
run;
```

```
title 'Orion Star Managers';
proc print data=work.salesmgmt;
   var ID Last Title HireDate Salary;
run;
title;
```

Solutions to Student Activities (Polls/Quizzes)

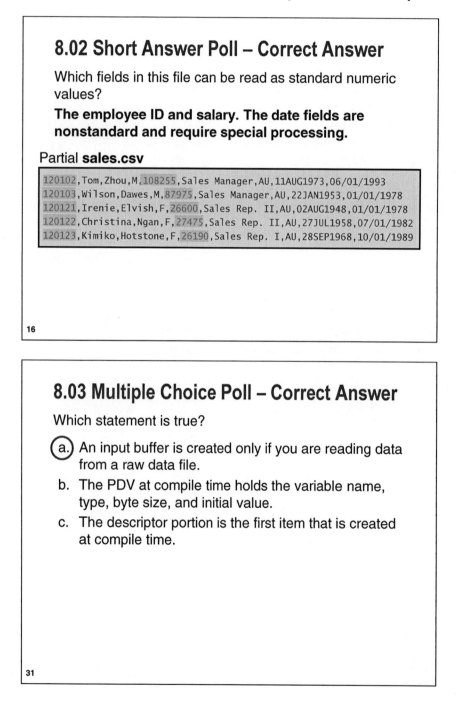

8.02 Short Answer Poll – Correct Answer

Which fields in this file can be read as standard numeric values?

The employee ID and salary. The date fields are nonstandard and require special processing.

Partial **sales.csv**

```
120102,Tom,Zhou,M,108255,Sales Manager,AU,11AUG1973,06/01/1993
120103,Wilson,Dawes,M,87975,Sales Manager,AU,22JAN1953,01/01/1978
120121,Irenie,Elvish,F,26600,Sales Rep. II,AU,02AUG1948,01/01/1978
120122,Christina,Ngan,F,27475,Sales Rep. II,AU,27JUL1958,07/01/1982
120123,Kimiko,Hotstone,F,26190,Sales Rep. I,AU,28SEP1968,10/01/1989
```

16

8.03 Multiple Choice Poll – Correct Answer

Which statement is true?

(a.) An input buffer is created only if you are reading data from a raw data file.

b. The PDV at compile time holds the variable name, type, byte size, and initial value.

c. The descriptor portion is the first item that is created at compile time.

31

8.04 Short Answer Poll – Correct Answer

Suppose you want the order of the variables to match the order of the fields. You can include the numeric variables in the LENGTH statement. Which of the following produces the correct results?

a.
```
length Employee_ID First_Name $ 12
       Last_Name $ 18 Gender $ 1
       Salary Job_Title $ 25
       Country $ 2;
```

(b.)
```
length Employee_ID 8 First_Name $ 12
       Last_Name $ 18 Gender $ 1
       Salary 8 Job_Title $ 25
       Country $ 2;
```

56

8.05 Short Answer Poll – Correct Answer

What problems do you see with the data values for the last two data fields, **Salary** and **Country**?

Partial **sales3inv.csv**

```
120102,Tom,Zhou,Manager,108255,AU
120103,Wilson,Dawes,Manager,87975,AU
120121,Irenie,Elvish,Rep. II,26600,AU
120122,Christina,Ngan,Rep. II,n/a,AU
120123,Kimiko,Hotstone,Rep. I,26190,AU
120124,Lucian,Daymond,Rep. I,26480,12
120125,Fong,Hofmeister,Rep. IV,32040,AU
```

63

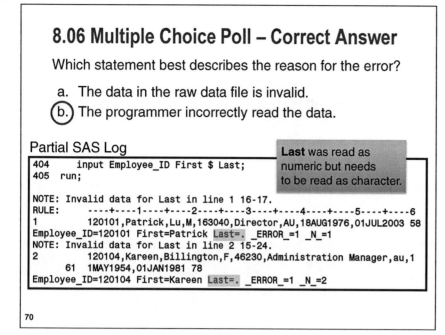

8.06 Multiple Choice Poll – Correct Answer

Which statement best describes the reason for the error?

a. The data in the raw data file is invalid.
b. The programmer incorrectly read the data.

Partial SAS Log

Last was read as numeric but needs to be read as character.

```
404      input Employee_ID First $ Last;
405   run;

NOTE: Invalid data for Last in line 1 16-17.
RULE:      ----+----1----+----2----+----3----+----4----+----5----+----6
1            120101,Patrick,Lu,M,163040,Director,AU,18AUG1976,01JUL2003 58
Employee_ID=120101 First=Patrick Last=. _ERROR_=1 _N_=1
NOTE: Invalid data for Last in line 2 15-24.
2            120104,Kareen,Billington,F,46230,Administration Manager,au,1
     61   1MAY1954,01JAN1981 78
Employee_ID=120104 First=Kareen Last=. _ERROR_=1 _N_=2
```

70

8.07 Short Answer Poll – Correct Answer

A *format* is an instruction that tells SAS how to display data values. What formats could you specify to display a SAS date in the styles shown below?

a) 01JAN2000   ⇨   **DATE9.**

b) 01/16/2000   ⇨   **MMDDYY10.**

81

8.08 Short Answer Poll – Correct Answer

Use the SAS Help Facility or documentation to investigate the **DATE***w.* informat and answer the following questions:

a) What does the *w* represent?
   the width of the input field

b) What is the default width of this informat?
   The default width is 7.

88

8.09 Short Answer Poll – Correct Answer

Submit **p108a03 and e**xamine the log and output.

How many input records were read and how many observations were created? **five read, three created**

Does the output look correct? **no**

```
NOTE: 5 records were read from the infile "S:\workshop\phone2.csv".
      The minimum record length was 31.
      The maximum record length was 44.
NOTE: SAS went to a new line when INPUT statement reached past the
end of a line.
NOTE: The data set WORK.CONTACTS has 3 observations and 3 variables.
```

Name	Phone	Mobile
James Kvarniq	(704) 293-8126	(701) 281-8923
Sandrina Stephano	(919) 871-7830	Cornelia Krahl
Karen Ballinger	(714) 344-4321	Elke Wallstab

109

Chapter 9   Manipulating Data

9.1 Using SAS Functions

Objectives

- Use SAS functions to create data values.

3

Business Scenario

Orion Star management plans to give a $500 bonus to each employee in his or her hire month.

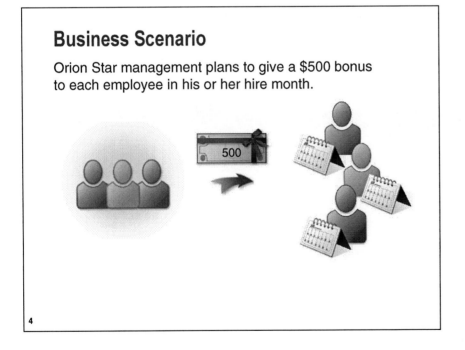

4

Considerations

Create a new data set with three new variables.

- **Bonus**, which is a constant 500
- **Compensation**, which is the sum of **Salary** and **Bonus**
- **BonusMonth**, which is the month in which the employee was hired

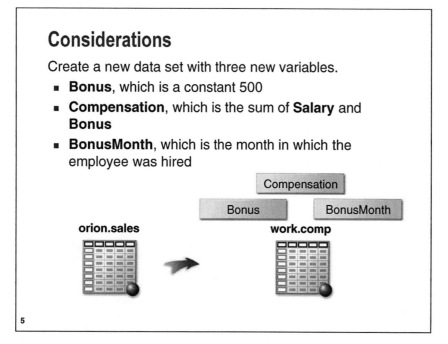

5

Considerations

Partial **orion.sales**

Employee _ID	First _Name	Last _Name	Gender	Salary	Job_Title	Country	Birth_ Date	Hire_ Date
120102	Tom	Zhou	M	108255	Sales Manager	AU	3510	10744
120103	Wilson	Dawes	M	87975	Sales Manager	AU	-3996	5114
120121	Irenie	Elvish	F	26600	Sales Rep. II	AU	-5630	5114

Partial **work.comp**

Employee _ID	First _Name	Last _Name	Bonus	Compensation	Bonus Month
120102	Tom	Zhou	500	108755	6
120103	Wilson	Dawes	500	88475	1
120121	Irenie	Elvish	500	27100	1

Drop **Gender, Salary, Job_Title, Country, Birth_Date,** and **Hire_Date** from **work.comp**.

6

9.01 Multiple Choice Poll

Which of the following statements creates a numeric
variable, **Bonus**, with a value of 500?

a. Bonus=$500;

b. Bonus=500;

c. label Bonus='500';

d. format Bonus 500.;

Partial **work.comp**

Bonus	Compensation	Bonus Month
500	108755	6
500	88475	1
500	27100	1

7

SAS Functions

SAS functions can be used in an assignment statement.
A *function* is a routine that accepts arguments and returns
a value.

```
variable=function-name(argument1, argument2, ...);
```

Some functions manipulate character values, compute
descriptive statistics, or manipulate SAS date values.

- Arguments are enclosed in parentheses and
  separated by commas.
- A function can return a numeric or character result.

9

SUM Function

Use the *SUM function* to create **Compensation**. The SUM function is a descriptive statistics function that returns the sum of its arguments.

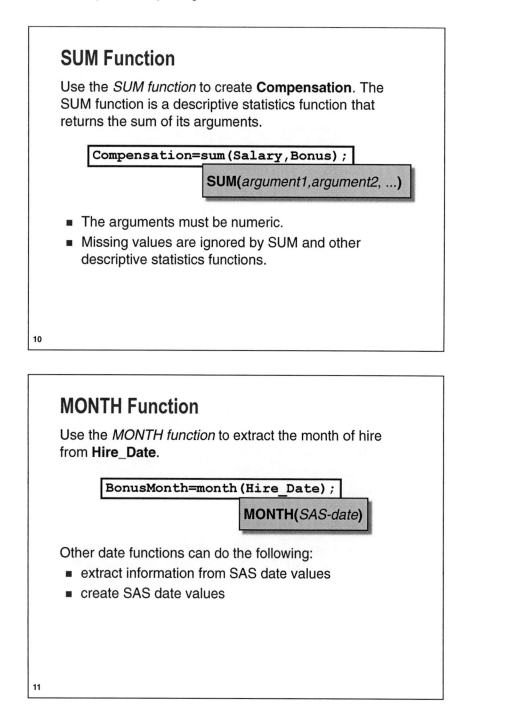

```
Compensation=sum(Salary,Bonus);
```

SUM(*argument1,argument2, ...*)

- The arguments must be numeric.
- Missing values are ignored by SUM and other descriptive statistics functions.

10

MONTH Function

Use the *MONTH function* to extract the month of hire from **Hire_Date**.

```
BonusMonth=month(Hire_Date);
```

MONTH(*SAS-date*)

Other date functions can do the following:
- extract information from SAS date values
- create SAS date values

11

Date Functions: Extracting Values

Syntax	Description
YEAR(*SAS-date*)	Extracts the year from a SAS date and returns a four-digit year.
QTR(*SAS-date*)	Extracts the calendar quarter from a SAS date and returns a number from 1 to 4.
MONTH(*SAS-date*)	Extracts the month from a SAS date and returns a number from 1 to 12.
DAY(*SAS-date*)	Extracts the day of the month from a SAS date and returns a number from 1 to 31.
WEEKDAY(*SAS-date*)	Extracts the day of the week from a SAS date and returns a number from 1 to 7, where 1 represents Sunday.

12

Date Functions: Creating SAS Dates

Syntax	Description
TODAY() DATE()	Returns the current date as a SAS date value.
MDY(*month,day,year*)	Returns a SAS date value from numeric month, day, and year values.

Examples
CurrentDate=today();
y2k=mdy(01,1,2000);
NewYear=mdy(Mon,Day,2013);

13

Using SAS Functions

A function call can be used alone in an assignment statement.

```
BonusMonth=month(Hire_Date);
AnnivBonus=mdy(BonusMonth,15,2008);
```

A function call can be part of any SAS expression.

```
if month(Hire_Date)=12;
```

A function call can be an argument to another function.

```
AnnivBonus=mdy(month(Hire_Date),15,2012);
```

14

Using SAS Functions

Create **Bonus**, **Compensation**, and **BonusMonth**.

```
data work.comp;
   set orion.sales;
   Bonus=500;
   Compensation=sum(Salary,Bonus);
   BonusMonth=month(Hire_Date);
run;
```

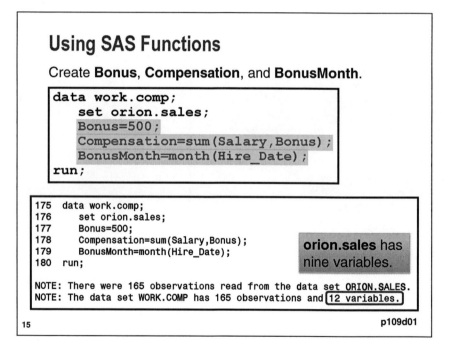

```
175   data work.comp;
176      set orion.sales;
177      Bonus=500;
178      Compensation=sum(Salary,Bonus);
179      BonusMonth=month(Hire_Date);
180   run;
```

orion.sales has nine variables.

```
NOTE: There were 165 observations read from the data set ORION.SALES.
NOTE: The data set WORK.COMP has 165 observations and 12 variables.
```

15   p109d01

Viewing the Output

```
proc print data=work.comp noobs;
   var Employee_ID First_Name Last_Name
       Bonus Compensation BonusMonth;
run;
```

Partial PROC PRINT Output

Employee_ID	First_ Name	Last_Name	Bonus	Compensation	Bonus Month
120102	Tom	Zhou	500	108755	6
120103	Wilson	Dawes	500	88475	1
120121	Irenie	Elvish	500	27100	1
120122	Christina	Ngan	500	27975	7
120123	Kimiko	Hotstone	500	26690	10

16

p109d01

9.02 Short Answer Poll

A DROP statement was added to this DATA step. Can the program calculate **Compensation** and **BonusMonth** correctly?

```
data work.comp;
   set orion.sales;
   drop Gender Salary Job_Title Country
       Birth_Date Hire_Date;
   Bonus=500;
   Compensation=sum(Salary,Bonus);
   BonusMonth=month(Hire_Date);
run;
```

17

p109a01

Viewing the Output

```
proc print data=work.comp noobs;
run;
```

Partial PROC PRINT Output

Employee_ID	First_Name	Last_Name	Bonus	Compensation	Bonus Month
120102	Tom	Zhou	500	108755	6
120103	Wilson	Dawes	500	88475	1
120121	Irenie	Elvish	500	27100	1
120122	Christina	Ngan	500	27975	7
120123	Kimiko	Hotstone	500	26690	10

19   p109a01

Exercises

If you restarted your SAS session since the last exercise, open and submit the **libname.sas** program that can be found in the data folder.

Level 1

1. **Creating New Variables**

   a. Retrieve the starter program **p109e01**.

   b. In the DATA step, create three new variables:
      - **Increase**, which is **Salary** multiplied by 0.10
      - **NewSalary**, which is **Salary** added to **Increase**
      - **BdayQtr**, which is the quarter in which the employee was born

   c. The new data set should include only **Employee_ID**, **Salary**, **Birth_Date**, and the three new variables.

   d. Store permanent formats to display **Salary**, **Increase**, and **NewSalary** with commas.

   e. Modify the program to create the report below, including labels. The results should contain 424 observations.

Partial PROC PRINT Output

Obs	Employee ID	Employee Annual Salary	Employee Birth Date	Increase	NewSalary	Bday Qtr
1	120101	163,040	18AUG1980	16,304	179,344	3
2	120102	108,255	11AUG1973	10,826	119,081	3
3	120103	87,975	22JAN1953	8,798	96,773	1
4	120104	46,230	11MAY1958	4,623	50,853	2
5	120105	27,110	21DEC1978	2,711	29,821	4

Level 2

2. **Creating New Variables**

   a. Write a DATA step that reads **orion.customer** to create **work.birthday**.

   b. In the DATA step, create three new variables: **Bday2012**, **BdayDOW2012**, and **Age2012**.
      - **Bday2012** is the combination of the month of **Birth_Date**, the day of **Birth_Date**, and the constant of **2012** in the MDY function.
      - **BdayDOW2012** is the day of the week of **Bday2012**.
      - **Age2012** is the age of the customer in 2012. Subtract **Birth_Date** from **Bday2012** and divide the result by 365.25.

   c. Include only the following variables in the new data set: **Customer_Name**, **Birth_Date**, **Bday2012**, **BdayDOW2012**, and **Age2012**.

   d. Format **Bday2012** to appear in the form 01Jan2012. **Age2012** should be formatted to appear with no decimal places.

   e. Write a PROC PRINT step to create the report below. The results should contain 77 observations.

   Partial PROC PRINT Output

Obs	Customer_Name	Birth_Date	Bday2012	Bday DOW2012	Age2012
1	James Kvarniq	27JUN1978	27JUN2012	4	34
2	Sandrina Stephano	09JUL1983	09JUL2012	2	29
3	Cornelia Krahl	27FEB1978	27FEB2012	2	34
4	Karen Ballinger	18OCT1988	18OCT2012	5	24
5	Elke Wallstab	16AUG1978	16AUG2012	5	34

Challenge

3. **Using the CATX and INTCK Functions to Create Variables**

   a. Write a DATA step that reads **orion.sales** to create **work.employees**.

   In the DATA step, create a new variable, **FullName**. This variable is the combination of **First_Name**, a space, and **Last_Name**. Use the CATX function. You can find documentation about CATX in the SAS Help Facility or in the online documentation.

In the DATA step, create a new variable, **Yrs2012**. This variable is the number of years between January 1, 2012, and **Hire_Date**. Use the INTCK function. Documentation about INTCK can be found in the SAS Help Facility or in the online documentation.

b. Format **Hire_Date** to appear in the form 31/01/2012.

c. Give **Yrs2012** a label of **Years of Employment as of 2012**.

d. Create the report shown below. The results should contain 165 observations.

Partial PROC PRINT Output

			Years of Employment
Obs	FullName	Hire_Date	as of 2012
1	Tom Zhou	01/06/1993	19
2	Wilson Dawes	01/01/1978	34
3	Irenie Elvish	01/01/1978	34
4	Christina Ngan	01/07/1982	30
5	Kimiko Hotstone	01/10/1989	23

9.2 Conditional Processing

Objectives

- Use IF-THEN/ELSE statements to process data conditionally.
- Use DO and END statements to execute multiple statements conditionally.
- Use the LENGTH statement to control the length of character variables.

23

Business Scenario

Orion Star management plans to give each sales employee a bonus based on his or her job title.

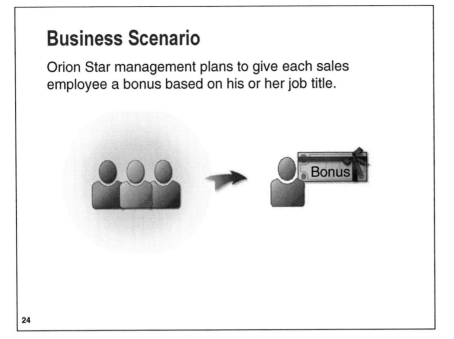

24

Considerations

Create a new data set, **work.comp**. Use **orion.sales** as input. Include a new variable, **Bonus**, with a value that is based on **Job_Title**.

Job_Title	Bonus
Sales Rep. IV	1000
Sales Manager	1500
Senior Sales Manager	2000
Chief Sales Officer	2500

25

IF-THEN Statements

The IF-THEN statement executes a SAS statement for observations that meet a specific condition.

```
data work.comp;
   set orion.sales;
   if Job_Title='Sales Rep. IV' then
      Bonus=1000;
   ...
run;
```

> **IF** *expression* **THEN** *statement*;

- *expression* defines a condition.
- *statement* can be any executable SAS statement.
- If *expression* is true, then *statement* executes.

26

Conditional Processing

The value assigned to **Bonus** is determined by testing for various values of **Job_Title**.

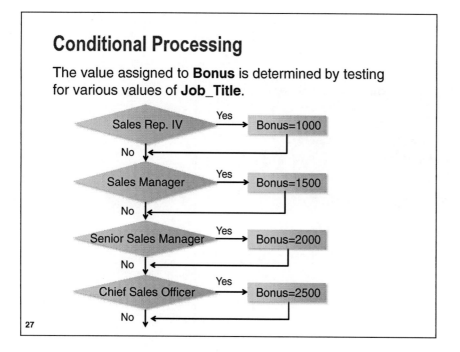

27

Conditional Processing

```
data work.comp;
   set orion.sales;
   if Job_Title='Sales Rep. IV' then
      Bonus=1000;
   if Job_Title='Sales Manager' then
      Bonus=1500;
   if Job_Title='Senior Sales Manager'
      then Bonus=2000;
   if Job_Title='Chief Sales Officer'
      then Bonus=2500;
run;
```

PDV

Employee_ID	Last_Name		Job_Title	Bonus
120102	Zhou	⋯	Sales Manager	.

28   p109d02
                                                              ⋯

Conditional Processing

```
data work.comp;
   set orion.sales;        ┌─────┐
   if Job_Title='Sales Rep. IV' then    false
      Bonus=1000;
   if Job_Title='Sales Manager' then
      Bonus=1500;
   if Job_Title='Senior Sales Manager'
      then Bonus=2000;
   if Job_Title='Chief Sales Officer'
      then Bonus=2500;
run;
```

PDV

Employee_ID	Last_Name		Job_Title	Bonus
120102	Zhou	⋯	Sales Manager	.

29   ⋯

Conditional Processing

```
data work.comp;
   set orion.sales;
   if Job_Title='Sales R      V' then
      Bonus=1000;
   if Job_Title='Sales Manager' then
      Bonus=1500;
   if Job_Title='Senior Sales Manager'
      then Bonus=2000;
   if Job_Title='Chief Sales Officer'
      then Bonus=2500;
run;
```

PDV

Employee_ID	Last_Name		Job_Title	Bonus
120102	Zhou	...	Sales Manager	.

30

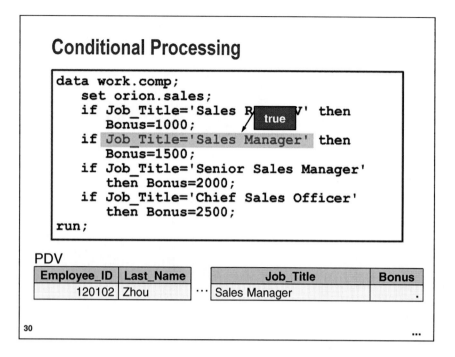

Conditional Processing

```
data work.comp;
   set orion.sales;
   if Job_Title='Sales Rep. IV' then
      Bonus=1000;
   if Job_Title='Sales Manager' then
      Bonus=1500;
   if Job_Title='Senior Sales Manager'
      then Bonus=2000;
   if Job_Title='Chief Sales Officer'
      then Bonus=2500;
run;
```

PDV

Employee_ID	Last_Name		Job_Title	Bonus
120102	Zhou	...	Sales Manager	1500

31

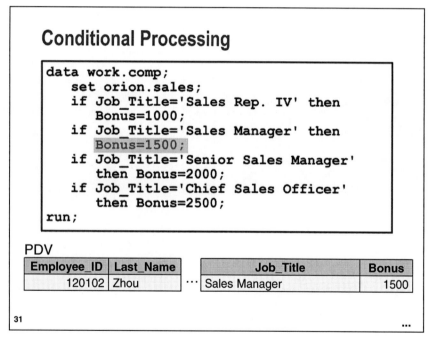

Conditional Processing

```
data work.comp;
   set orion.sales;
   if Job_Title='Sales Rep. IV' then
      Bonus=1000;
   if Job_Title='Sales Manager' then
      Bonus=1500;
   if Job_Title='Senior Sales Manager'
      then Bonus=2000;
   if Job_Title='Chief Sales Officer'
      then Bonus=2500;
run;
```

PDV

Employee_ID	Last_Name		Job_Title	Bonus
120102	Zhou	⋯	Sales Manager	1500

32

Conditional Processing

```
data work.comp;
   set orion.sales;
   if Job_Title='Sales Rep. IV' then
      Bonus=1000;
   if Job_Title='Sales Manager' then
      Bonus=1500;
   if Job_Title='Senior Sales Manager'
      then Bonus=2000;
   if Job_Title='Chief Sales Officer'
      then Bonus=2500;
run;
```

PDV

Employee_ID	Last_Name		Job_Title	Bonus
120102	Zhou	⋯	Sales Manager	1500

33

Conditional Processing

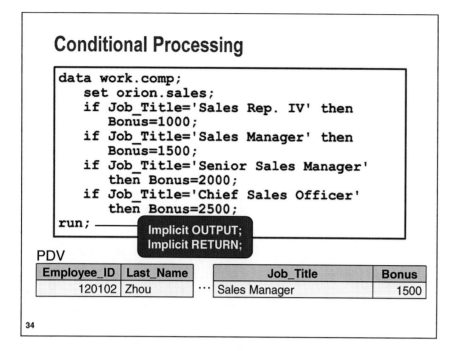

```
data work.comp;
   set orion.sales;
   if Job_Title='Sales Rep. IV' then
      Bonus=1000;
   if Job_Title='Sales Manager' then
      Bonus=1500;
   if Job_Title='Senior Sales Manager'
      then Bonus=2000;
   if Job_Title='Chief Sales Officer'
      then Bonus=2500;
run;
```

Implicit OUTPUT;
Implicit RETURN;

PDV

Employee_ID	Last_Name		Job_Title	Bonus
120102	Zhou	...	Sales Manager	1500

34

Conditional Processing

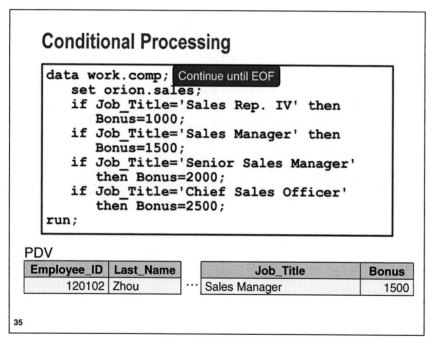

```
data work.comp;
   set orion.sales;
   if Job_Title='Sales Rep. IV' then
      Bonus=1000;
   if Job_Title='Sales Manager' then
      Bonus=1500;
   if Job_Title='Senior Sales Manager'
      then Bonus=2000;
   if Job_Title='Chief Sales Officer'
      then Bonus=2500;
run;
```

Continue until EOF

PDV

Employee_ID	Last_Name		Job_Title	Bonus
120102	Zhou	...	Sales Manager	1500

35

Viewing the Output

```
proc print data=work.comp;
   var Last_Name Job_Title Bonus;
run;
```

Partial PROC PRINT Output

Obs	Last_Name	Job_Title	Bonus
1	Zhou	Sales Manager	1500
2	Dawes	Sales Manager	1500
3	Elvish	Sales Rep. II	.
4	Ngan	Sales Rep. II	.
5	Hotstone	Sales Rep. I	.
6	Daymond	Sales Rep. I	.
7	Hofmeister	Sales Rep. IV	1000
8	Denny	Sales Rep. II	.
9	Clarkson	Sales Rep. II	.
10	Kletschkus	Sales Rep. IV	1000
11	Roebuck	Sales Rep. III	.
12	Lyon	Sales Rep. I	.

36   p109d02

9.03 Multiple Choice Poll

In the previous program, is it possible for more than one condition to be true for a single observation?

a. Yes, more than one condition can be true.

b. No, the conditions are mutually exclusive, so only one condition can be true.

37

Using the ELSE Statement

Use the *ELSE statement* when you test mutually exclusive conditions.

```
data work.comp;
   set orion.sales;
   if Job_Title='Sales Rep. IV'
      then Bonus=1000;
   else if Job_Title='Sales Manager'
      then Bonus=1500;
   else if Job_Title='Senior Sales Manager'
      then Bonus=2000;
   else if Job_Title='Chief Sales Officer'
      then Bonus=2500;
run;
```

IF *expression* **THEN** *statement*;
<ELSE IF *expression* **THEN** *statement*;**>**
<ELSE IF *expression* **THEN** *statement*;**>**

39   p109d03

Conditional Processing

When an expression is true, the associated statement is executed and subsequent ELSE statements are skipped.

40

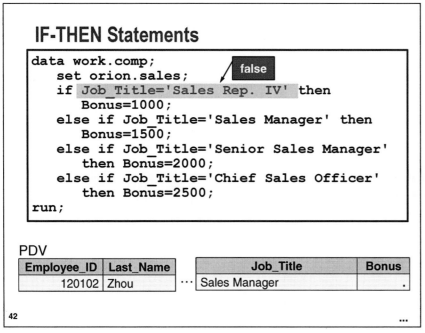

IF-THEN Statements

```
data work.comp;
   set orion.sales;
   if Job_Title='Sales Rep.         en
      Bonus=1000;                 true
   else if Job_Title='Sales Manager' then
      Bonus=1500;
   else if Job_Title='Senior Sales Manager'
      then Bonus=2000;
   else if Job_Title='Chief Sales Officer'
      then Bonus=2500;
run;
```

PDV

Employee_ID	Last_Name		Job_Title	Bonus
120102	Zhou	⋯	Sales Manager	.

43   ⋯

IF-THEN Statements

```
data work.comp;
   set orion.sales;
   if Job_Title='Sales Rep. IV' then
      Bonus=1000;
   else if Job_Title='Sales Manager' then
      Bonus=1500;
   else if Job_Title='Senior Sales Manager'
      then Bonus=2000;
   else if Job_Title='Chief Sales Officer'
      then Bonus=2500;
run;
```

PDV

Employee_ID	Last_Name		Job_Title	Bonus
120102	Zhou	⋯	Sales Manager	1500

44   ⋯

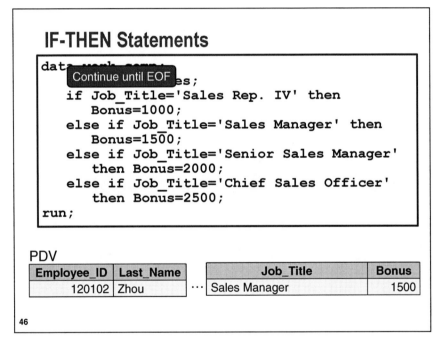

Viewing the Output

```
proc print data=work.comp;
    var Last_Name Job_Title Bonus;
run;
```

Partial PROC PRINT Output

Obs	Last_Name	Job_Title	Bonus
1	Zhou	Sales Manager	1500
2	Dawes	Sales Manager	1500
3	Elvish	Sales Rep. II	.
4	Ngan	Sales Rep. II	.
5	Hotstone	Sales Rep. I	.
6	Daymond	Sales Rep. I	.
7	Hofmeister	Sales Rep. IV	1000
8	Denny	Sales Rep. II	.
9	Clarkson	Sales Rep. II	.
10	Kletschkus	Sales Rep. IV	1000

47   p109d03

Business Scenario: Part 2

Orion Star management wants to modify the bonus plan as defined below.

Job_Title	Bonus
Sales Rep. III	1000
Sales Rep. IV	1000
Sales Manager	1500
Senior Sales Manager	2000
Chief Sales Officer	2500
All other titles	500

48

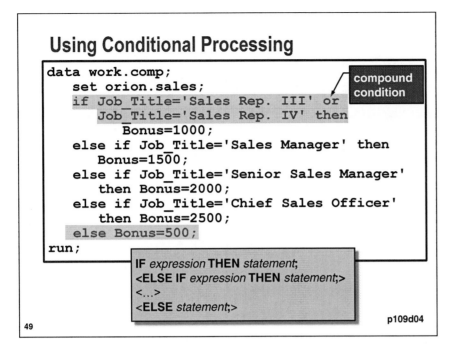

Using Conditional Processing

```
data work.comp;
   set orion.sales;
   if Job_Title='Sales Rep. III' or
      Job_Title='Sales Rep. IV' then
         Bonus=1000;
   else if Job_Title='Sales Manager' then
      Bonus=1500;
   else if Job_Title='Senior Sales Manager'
      then Bonus=2000;
   else if Job_Title='Chief Sales Officer'
      then Bonus=2500;
   else Bonus=500;
run;
```

compound condition

IF *expression* **THEN** *statement*;
<ELSE IF *expression* **THEN** *statement*;>
<...>
<ELSE *statement*;>

49   p109d04

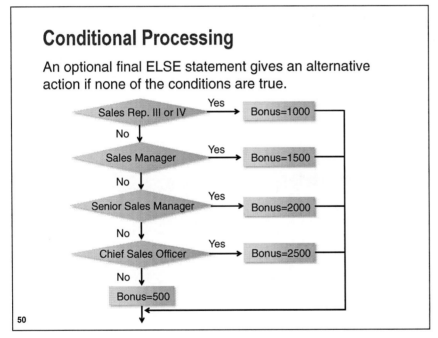

Conditional Processing

An optional final ELSE statement gives an alternative
action if none of the conditions are true.

50

Viewing the Output

```
proc print data=work.comp;
   var Last_Name Job_Title Bonus;
run;
```

Partial PROC PRINT Output

Obs	Last_Name	Job_Title	Bonus
1	Zhou	Sales Manager	1500
2	Dawes	Sales Manager	1500
3	Elvish	Sales Rep. II	500
4	Ngan	Sales Rep. II	500
5	Hotstone	Sales Rep. I	500
6	Daymond	Sales Rep. I	500
7	Hofmeister	Sales Rep. IV	1000
8	Denny	Sales Rep. II	500
9	Clarkson	Sales Rep. II	500
10	Kletschkus	Sales Rep. IV	1000

51   p109d04

Business Scenario

Orion Star managers are considering a country-based bonus. Create a new SAS data set named **work.bonus**. Use **orion.sales** as input. The value of the new variable, **Bonus**, is based on **Country**.

52

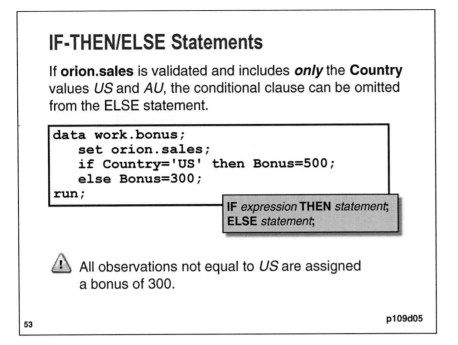

IF-THEN/ELSE Statements

If **orion.sales** is validated and includes *only* the **Country** values *US* and *AU*, the conditional clause can be omitted from the ELSE statement.

```
data work.bonus;
   set orion.sales;
   if Country='US' then Bonus=500;
   else Bonus=300;
run;
```

IF *expression* **THEN** *statement*;
ELSE *statement*;

⚠ All observations not equal to *US* are assigned a bonus of 300.

53   p109d05

You should use this technique only when you know that the final ELSE statement must be executed for all other observations.

Viewing the Output

```
proc print data=work.bonus;
   var First_Name Last_Name Country Bonus;
run;
```

Partial PROC PRINT Output

Obs	First_Name	Last_Name	Country	Bonus
60	Billy	Plested	AU	300
61	Matsuoka	Wills	AU	300
62	Vino	George	AU	300
63	Meera	Body	AU	300
64	Harry	Highpoint	US	500
65	Julienne	Magolan	US	500
66	Scott	Desanctis	US	500
67	Cherda	Ridley	US	500
68	Priscilla	Farren	US	500
69	Robert	Stevens	US	500

54   p109d05

9.04 Short Answer Poll

Program **p109a02** reads **orion.nonsales**, a non-validated data set. Open and submit the program and review the results. Why is **Bonus** set to 300 in observations 125, 197, and 200?

```
data work.bonus;
   set orion.nonsales;
   if Country='US' then Bonus=500;
   else Bonus=300;
run;
```

55

Testing for Invalid Data

You can test for multiple values of **Country**.

```
data work.bonus;
   set orion.nonsales;
   if Country in ('US','us')
      then Bonus=500;
   else Bonus=300;
run;
```

You can use the UPCASE function in the expression.

```
data work.bonus;
   set orion.nonsales;
   if upcase(Country)='US'
      then Bonus=500;
   else Bonus=300;
run;
```

57   p109a02s

Cleaning Invalid Data

You can clean the data before checking the value.

```
data work.bonus;
   set orion.nonsales;
   Country=upcase(Country);
   if Country='US'
      then Bonus=500;
   else Bonus=300;
run;
```

✎ It is a best practice to clean the data at the source, but in some cases, that is not possible. With this method, you are creating a clean data set.

58   p109d06

Business Scenario

Orion Star employees receive a bonus once or twice a year. In addition to **Bonus**, add a new variable, **Freq**, that is equal to the following:

- *Once a Year* for United States employees
- *Twice a Year* for Australian employees

Once a Year   Twice a Year

60

IF-THEN/ELSE Statements

Only **one** executable statement is allowed
in IF-THEN and ELSE statements.

IF *expression* **THEN** *statement*;
ELSE IF *expression* **THEN** *statement*;
ELSE *statement*;

For this business scenario, **two** statements must be
executed for each true expression.

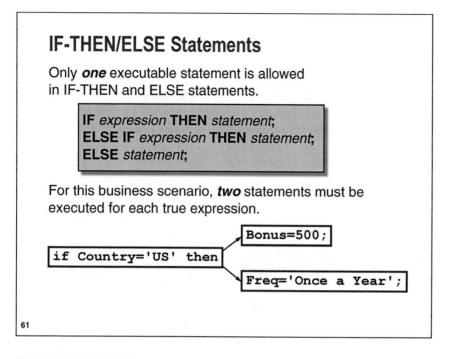

61

DO Group

Multiple statements are permitted in a *DO group*.

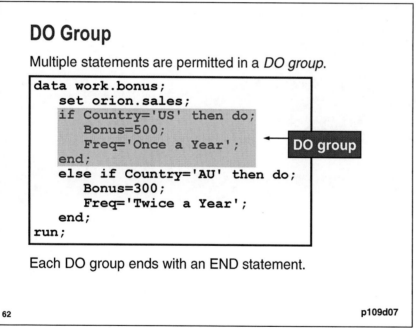

Each DO group ends with an END statement.

62   p109d07

IF-THEN DO/ELSE DO Statements

Multiple statements are also permitted in an ELSE DO group.

63

Viewing the Output

```
proc print data=work.bonus;
    var First_Name Last_Name Country Bonus
        Freq;
run;
```

Partial PROC PRINT Output

Obs	First_Name	Last_Name	Country	Bonus	Freq
60	Billy	Plested	AU	300	Twice a Yea
61	Matsuoka	Wills	AU	300	Twice a Yea
62	Vino	George	AU	300	Twice a Yea
63	Meera	Body	AU	300	Twice a Yea
64	Harry	Highpoint	US	500	Once a Year
65	Julienne	Magolan	US	500	Once a Year
66	Scott	Desanctis	US	500	Once a Year
67	Cherda	Ridley	US	500	Once a Year
68	Priscilla	Farren	US	500	Once a Year
69	Robert	Stevens	US	500	Once a Year

truncation

p109d07

64

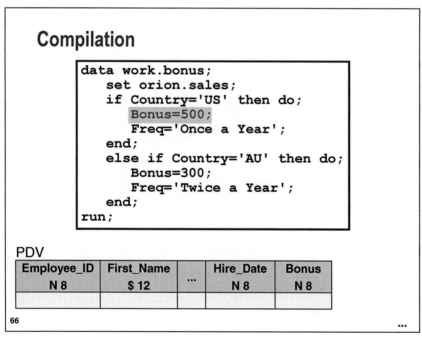

Compilation

```
data work.bonus;
   set orion.sales;
   if Country='US' then do;
      Bonus=500;
      Freq='Once a Year';
   end;
   else if C[ 11 characters ]  then do;
      Bonus=300;
      Freq='Twice a Year';
   end;
run;
```

11 characters

PDV

Employee_ID	First_Name	...	Hire_Date	Bonus	Freq
N 8	$ 12		N 8	N 8	$ 11

67   ...

Compilation

```
data work.bonus;
   set orion.sales;
   if Country='US' then do;
      Bonus=500;
      Freq='Once a Year';
   end;
   else if Country='AU' then do;
      Bonus=300;
      Freq='Twice a Year';
   end;
run;
```

12 characters

Length does not change.

PDV

Employee_ID	First_Name	...	Hire_Date	Bonus	Freq
N 8	$ 12		N 8	N 8	$ 11

68

9.05 Short Answer Poll

How would you prevent **Freq** from being truncated?

69

Defining Character Variables

Set the length of the variable **Freq** to avoid truncation.

```
data work.bonus;
   set orion.sales;
   length Freq $ 12;
   if Country='US' then do;
      Bonus=500;
      Freq='Once a Year';
   end;
   else if Country='AU' then do;
      Bonus=300;
      Freq='Twice a Year';
   end;
run;
```

LENGTH *variable(s)* <$> *length*;

✐ It is a good practice to use a LENGTH statement anytime that you create a new character variable.

71   p109d08

✐   The LENGTH statement is usually placed at or near the top of the DATA step.

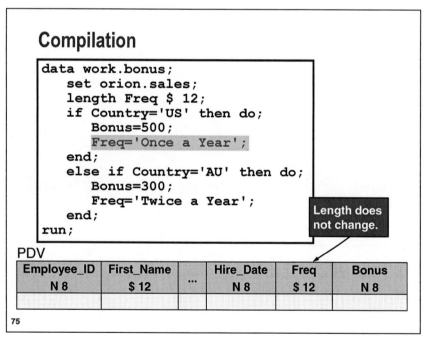

Viewing the Output

```
proc print data=work.bonus;
    var First_Name Last_Name Country
        Bonus Freq;
run;
```

Partial PROC PRINT Output

Obs	First_Name	Last_Name	Country	Bonus	Freq
60	Billy	Plested	AU	300	Twice a Year
61	Matsuoka	Wills	AU	300	Twice a Year
62	Vino	George	AU	300	Twice a Year
63	Meera	Body	AU	300	Twice a Year
64	Harry	Highpoint	US	500	Once a Year
65	Julienne	Magolan	US	500	Once a Year
66	Scott	Desanctis	US	500	Once a Year
67	Cherda	Ridley	US	500	Once a Year
68	Priscilla	Farren	US	500	Once a Year
69	Robert	Stevens	US	500	Once a Year

no truncation

76   p109d08

Exercises

If you restarted your SAS session since the last exercise, open and submit the **libname.sas** program that can be found in the data folder.

Level 1

4. **Using Conditional Processing**

    a. Retrieve the starter program **p109e04**.

    b. In the DATA step, create a new variable, **Method**, and assign a value based on **Order_Type**.

    If **Order_Type** is equal to 1, then **Method** equals *Retail*.

    If **Order_Type** is equal to 2, then **Method** equals *Catalog*.

    If **Order_Type** is equal to 3, then **Method** equals *Internet*.

    For any other values of **Order_Type**, **Method** equals *Unknown*.

    c. Modify the PROC PRINT step to display the report below. The results should contain 490 observations.

Partial PROC PRINT Output

```
                        Order_
Obs      Order_ID       Type       Method

 1      1230058123        1         Retail
 2      1230080101        2         Catalog
 3      1230106883        2         Catalog
 4      1230147441        1         Retail
 5      1230315085        1         Retail
```

5. **Using Conditional Processing with DO Groups**

   a. Retrieve the starter program **p109e05**.

   b. Modify the DATA step to create three new variables: **Discount**, **DiscountType**, and **Region**. Assign values to the new variables based on **Country**.

   If **Country** is equal to *CA* or *US*, then the listed variables equal the following values:
   Discount is equal to 0.10.
   DiscountType is equal to *Required*.
   Region is equal to *North America*.

   If **Country** is equal to any other value, then the listed variables equal the following values:
   Discount is equal to 0.05.
   DiscountType is equal to *Optional*.
   Region is equal to *Not North America*.

   c. The new data set should include only **Supplier_Name**, **Country**, **Discount**, **DiscountType**, and **Region**.

   d. Submit the program to create the report below. The results should contain 52 observations.

   Partial PROC PRINT Output

```
                                                                               Discount
Obs    Supplier_Name               Country     Region             Discount     Type

 1     Scandinavian Clothing A/S     NO       Not North America      0.05       Optional
 2     Petterson AB                  SE       Not North America      0.05       Optional
 3     Prime Sports Ltd              GB       Not North America      0.05       Optional
 4     Top Sports                    DK       Not North America      0.05       Optional
 5     AllSeasons Outdoor Clothing   US       North America          0.10       Required
```

Level 2

6. **Creating Multiple Variables in Conditional Processing**

   a. Write a DATA step that reads **orion.customer_dim** to create **work.season**.

   b. Create two new variables: **Promo** and **Promo2**.

   The value of **Promo** is based on the quarter in which the customer was born.

   - If the customer was born in the first quarter, then **Promo** is equal to *Winter*.

   - If the customer was born in the second quarter, then **Promo** is equal to *Spring*.

- If the customer was born in the third quarter, then **Promo** is equal to *Summer*.
- If the customer was born in the fourth quarter, then **Promo** is equal to *Fall*.

The value of **Promo2** is based on the customer's age.

- For young adults, whose age is between 18 and 25, set **Promo2** equal to *YA*.
- For seniors, aged 65 or older, set **Promo2** equal to *Senior*.

Promo2 should have a missing value for all other customers.

c. The new data set should include only **Customer_FirstName**, **Customer_LastName**, **Customer_BirthDate**, **Customer_Age**, **Promo**, and **Promo2**.

d. Create the report below. The results should include 77 observations.

Partial PROC PRINT Output

Obs	Customer_ FirstName	Customer_ LastName	Customer_ BirthDate	Promo	Customer_ Age	Promo2
1	James	Kvarniq	27JUN1978	Spring	33	
2	Sandrina	Stephano	09JUL1983	Summer	28	
3	Cornelia	Krahl	27FEB1978	Winter	33	
4	Karen	Ballinger	18OCT1988	Fall	23	YA
5	Elke	Wallstab	16AUG1978	Summer	33	
6	David	Black	12APR1973	Spring	38	
7	Markus	Sepke	21JUL1992	Summer	19	YA
8	Ulrich	Heyde	16JAN1943	Winter	68	Senior

7. **Creating Variables Unconditionally and Conditionally**

a. Write a DATA step that reads **orion.orders** to create **work.ordertype**.

b. Create a new variable, **DayOfWeek**, that is equal to the weekday of **Order_Date**.

c. Create the new variable **Type**, which is equal to the following:
- *Retail Sale* if **Order_Type** is equal to *1*
- *Catalog Sale* if **Order_Type** is equal to *2*
- *Internet Sale* if **Order_Type** is equal to *3*.

d. Create the new variable **SaleAds**, which is equal to the following:
- *Mail* if **Order_Type** is equal to *2*
- *Email* if **Order_Type** is equal to *3*.

e. Do not include **Order_Type**, **Employee_ID**, and **Customer_ID** in the new data set.

f. Create the report below. The results should contain 490 observations.

Partial PROC PRINT Output

Obs	Order_ID	Order_ Date	Delivery_ Date	Type	Sale Ads	Day Of Week
1	1230058123	11JAN2007	11JAN2007	Retail Sale		5
2	1230080101	15JAN2007	19JAN2007	Catalog Sale	Mail	2
3	1230106883	20JAN2007	22JAN2007	Catalog Sale	Mail	7
4	1230147441	28JAN2007	28JAN2007	Retail Sale		1
5	1230315085	27FEB2007	27FEB2007	Retail Sale		3

Challenge

8. **Using WHEN Statements in a SELECT Group to Create Variables Conditionally**

   a. Write a DATA step that reads **orion.nonsales** to create **work.gifts**.

   b. Create two new variables, **Gift1** and **Gift2**. Use a SELECT group with WHEN statements. You can find documentation about the SELECT group with WHEN statements in the SAS Help Facility or in the online documentation.

   If **Gender** is equal to *F*, then the listed variables equal the following values:
   Gift1 is equal to *Scarf.*
   Gift2 is equal to *Pedometer.*

   If **Gender** is equal to *M*, then the listed variables equal the following values:
   Gift1 is equal to *Gloves.*
   Gift2 is equal to *Money Clip.*

   If **Gender** is not equal to *F* or *M*, then the listed variables equal the following values:
   Gift1 is equal to *Coffee.*
   Gift2 is equal to *Calendar.*

   c. The new data set should include only **Employee_ID**, **First**, **Last**, **Gender**, **Gift1**, and **Gift2**.

   d. Create the report below. The results should contain 235 observations.

   Partial PROC PRINT Output

Employee_ID	First	Last	Gender	Gift1	Gift2
120101	Patrick	Lu	M	Gloves	Money Clip
120104	Kareen	Billington	F	Scarf	Pedometer
120105	Liz	Povey	F	Scarf	Pedometer
120106	John	Hornsey	M	Gloves	Money Clip
120107	Sherie	Sheedy	F	Scarf	Pedometer

9.3 Solutions

Solutions to Exercises

1. **Creating New Variables**

```
data work.increase;
   set orion.staff;
   Increase=Salary*0.10;
   NewSalary=sum(Salary,Increase);
 /* alternate statement is */
 /* NewSalary=Salary+Increase; */
   BdayQtr=qtr(Birth_Date);
   keep Employee_ID Birth_Date Salary Increase NewSalary BdayQtr;
   format Salary Increase NewSalary comma8.;
run;


proc print data=work.increase label;
run;
```

2. **Creating New Variables**

```
data work.birthday;
   set orion.customer;
   Bday2012=mdy(month(Birth_Date),day(Birth_Date),2012);
   BdayDOW2012=weekday(Bday2012);
   Age2012=(Bday2012-Birth_Date)/365.25;
   keep Customer_Name Birth_Date Bday2012 BdayDOW2012 Age2012;
   format Bday2012 date9. Age2012 3.;
run;


proc print data=work.birthday;
run;
```

3. **Using the CATX and INTCK Functions to Create Variables**

```
data work.employees;
   set orion.sales;
   FullName=catx(' ',First_Name,Last_Name);
   Yrs2012=intck('year',Hire_Date,'01JAN2012'd);
   format Hire_Date ddmmyy10.;
   label Yrs2012='Years of Employment in 2012';
run;

proc print data=work.employees label;
   var FullName Hire_Date Yrs2012;
run;
```

4. Using Conditional Processing

```
data work.ordertype;
   set orion.orders;
   length Method $ 8;
   if Order_Type=1 then Method='Retail';
   else if Order_Type=2 then Method='Catalog';
   else if Order_type=3 then Method='Internet';
   else Method='Unknown';
run;

proc print data=work.ordertype;
   var Order_ID Order_Type Method;
run;
```

5. Using Conditional Processing with DO Groups

```
data work.region;
   set orion.supplier;
   length Region $ 17;
   if Country in ('CA','US') then do;
      Discount=0.10;
      DiscountType='Required';
      Region='North America';
   end;
   else do;
      Discount=0.05;
      DiscountType='Optional';
      Region='Not North America';
   end;
   keep Supplier_Name Country
        Discount DiscountType Region;
run;

proc print data=work.region;
run;
```

6. Creating Multiple Variables in Conditional Processing

```
data work.season;
   set orion.customer_dim;
   length Promo2 $ 6;
   Quarter=qtr(Customer_BirthDate);
   if Quarter=1 then Promo='Winter';
   else if Quarter=2 then Promo='Spring';
   else if Quarter=3 then Promo='Summer';
   else if Quarter=4 then Promo='Fall';
   if Customer_Age>=18 and Customer_Age<=25 then  Promo2='YA';
   else if Customer_Age>=65 then  Promo2='Senior';
   keep Customer_FirstName Customer_LastName Customer_BirthDate
        Customer_Age Promo Promo2;
run;
```

```
proc print data=work.season;
    var Customer_FirstName Customer_LastName Customer_BirthDate Promo
        Customer_Age Promo2;
run;
```

7. **Creating Variables Unconditionally and Conditionally**

```
data work.ordertype;
    set orion.orders;
    length Type $ 13 SaleAds $ 5;
    DayOfWeek=weekday(Order_Date);
    if Order_Type=1 then
        Type='Retail Sale';
    else if Order_Type=2 then do;
        Type='Catalog Sale';
        SaleAds='Mail';
    end;
    else if Order_Type=3 then do;
        Type='Internet Sale';
        SaleAds='Email';
    end;
    drop Order_Type Employee_ID Customer_ID;
run;

proc print data=work.ordertype;
run;
```

8. **Using WHEN Statements in a SELECT Group to Create Variables Conditionally**

```
data work.gifts;
    set orion.nonsales;
    length Gift1 $ 6 Gift2 $ 10;
    select(Gender);
        when('F') do;
            Gift1='Scarf';
            Gift2='Pedometer';
        end;
        when('M') do;
            Gift1='Gloves';
            Gift2='Money Clip';
        end;
        otherwise do;
            Gift1='Coffee';
            Gift2='Calendar';
        end;
        end;
        keep Employee_ID First Last Gender Gift1 Gift2;
run;

proc print data=work.gifts noobs;
run;
```

Solutions to Student Activities (Polls/Quizzes)

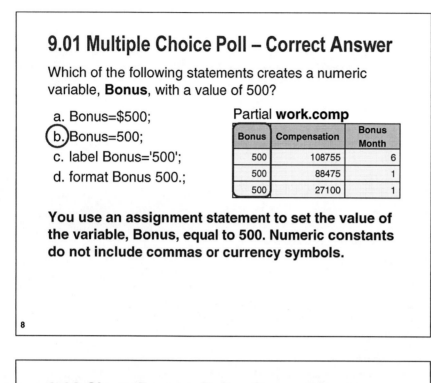

9.01 Multiple Choice Poll – Correct Answer

Which of the following statements creates a numeric variable, **Bonus**, with a value of 500?

a. Bonus=$500;
b. Bonus=500;
c. label Bonus='500';
d. format Bonus 500.;

Partial **work.comp**

Bonus	Compensation	Bonus Month
500	108755	6
500	88475	1
500	27100	1

You use an assignment statement to set the value of the variable, Bonus, equal to 500. Numeric constants do not include commas or currency symbols.

8

9.02 Short Answer Poll – Correct Answer

A DROP statement was added to this DATA step. Can the program calculate **Compensation** and **BonusMonth** correctly?

```
23   data work.comp;
24      set orion.sales;
25      drop Gender Salary Job_Title Country
26              Birth_Date Hire_Date;
27      Bonus=500;
28      Compensation=sum(Salary,Bonus);
29      BonusMonth=month(Hire_Date);
30   run;
NOTE: There were 165 observations read from the data set ORION.SALES.
NOTE: The data set WORK.COMP has 165 observations and 6 variables.
```

Yes. A drop flag is set for the dropped variables, but the variables are in the PDV and therefore available for processing. DROP is a compile-time only statement.

18

9.03 Multiple Choice Poll – Correct Answer

In the previous program, is it possible for more than one condition to be true for a single observation?

  a. Yes, more than one condition can be true.
  (b.) No, the conditions are mutually exclusive,
      so only one condition can be true.

For each observation, there is only one value for Job_Title. If that value matches one of the conditions, then it cannot match any other condition.

38

9.04 Short Answer Poll – Correct Answer

Program **p109a02** reads **orion.nonsales**, a non-validated data set. Open and submit the program and review the results. Why is **Bonus** set to 300 in observations 125, 197, and 200?

```
data work.bonus;
   set orion.nonsales;
   if Country='US' then Bonus=500;
   else Bonus=300;
run;
```

The Country variable has some mixed case values in orion.nonsales. Observations with a country value of *US* are assigned 500. All others are assigned 300, including *us*.

56

9.05 Short Answer Poll – Correct Answer

How would you prevent **Freq** from being truncated?

Possible solutions:

- **Pad the first occurrence of the Freq value with blanks to be the length of the longest possible value.**
- **Switch conditional statements to place the longest value of Freq in the first conditional statement.**
- **Add a LENGTH statement to declare the byte size of the variable up front.**

70

Chapter 10   Combining Data Sets

10.1   Concatenating Data Sets

Objectives

- Concatenate two or more SAS data sets.
  Use the SET statement in a DATA step.
- Change the names of variables. Use the
  RENAME= data set option.

3

Business Scenario

You were asked to combine the data sets that contain
information about Orion Star employees from Denmark
and France into a new data set.

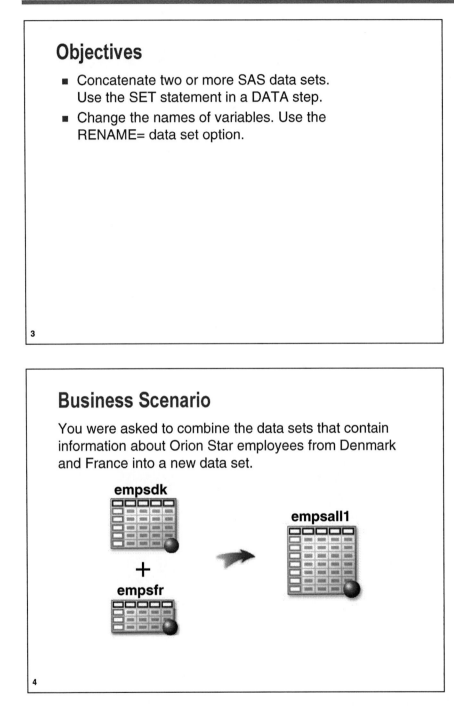

4

Considerations

Concatenate like-structured data sets, **empsdk** and
empsfr, to create a new data set named **empsall1**.

empsdk

First	Gender	Country
Lars	M	Denmark
Kari	F	Denmark
Jonas	M	Denmark

empsfr

First	Gender	Country
Pierre	M	France
Sophie	F	France

empsall1

First	Gender	Country
Lars	M	Denmark
Kari	F	Denmark
Jonas	M	Denmark
Pierre	M	France
Sophie	F	France

Both data sets contain the same variables.

5

Using a DATA Step

Use a DATA step to concatenate the data sets.
List the data sets in the SET statement.

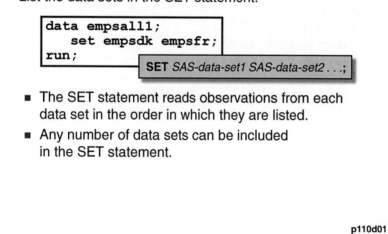

```
data empsall1;
   set empsdk empsfr;
run;
```

SET *SAS-data-set1 SAS-data-set2 . . .;*

- The SET statement reads observations from each
  data set in the order in which they are listed.
- Any number of data sets can be included
  in the SET statement.

6   p110d01

Compilation

empsdk

First	Gender	Country
Lars	M	Denmark
Kari	F	Denmark
Jonas	M	Denmark

empsfr

First	Gender	Country
Pierre	M	France
Sophie	F	France

```
data empsall1;
    set empsdk empsfr;
run;
```

PDV

First	Gender	Country

empsall1

First	Gender	Country

p110d01

7   ...

Execution

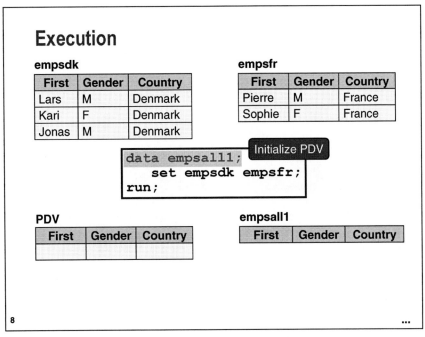

empsdk

First	Gender	Country
Lars	M	Denmark
Kari	F	Denmark
Jonas	M	Denmark

empsfr

First	Gender	Country
Pierre	M	France
Sophie	F	France

```
data empsall1;          Initialize PDV
    set empsdk empsfr;
run;
```

PDV

First	Gender	Country

empsall1

First	Gender	Country

8   ...

Execution

empsdk

First	Gender	Country
Lars	M	Denmark
Kari	F	Denmark
Jonas	M	Denmark

empsfr

First	Gender	Country
Pierre	M	France
Sophie	F	France

```
data empsall1;
    set empsdk empsfr;
run;
```

PDV

First	Gender	Country
Jonas	M	Denmark

empsall1

First	Gender	Country
Lars	M	Denmark
Kari	F	Denmark

15   ...

Execution

empsdk

First	Gender	Country
Lars	M	Denmark
Kari	F	Denmark
Jonas	M	Denmark

empsfr

First	Gender	Country
Pierre	M	France
Sophie	F	France

```
data empsall1;
    set empsdk empsfr;
run;
```

Implicit OUTPUT;
Implicit RETURN;

PDV

First	Gender	Country
Jonas	M	Denmark

empsall1

First	Gender	Country
Lars	M	Denmark
Kari	F	Denmark
Jonas	M	Denmark

16   ...

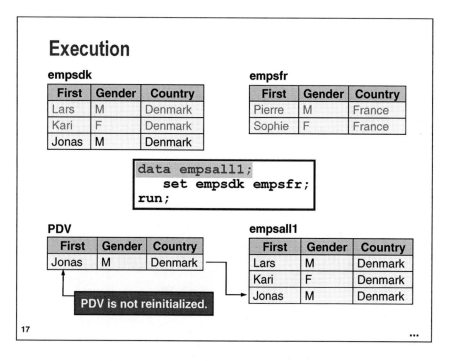

Execution

empsdk

First	Gender	Country
Lars	M	Denmark
Kari	F	Denmark
Jonas	M	Denmark

empsfr

First	Gender	Country
Pierre	M	France
Sophie	F	France

```
data empsall1;
    set empsdk empsfr;
run;
```

PDV

First	Gender	Country
Jonas	M	Denmark

PDV is not reinitialized.

empsall1

First	Gender	Country
Lars	M	Denmark
Kari	F	Denmark
Jonas	M	Denmark

17   ...

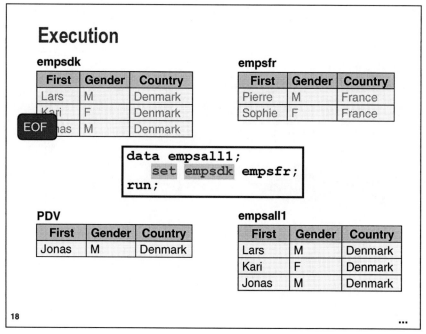

Execution

empsdk

First	Gender	Country
Lars	M	Denmark
Kari	F	Denmark
Jonas	M	Denmark

EOF

empsfr

First	Gender	Country
Pierre	M	France
Sophie	F	France

```
data empsall1;
    set empsdk empsfr;
run;
```

PDV

First	Gender	Country
Jonas	M	Denmark

empsall1

First	Gender	Country
Lars	M	Denmark
Kari	F	Denmark
Jonas	M	Denmark

18   ...

Execution

empsdk

First	Gender	Country
Lars	M	Denmark
Kari	F	Denmark
Jonas	M	Denmark

empsfr

First	Gender	Country
Pierre	M	France
Sophie	F	France

```
data empsall1;      Reinitialize PDV
    set empsdk empsfr;
run;
```

PDV

First	Gender	Country

↑ PDV is reinitialized before processing the next data set.

empsall1

First	Gender	Country
Lars	M	Denmark
Kari	F	Denmark
Jonas	M	Denmark

19   ...

When concatenating data sets, SAS reinitializes the entire PDV before it begins reading the next data set that is listed in the SET statement.

Execution

empsdk

First	Gender	Country
Lars	M	Denmark
Kari	F	Denmark
Jonas	M	Denmark

empsfr

First	Gender	Country
Pierre	M	France
Sophie	F	France

```
data empsall1;
    set empsdk empsfr;
run;
```

PDV

First	Gender	Country
Pierre	M	France

empsall1

First	Gender	Country
Lars	M	Denmark
Kari	F	Denmark
Jonas	M	Denmark

20   ...

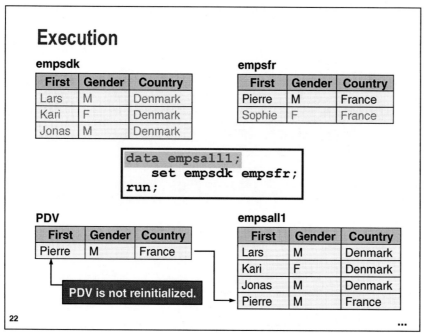

Execution

empsdk

First	Gender	Country
Lars	M	Denmark
Kari	F	Denmark
Jonas	M	Denmark

empsfr

First	Gender	Country
Pierre	M	France
Sophie	F	France

```
data empsall1;
    set empsdk empsfr;
run;
```

PDV

First	Gender	Country
Sophie	F	France

empsall1

First	Gender	Country
Lars	M	Denmark
Kari	F	Denmark
Jonas	M	Denmark
Pierre	M	France

23   ...

Execution

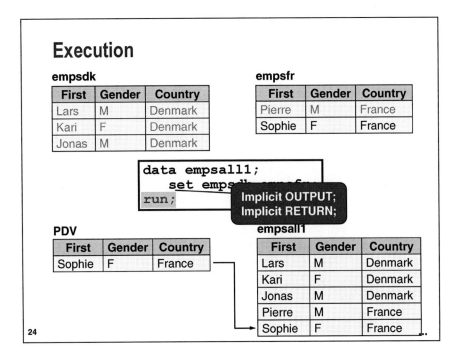

empsdk

First	Gender	Country
Lars	M	Denmark
Kari	F	Denmark
Jonas	M	Denmark

empsfr

First	Gender	Country
Pierre	M	France
Sophie	F	France

```
data empsall1;
    set emps
run;
```

Implicit OUTPUT;
Implicit RETURN;

PDV

First	Gender	Country
Sophie	F	France

empsall1

First	Gender	Country
Lars	M	Denmark
Kari	F	Denmark
Jonas	M	Denmark
Pierre	M	France
Sophie	F	France

24

Execution

empsdk

First	Gender	Country
Lars	M	Denmark
Kari	F	Denmark
Jonas	M	Denmark

empsfr

First	Gender	Country
Pierre	M	France
Sophie	F	France

```
data empsall1;
    set empsdk empsfr;
run;
```

PDV

First	Gender	Country
Sophie	F	France

PDV is not reinitialized.

empsall1

First	Gender	Country
Lars	M	Denmark
Kari	F	Denmark
Jonas	M	Denmark
Pierre	M	France
Sophie	F	France

25

Execution

empsdk

First	Gender	Country
Lars	M	Denmark
Kari	F	Denmark
Jonas	M	Denmark

empsfr

First	Gender	Country
Pierre	M	France
Sophie	F	France

EOF

```
data empsall1;
    set empsdk empsfr;
run;
```

PDV

First	Gender	Country
Sophie	F	France

empsall1

First	Gender	Country
Lars	M	Denmark
Kari	F	Denmark
Jonas	M	Denmark
Pierre	M	France
Sophie	F	France

26

Viewing the Log

Partial SAS Log

```
145  data empsall1;
146     set empsdk empsfr;
147  run;

NOTE: There were 3 observations read from the data set WORK.EMPSDK.
NOTE: There were 2 observations read from the data set WORK.EMPSFR.
NOTE: The data set WORK.EMPSALL1 has 5 observations and 3
variables.
```

27

Unlike-Structured Data Sets

Concatenate **empscn** and **empsjp** to create a new data set named **empsall2**.

empscn

First	Gender	Country
Chang	M	China
Li	M	China
Ming	F	China

empsjp

First	Gender	Region
Cho	F	Japan
Tomi	M	Japan

The data sets do not contain the same variables.

```
data empsall2;
    set empscn empsjp;
run;
```

28

p110d02

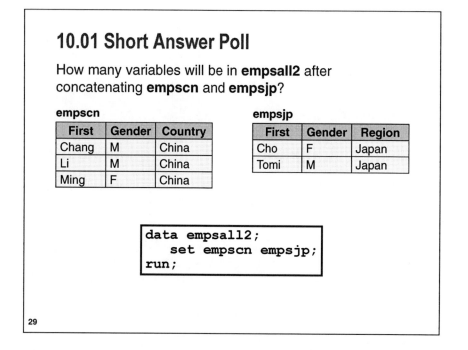

10.01 Short Answer Poll

How many variables will be in **empsall2** after concatenating **empscn** and **empsjp**?

empscn

First	Gender	Country
Chang	M	China
Li	M	China
Ming	F	China

empsjp

First	Gender	Region
Cho	F	Japan
Tomi	M	Japan

```
data empsall2;
   set empscn empsjp;
run;
```

29

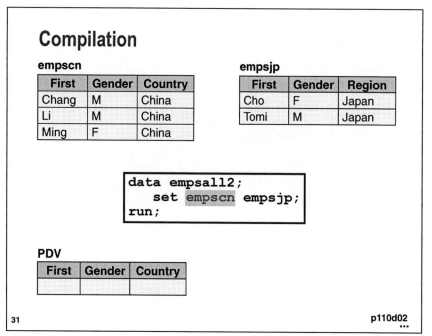

Compilation

empscn

First	Gender	Country
Chang	M	China
Li	M	China
Ming	F	China

empsjp

First	Gender	Region
Cho	F	Japan
Tomi	M	Japan

```
data empsall2;
   set empscn empsjp;
run;
```

PDV

First	Gender	Country

31

p110d02

...

Compilation

empscn

First	Gender	Country
Chang	M	China
Li	M	China
Ming	F	China

empsjp

First	Gender	Region
Cho	F	Japan
Tomi	M	Japan

```
data empsall2;
    set empscn empsjp;
run;
```

PDV

First	Gender	Country	Region

32

Final Results

empsall2

First	Gender	Country	Region
Chang	M	China	
Li	M	China	
Ming	F	China	
Cho	F		Japan
Tomi	M		Japan

- **Region** has missing values due to PDV initialization.
- **Country** has missing values due to PDV reinitialization before processing the second data set.

33

Business Scenario

Rename variables in one or more data sets to align columns.

RENAME= Data Set Option

The *RENAME= data set option* changes the name of a variable.

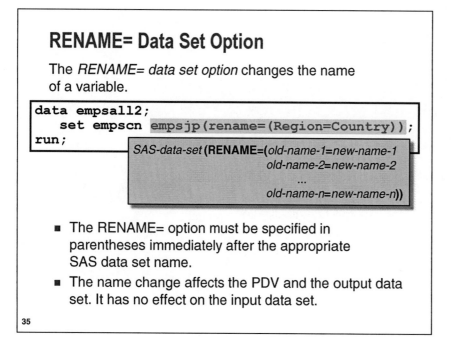

- The RENAME= option must be specified in parentheses immediately after the appropriate SAS data set name.
- The name change affects the PDV and the output data set. It has no effect on the input data set.

RENAME= Data Set Option

Multiples variables can be renamed in one
or more data sets.

```
set empscn(rename=(Country=Region))
    empsjp;
```

```
set empscn(rename=(First=Fname
                   Country=Region))
    empsjp(rename=(First=Fname));
```

```
set empscn
    empsjp(rename=(Region=Country));
```

36

10.02 Short Answer Poll

Which statement has correct syntax?

a.
```
set empscn(rename(Country=Location))
    empsjp(rename(Region=Location));
```

b.
```
set empscn(rename=(Country=Location))
    empsjp(rename=(Region=Location));
```

c.
```
set empscn rename=(Country=Location)
    empsjp rename=(Region=Location);
```

37

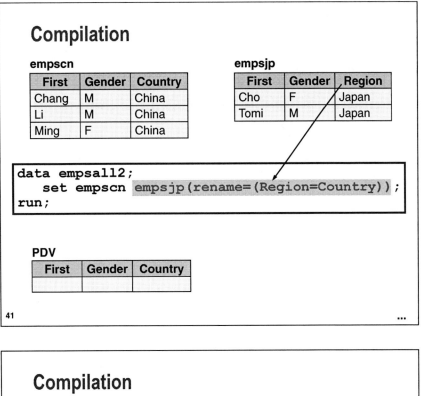

Compilation

empscn

First	Gender	Country
Chang	M	China
Li	M	China
Ming	F	China

empsjp

First	Gender	Region
Cho	F	Japan
Tomi	M	Japan

```
data empsall2;
   set empscn empsjp(rename=(Region=Country));
run;
```

PDV

First	Gender	Country

41   ...

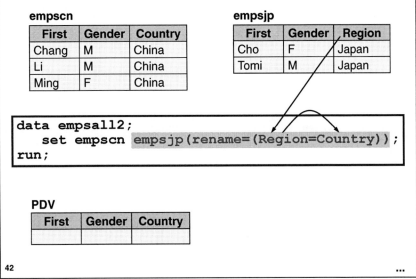

Compilation

empscn

First	Gender	Country
Chang	M	China
Li	M	China
Ming	F	China

empsjp

First	Gender	Region
Cho	F	Japan
Tomi	M	Japan

```
data empsall2;
   set empscn empsjp(rename=(Region=Country));
run;
```

PDV

First	Gender	Country

42   ...

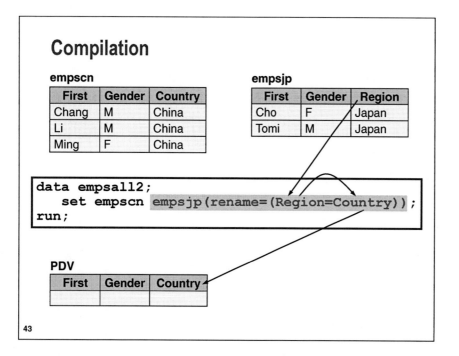

Compilation

empscn

First	Gender	Country
Chang	M	China
Li	M	China
Ming	F	China

empsjp

First	Gender	Region
Cho	F	Japan
Tomi	M	Japan

```
data empsall2;
   set empscn empsjp(rename=(Region=Country));
run;
```

PDV

First	Gender	Country

43

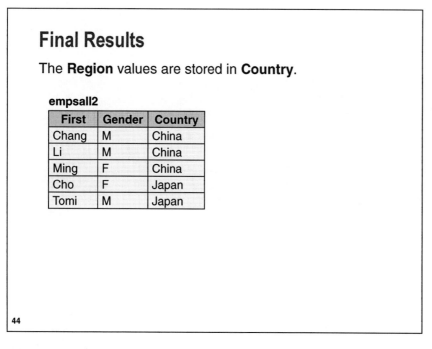

Final Results

The **Region** values are stored in **Country**.

empsall2

First	Gender	Country
Chang	M	China
Li	M	China
Ming	F	China
Cho	F	Japan
Tomi	M	Japan

44

Exercises

If you restarted your SAS session since the last exercise, open and submit the **libname.sas** program that can be found in the data folder.

Level 1

1. Concatenating Like-Structured Data Sets

a. Write and submit a DATA step to concatenate **orion.mnth7_2011**, **orion.mnth8_2011**, and **orion.mnth9_2011** to create a new data set, **work.thirdqtr**.

How many observations in **work.thirdqtr** are from **orion.mnth7_2011**? _____

How many observations in **work.thirdqtr** are from **orion.mnth8_2011**? _____

How many observations in **work.thirdqtr** are from **orion.mnth9_2011**? _____

b. Write a PROC PRINT step to create the report below. The results should contain 32 observations.

Partial PROC PRINT Output

Obs	Order_ID	Order_Type	Employee_ID	Customer_ID	Order_Date	Delivery_Date
1	1242691897	2	99999999	90	02JUL2011	04JUL2011
2	1242736731	1	121107	10	07JUL2011	07JUL2011
3	1242773202	3	99999999	24	11JUL2011	14JUL2011
4	1242782701	3	99999999	27	12JUL2011	17JUL2011
5	1242827683	1	121105	10	17JUL2011	17JUL2011

2. Concatenating Unlike-Structured Data Sets

Open **p110e02**. Submit the two PROC CONTENTS steps or explore the data sets interactively to compare the variables in the two data sets. What are the names of the two variables that are different in the two data sets?

orion.sales	orion.nonsales

a. Add a DATA step after the PROC CONTENTS steps to concatenate **orion.sales** and **orion.nonsales** to create a new data set, **work.allemployees**.

Use a RENAME= data set option to change the names of the different variables in **orion.nonsales**.

The new data set should include only **Employee_ID**, **First_Name**, **Last_Name**, **Job_Title**, and **Salary**.

b. Add a PROC PRINT step to create the report below. The results should contain 400 observations.

Partial PROC PRINT Output

Obs	Employee_ID	First_Name	Last_Name	Salary	Job_Title
1	120102	Tom	Zhou	108255	Sales Manager
2	120103	Wilson	Dawes	87975	Sales Manager
3	120121	Irenie	Elvish	26600	Sales Rep. II
4	120122	Christina	Ngan	27475	Sales Rep. II
5	120123	Kimiko	Hotstone	26190	Sales Rep. I

Level 2

3. **Concatenating Data Sets with Variables of Different Lengths and Types**

    a. Open **p110e03**. Submit the PROC CONTENTS steps or explore the data sets interactively to complete the table below. Fill in attribute information for each variable in each data set.

	Code		Company		ContactType	
	Type	Length	Type	Length	Type	Length
orion.charities						
orion.us_suppliers						
orion.consultants						

    b. Write a DATA step to concatenate **orion.charities** and **orion.us_suppliers** and create a temporary data set, **contacts**.

    c. Submit a PROC CONTENTS step to examine **work.contacts**. From which input data set were the variable attributes assigned? _____

    d. Write a DATA step to concatenate **orion.us_suppliers** and **orion.charities** and create a temporary data set, **contacts2**. Notice that these are the same data sets as in the previous program, but they are in reverse order.

    e. Submit a PROC CONTENTS step to examine **work.contacts2**. From which input data set were the variable attributes assigned? _____

    f. Write a DATA step to concatenate **orion.us_suppliers** and **orion.consultants** and create a temporary data set, **contacts3**.

    Why did the DATA step fail? _____

10.2 Merging Data Sets One-to-One

Objectives

- Prepare data sets for merging. Use the SORT procedure.
- Merge SAS data sets one-to-one based on a common variable.

48

Match-Merging

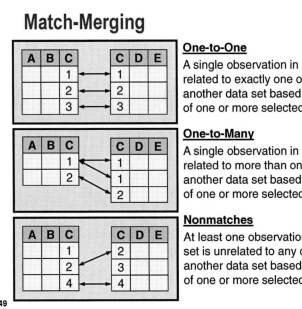

One-to-One

A single observation in one data set is related to exactly one observation in another data set based on the values of one or more selected variables.

One-to-Many

A single observation in one data set is related to more than one observation in another data set based on the values of one or more selected variables.

Nonmatches

At least one observation in one data set is unrelated to any observation in another data set based on the values of one or more selected variables.

49

Match-Merging: Sorting the Data Sets

The data sets in a match-merge must be sorted by the common variable or variables that are being matched.

```
PROC SORT  DATA=input-SAS-data-set
             <OUT=output-SAS-data-set>;
      BY <DESCENDING> by-variable(s);
RUN;
```

50

10.03 Multiple Choice Poll

Which of the following BY statements correctly sorts by descending **salary** within **gender**?

a. by descending salary within gender;
b. by descending salary gender;
c. by gender descending salary;
d. by gender salary descending;

51

Business Scenario

Merge the Australian employee data set with a phone data set to obtain each employee's home phone number. Store the results in a new data set.

53

Match-Merging

The *MERGE statement* in a DATA step joins observations from two or more SAS data sets into single observations.

A *BY statement* indicates a match-merge and lists the variable or variables to match.

54

p110d04

MERGE and BY Statements

Requirements for match-merging:

- Two or more data sets are listed in the MERGE statement.
- The variables in the BY statement must be common to all data sets.
- The data sets must be sorted by the variables listed in the BY statement.

55

One-to-One Merge

One observation in **empsau** matches exactly one observation in **phoneh**.

empsau

First	Gender	EmpID
Togar	M	121150
Kylie	F	121151
Birin	M	121152

phoneh

EmpID	Phone
121150	+61(2)5555-1793
121151	+61(2)5555-1849
121152	+61(2)5555-1665

The data sets are sorted by **EmpID**.

56

Final Results

empsau

First	Gender	EmpID
Togar	M	121150
Kylie	F	121151
Birin	M	121152

phoneh

EmpID	Phone
121150	+61(2)5555-1793
121151	+61(2)5555-1849
121152	+61(2)5555-1665

empsauh

First	Gender	EmpID	Phone
Togar	M	121150	+61(2)5555-1793
Kylie	F	121151	+61(2)5555-1849
Birin	M	121152	+61(2)5555-1665

57

10.04 Short Answer Poll

Complete program **p110a01 t**o match-merge the sorted
SAS data sets referenced in the PROC SORT steps.

Submit the program. Correct and resubmit it, if necessary.

What are the modified, completed statements?

58

10.3   Merging Data Sets One-to-Many

Objectives

- Merge SAS data sets one-to-many based on a common variable.

62

Business Scenario

Merge the Australian employee information data set with the **phones** data set to obtain the phone numbers for each employee.

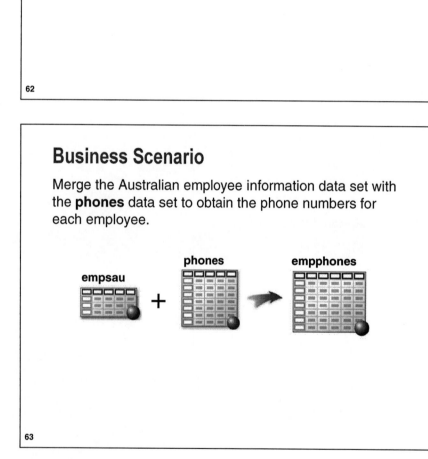

63

Considerations

In this one-to-many merge, one observation in **empsau** matches one or more observations in **phones**.

The data sets are sorted by **EmpID**.

64

Match-Merging

Merge the two data sets by **EmpID** and create a new data set named **empphones**.

```
data empphones;
   merge empsau phones;
   by EmpID;
run;
```

65   p110d05

Match-Merging

empsau

First	Gender	EmpID
Togar	M	121150
Kylie	F	121151
Birin	M	121152

phones

EmpID	Type	Phone
121150	Home	+61(2)5555-1793
121150	Work	+61(2)5555-1794
121151	Home	+61(2)5555-1849
121152	Work	+61(2)5555-1850
121152	Home	+61(2)5555-1665
121152	Cell	+61(2)5555-1666

- The common variable is called the *BY variable*.
- The value of the BY variable is the *BY value*.
- A group of observations with the same BY value is a *BY group*.

66

Execution

empsau

First	Gender	EmpID
Togar	M	121150
Kylie	F	121151
Birin	M	121152

phones

EmpID	Type	Phone
121150	Home	+61(2)5555-1793
121150	Work	+61(2)5555-1794
121151	Home	+61(2)5555-1849
121152	Work	+61(2)5555-1850
121152	Home	+61(2)5555-1665
121152	Cell	+61(2)5555-1666

Initialize PDV

```
data empphones;
   merge empsau phones;
   by EmpID;
run;
```

PDV

First	Gender	EmpID	Type	Phone
		.		

67   p110d05
                                                                    ...

Execution

empsau

First	Gender	EmpID
Togar	M	121150
Kylie	F	121151
Birin	M	121152

phones

EmpID	Type	Phone
121150	Home	+61(2)5555-1793
121150	Work	+61(2)5555-1794
121151	Home	+61(2)5555-1849
121152	Work	+61(2)5555-1850
121152	Home	+61(2)5555-1665
121152	Cell	+61(2)5555-1666

```
data empphones;
   merge empsau phones;
   by EmpID;
run;
```

Do the **EmpID** values match?

Yes

PDV

First	Gender	EmpID	Type	Phone
		.		

68 ...

Execution

empsau

First	Gender	EmpID
Togar	M	121150
Kylie	F	121151
Birin	M	121152

phones

EmpID	Type	Phone
121150	Home	+61(2)5555-1793
121150	Work	+61(2)5555-1794
121151	Home	+61(2)5555-1849
121152	Work	+61(2)5555-1850
121152	Home	+61(2)5555-1665
121152	Cell	+61(2)5555-1666

```
data empphones;
   merge empsau phones;
   by EmpID;
run;
```

Reads both observations into the PDV.

PDV

First	Gender	EmpID	Type	Phone
Togar	M	121150	Home	+61(2)5555-1793

69 ...

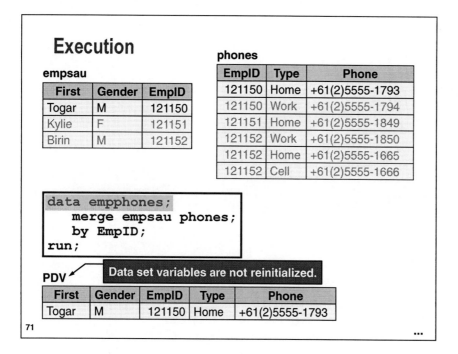

Execution

empsau

First	Gender	EmpID
Togar	M	121150
Kylie	F	121151
Birin	M	121152

phones

EmpID	Type	Phone
121150	Home	+61(2)5555-1793
121150	Work	+61(2)5555-1794
121151	Home	+61(2)5555-1849
121152	Work	+61(2)5555-1850
121152	Home	+61(2)5555-1665
121152	Cell	+61(2)5555-1666

```
data empphones;
   merge empsau phones;
   by EmpID;
run;
```

Implicit OUTPUT;
Implicit RETURN;

PDV

First	Gender	EmpID	Type	Phone
Togar	M	121150	Home	+61(2)5555-1793

70   ...

Execution

empsau

First	Gender	EmpID
Togar	M	121150
Kylie	F	121151
Birin	M	121152

phones

EmpID	Type	Phone
121150	Home	+61(2)5555-1793
121150	Work	+61(2)5555-1794
121151	Home	+61(2)5555-1849
121152	Work	+61(2)5555-1850
121152	Home	+61(2)5555-1665
121152	Cell	+61(2)5555-1666

```
data empphones;
   merge empsau phones;
   by EmpID;
run;
```

Data set variables are not reinitialized.

PDV

First	Gender	EmpID	Type	Phone
Togar	M	121150	Home	+61(2)5555-1793

71   ...

Execution

empsau

First	Gender	EmpID
Togar	M	121150
Kylie	F	121151
Birin	M	121152

phones

EmpID	Type	Phone
121150	Home	+61(2)5555-1793
121150	Work	+61(2)5555-1794
121151	Home	+61(2)5555-1849
121152	Work	+61(2)5555-1850
121152	Home	+61(2)5555-1665
121152	Cell	+61(2)5555-1666

```
data empphones;
   merge empsau phones;
   by EmpID;
run;
```

Do the **EmpID** values match?

No

PDV

First	Gender	EmpID	Type	Phone
Togar	M	121150	Home	+61(2)5555-1793

72   ...

Execution

empsau

First	Gender	EmpID
Togar	M	121150
Kylie	F	121151
Birin	M	121152

phones

EmpID	Type	Phone
121150	Home	+61(2)5555-1793
121150	Work	+61(2)5555-1794
121151	Home	+61(2)5555-1849
121152	Work	+61(2)5555-1850
121152	Home	+61(2)5555-1665
121152	Cell	+61(2)5555-1666

```
data empphones;
   merge empsau phones;
   by EmpID;
run;
```

Did **EmpID** change?

No

PDV

First	Gender	EmpID	Type	Phone
Togar	M	121150	Home	+61(2)5555-1793

73   ...

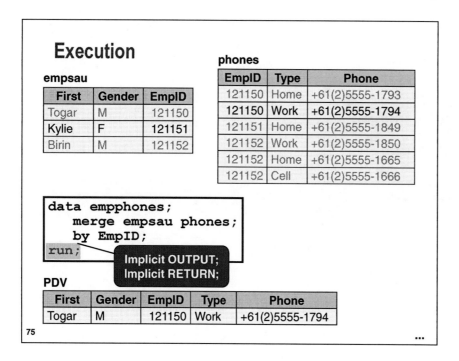

Execution

empsau

First	Gender	EmpID
Togar	M	121150
Kylie	F	121151
Birin	M	121152

phones

EmpID	Type	Phone
121150	Home	+61(2)5555-1793
121150	Work	+61(2)5555-1794
121151	Home	+61(2)5555-1849
121152	Work	+61(2)5555-1850
121152	Home	+61(2)5555-1665
121152	Cell	+61(2)5555-1666

```
data empphones;
   merge empsau phones;
   by EmpID;
run;
```

Do the **EmpID** values match?

Yes

PDV

First	Gender	EmpID	Type	Phone
Togar	M	121150	Work	+61(2)5555-1794

76

...

Execution

empsau

First	Gender	EmpID
Togar	M	121150
Kylie	F	121151
Birin	M	121152

phones

EmpID	Type	Phone
121150	Home	+61(2)5555-1793
121150	Work	+61(2)5555-1794
121151	Home	+61(2)5555-1849
121152	Work	+61(2)5555-1850
121152	Home	+61(2)5555-1665
121152	Cell	+61(2)5555-1666

```
data empphones;
   merge empsau phones;
   by EmpID;
run;
```

Did **EmpID** change?

Yes

PDV

First	Gender	EmpID	Type	Phone
Togar	M	121150	Work	+61(2)5555-1794

77

...

Execution

empsau

First	Gender	EmpID
Togar	M	121150
Kylie	F	121151
Birin	M	121152

phones

EmpID	Type	Phone
121150	Home	+61(2)5555-1793
121150	Work	+61(2)5555-1794
121151	Home	+61(2)5555-1849
121152	Work	+61(2)5555-1850
121152	Home	+61(2)5555-1665
121152	Cell	+61(2)5555-1666

```
data empphones;
   merge empsau phones;
   by EmpID;
run;
```
Reinitialize PDV

PDV

First	Gender	EmpID	Type	Phone
			.	

78

SAS reinitializes the entire program data vector before processing a different BY group.

Execution

empsau

First	Gender	EmpID
Togar	M	121150
Kylie	F	121151
Birin	M	121152

phones

EmpID	Type	Phone
121150	Home	+61(2)5555-1793
121150	Work	+61(2)5555-1794
121151	Home	+61(2)5555-1849
121152	Work	+61(2)5555-1850
121152	Home	+61(2)5555-1665
121152	Cell	+61(2)5555-1666

```
data empphones;
   merge empsau phones;
   by EmpID;
run;
```
Reads both observations into the PDV.

PDV

First	Gender	EmpID	Type	Phone
Kylie	F	121151	Home	+61(2)5555-1849

79

Execution

empsau

First	Gender	EmpID
Togar	M	121150
Kylie	F	121151
Birin	M	121152

phones

EmpID	Type	Phone
121150	Home	+61(2)5555-1793
121150	Work	+61(2)5555-1794
121151	Home	+61(2)5555-1849
121152	Work	+61(2)5555-1850
121152	Home	+61(2)5555-1665
121152	Cell	+61(2)5555-1666

```
data empphones;
   merge empsau phones;
   by EmpID;
run;
```

Implicit OUTPUT;
Implicit RETURN;

PDV

First	Gender	EmpID	Type	Phone
Kylie	F	121151	Home	+61(2)5555-1849

80

...

Execution

empsau

First	Gender	EmpID
Togar	M	121150
Kylie	F	121151
Birin	M	121152

phones

EmpID	Type	Phone
121150	Home	+61(2)5555-1793
121150	Work	+61(2)5555-1794
121151	Home	+61(2)5555-1849
121152	Work	+61(2)5555-1850
121152	Home	+61(2)5555-1665
121152	Cell	+61(2)5555-1666

```
data empphones;
   merge empsau phones;
   by EmpID;
run;
```

Do the **EmpID** values match?

Yes

PDV

First	Gender	EmpID	Type	Phone
Kylie	F	121151	Home	+61(2)5555-1849

81

...

Execution

empsau

First	Gender	EmpID
Togar	M	121150
Kylie	F	121151
Birin	M	121152

phones

EmpID	Type	Phone
121150	Home	+61(2)5555-1793
121150	Work	+61(2)5555-1794
121151	Home	+61(2)5555-1849
121152	Work	+61(2)5555-1850
121152	Home	+61(2)5555-1665
121152	Cell	+61(2)5555-1666

```
data empphones;
   merge empsau phones;
   by EmpID;
run;
```

Did **EmpID** change?

Yes

PDV

First	Gender	EmpID	Type	Phone
Kylie	F	121151	Home	+61(2)5555-1849

82

...

Execution

empsau

First	Gender	EmpID
Togar	M	121150
Kylie	F	121151
Birin	M	121152

phones

EmpID	Type	Phone
121150	Home	+61(2)5555-1793
121150	Work	+61(2)5555-1794
121151	Home	+61(2)5555-1849
121152	Work	+61(2)5555-1850
121152	Home	+61(2)5555-1665
121152	Cell	+61(2)5555-1666

Reinitialize PDV

```
data empphones;
   merge empsau phones;
   by EmpID;
run;
```

PDV

First	Gender	EmpID	Type	Phone
		.		

83

...

Execution

empsau

First	Gender	EmpID
Togar	M	121150
Kylie	F	121151
Birin	M	121152

phones

EmpID	Type	Phone
121150	Home	+61(2)5555-1793
121150	Work	+61(2)5555-1794
121151	Home	+61(2)5555-1849
121152	Work	+61(2)5555-1850
121152	Home	+61(2)5555-1665
121152	Cell	+61(2)5555-1666

```
data empphones;
   merge empsau phones;
   by EmpID;
run;
```

Reads both observations into the PDV.

PDV

First	Gender	EmpID	Type	Phone
Birin	M	121152	Work	+61(2)5555-1850

84   ...

Execution

empsau

First	Gender	EmpID
Togar	M	121150
Kylie	F	121151
Birin	M	121152

phones

EmpID	Type	Phone
121150	Home	+61(2)5555-1793
121150	Work	+61(2)5555-1794
121151	Home	+61(2)5555-1849
121152	Work	+61(2)5555-1850
121152	Home	+61(2)5555-1665
121152	Cell	+61(2)5555-1666

```
data empphones;
   merge empsau phones;
   by EmpID;
run;
```

Implicit OUTPUT;
Implicit RETURN;

PDV

First	Gender	EmpID	Type	Phone
Birin	M	121152	Work	+61(2)5555-1850

85   ...

Execution

empsau

First	Gender	EmpID
Togar	M	121150
Kylie	F	121151
Birin	M	121152

EOF

phones

EmpID	Type	Phone
121150	Home	+61(2)5555-1793
121150	Work	+61(2)5555-1794
121151	Home	+61(2)5555-1849
121152	Work	+61(2)5555-1850
121152	Home	+61(2)5555-1665
121152	Cell	+61(2)5555-1666

```
data empphones;
   merge empsau phones;
   by EmpID;
run;
```

Did **EmpID** change?

No

PDV

First	Gender	EmpID	Type	Phone
Birin	M	121152	Work	+61(2)5555-1850

86   ...

Execution

empsau

First	Gender	EmpID
Togar	M	121150
Kylie	F	121151
Birin	M	121152

EOF

phones

EmpID	Type	Phone
121150	Home	+61(2)5555-1793
121150	Work	+61(2)5555-1794
121151	Home	+61(2)5555-1849
121152	Work	+61(2)5555-1850
121152	Home	+61(2)5555-1665
121152	Cell	+61(2)5555-1666

```
data empphones;
   merge empsau phones;
   by EmpID;
run;
```

Reads the matching observation into the PDV.

PDV

First	Gender	EmpID	Type	Phone
Birin	M	121152	Home	+61(2)5555-1665

87   ...

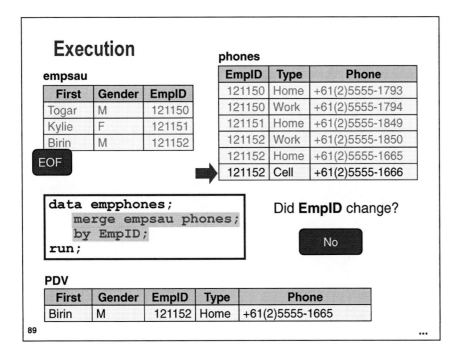

Execution

empsau

First	Gender	EmpID
Togar	M	121150
Kylie	F	121151
Birin	M	121152

EOF

phones

EmpID	Type	Phone
121150	Home	+61(2)5555-1793
121150	Work	+61(2)5555-1794
121151	Home	+61(2)5555-1849
121152	Work	+61(2)5555-1850
121152	Home	+61(2)5555-1665
121152	Cell	+61(2)5555-1666

```
data empphones;
   merge empsau phones;
   by EmpID;
run;
```

Implicit OUTPUT;
Implicit RETURN;

PDV

First	Gender	EmpID	Type	Phone
Birin	M	121152	Home	+61(2)5555-1665

88   ...

Execution

empsau

First	Gender	EmpID
Togar	M	121150
Kylie	F	121151
Birin	M	121152

EOF

phones

EmpID	Type	Phone
121150	Home	+61(2)5555-1793
121150	Work	+61(2)5555-1794
121151	Home	+61(2)5555-1849
121152	Work	+61(2)5555-1850
121152	Home	+61(2)5555-1665
121152	Cell	+61(2)5555-1666

```
data empphones;
   merge empsau phones;
   by EmpID;
run;
```

Did **EmpID** change?

No

PDV

First	Gender	EmpID	Type	Phone
Birin	M	121152	Home	+61(2)5555-1665

89   ...

Execution

empsau

First	Gender	EmpID
Togar	M	121150
Kylie	F	121151
Birin	M	121152

EOF

phones

EmpID	Type	Phone
121150	Home	+61(2)5555-1793
121150	Work	+61(2)5555-1794
121151	Home	+61(2)5555-1849
121152	Work	+61(2)5555-1850
121152	Home	+61(2)5555-1665
121152	Cell	+61(2)5555-1666

```
data empphones;
   merge empsau phones;
   by EmpID;
run;
```

Reads the matching observation into the PDV.

PDV

First	Gender	EmpID	Type	Phone
Birin	M	121152	Cell	+61(2)5555-1666

90 ...

Execution

empsau

First	Gender	EmpID
Togar	M	121150
Kylie	F	121151
Birin	M	121152

EOF

phones

EmpID	Type	Phone
121150	Home	+61(2)5555-1793
121150	Work	+61(2)5555-1794
121151	Home	+61(2)5555-1849
121152	Work	+61(2)5555-1850
121152	Home	+61(2)5555-1665
121152	Cell	+61(2)5555-1666

```
data empphones;
   merge empsau phones;
   by EmpID;
run;
```

Implicit OUTPUT;
Implicit RETURN;

PDV

First	Gender	EmpID	Type	Phone
Birin	M	121152	Cell	+61(2)5555-1666

91 ...

Execution

empsau

First	Gender	EmpID
Togar	M	121150
Kylie	F	121151
Birin	M	121152

EOF

phones

EmpID	Type	Phone
121150	Home	+61(2)5555-1793
121150	Work	+61(2)5555-1794
121151	Home	+61(2)5555-1849
121152	Work	+61(2)5555-1850
121152	Home	+61(2)5555-1665
121152	Cell	+61(2)5555-1666

EOF

```
data empphones;
   merge empsau phones;
   by EmpID;
run;
```

PDV

First	Gender	EmpID	Type	Phone
Birin	M	121152	Cell	+61(2)5555-1666

92

Final Results

empphones

First	Gender	EmpID	Type	Phone
Togar	M	121150	Home	+61(2)5555-1793
Togar	M	121150	Work	+61(2)5555-1794
Kylie	F	121151	Home	+61(2)5555-1849
Birin	M	121152	Work	+61(2)5555-1850
Birin	M	121152	Home	+61(2)5555-1665
Birin	M	121152	Cell	+61(2)5555-1666

93

10.05 Short Answer Poll

In a one-to-many merge, does it matter which data set is listed first in the MERGE statement?

- Open **p110a02** and submit the program.
- Reverse the order of the data sets and submit it again.
- Observe the results. How are they different?

95

Many-to-One Merge

One or more rows in one data set match exactly one row in the other data set.

```
data phones;
   merge phones empsau;
   by EmpID;
run;
```

97

p110d06

Viewing the Output

PROC PRINT Output

Obs	EmpID	Type	Phone	First	Gender
1	121150	Home	+61(2)5555-1793	Togar	M
2	121150	Work	+61(2)5555-1794	Togar	M
3	121151	Home	+61(2)5555-1849	Kylie	F
4	121152	Work	+61(2)5555-1850	Birin	M
5	121152	Home	+61(2)5555-1665	Birin	M
6	121152	Cell	+61(2)5555-1666	Birin	M

- The results are the same as the one-to-many merge.
- The order of variables is different.

98

Exercises

If you restarted your SAS session since the last exercise, open and submit the **libname.sas** program that can be found in the data folder.

Level 1

4. **Merging Two Sorted Data Sets in a One-to-Many Merge**

   a. Retrieve the starter program **p110e04**.

   b. Submit the two PROC CONTENTS steps or explore the data sets interactively to determine the common variable among the two data sets.

   c. Add a DATA step after the two PROC CONTENTS steps to merge **orion.orders** and **orion.order_item** by the common variable to create a new data set, **work.allorders**. A sort is not required because the data sets are already sorted by the common variable.

   d. Submit the program and confirm that **work.allorders** was created with 732 observations and 12 variables.

   e. Add a statement to subset the variables. The new data set should contain six variables: **Order_ID, Order_Item_Num, Order_Type, Order_Date, Quantity,** and **Total_Retail_Price**.

   f. Write a PROC PRINT step to create the report below. Include only those observations with a value for **Order_Date** in the fourth quarter of 2011. The results should contain 35 observations.

```
                Order_         Order_        Order_                     Total_Retail_
   Order_ID      Type          Date        Item_Num     Quantity           Price

  1243515588      1          01OCT2011        1            1              $251.80
  1243515588      1          01OCT2011        2            1              $114.20
  1243568955      1          07OCT2011        1            1              $172.50
  1243643970      1          16OCT2011        1            1              $101.50
  1243644877      3          16OCT2011        1            1               $14.60
```

Level 2

5. **Merging a Sorted Data Set and an Unsorted Data Set in a One-to-Many Merge**

   a. Sort **orion.product_list** by **Product_Level** to create a new data set, **work.product_list**.

   b. Merge **orion.product_level** with the sorted data set. Create a new data set, **work.listlevel**, which includes only **Product_ID**, **Product_Name**, **Product_Level**, and **Product_Level_Name**.

   c. Create the report below. Include only those observations with **Product Level** equal to *3*. The results should contain 13 observations.

   Partial PROC PRINT Output

```
  Product_       Product_Level_
   Level             Name            Product_ID      Product_Name

      3         Product Category     210100000000    Children Outdoors
      3         Product Category     210200000000    Children Sports
      3         Product Category     220100000000    Clothes
      3         Product Category     220200000000    Shoes
      3         Product Category     230100000000    Outdoors
```

Challenge

6. **Using the MERGENOBY Option**

   a. Use the SAS Help facility or online documentation to explore the MERGENOBY system option.

   What is the purpose of this option and why is it used? _____

   _____

   b. Complete the following table to include the values that this option can assume:

Value	Description	Default (Y/N)

10.4 Merging Data Sets with Nonmatches

Objectives

- Control the observations in the output data set by using the IN= data set option.

102

Business Scenario

An Orion Star manager in Australia requested an inventory of company phone numbers.

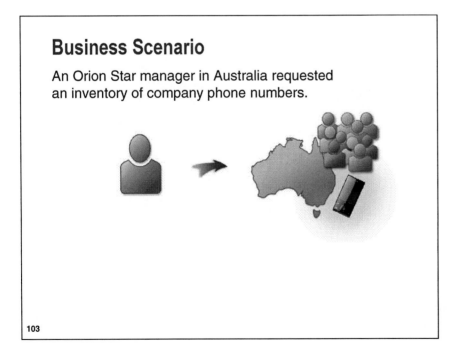

103

Merge with Nonmatches

There are observations in **empsau** that do not have a match in **phonec**, and some in **phonec** that do not match any observations in **empsau**.

empsau

First	Gender	EmpID
Togar	M	121150
Kylie	F	121151
Birin	M	121152

phonec

EmpID	Phone
121150	+61(2)5555-1795
121152	+61(2)5555-1667
121153	+61(2)5555-1348

The data sets are sorted by **EmpID**.

104

Match-Merging

Merge **empsau** and **phonec** by **EmpID** to create a new data set named **empsauc**.

```
data empsauc;
   merge empsau phonec;
   by EmpID;
run;
```

105   p110d07

Execution

empsau

First	Gender	EmpID
Togar	M	121150
Kylie	F	121151
Birin	M	121152

phonec

EmpID	Phone
121150	+61(2)5555-1795
121152	+61(2)5555-1667
121153	+61(2)5555-1348

```
data empsauc;
   merge empsau phonec;
   by EmpID;
run;
```

Do the **EmpID** values match?

No

PDV

First	Gender	EmpID	Phone
Togar	M	121150	+61(2)5555-1795

110   ...

Execution

empsau

First	Gender	EmpID
Togar	M	121150
Kylie	F	121151
Birin	M	121152

phonec

EmpID	Phone
121150	+61(2)5555-1795
121152	+61(2)5555-1667
121153	+61(2)5555-1348

```
data empsauc;
   merge empsau phonec;
   by EmpID;
run;
```

Did **EmpID** change?

Yes

PDV

First	Gender	EmpID	Phone
Togar	M	121150	+61(2)5555-1795

111   ...

Execution

empsau

First	Gender	EmpID
Togar	M	121150
Kylie	F	121151
Birin	M	121152

phonec

EmpID	Phone
121150	+61(2)5555-1795
121152	+61(2)5555-1667
121153	+61(2)5555-1348

Reinitialize PDV

```
data empsauc;
   merge empsau phonec;
   by EmpID;
run;
```

PDV

First	Gender	EmpID	Phone
		.	

112   ...

Execution

empsau

First	Gender	EmpID
Togar	M	121150
Kylie	F	121151
Birin	M	121152

phonec

EmpID	Phone
121150	+61(2)5555-1795
121152	+61(2)5555-1667
121153	+61(2)5555-1348

```
data empsauc;
   merge empsau phonec;
   by EmpID;
run;
```

Which **EmpID** value
sequentially comes first?

121151

PDV

First	Gender	EmpID	Phone
		.	

113   ...

Execution

empsau

First	Gender	EmpID
Togar	M	121150
Kylie	F	121151
Birin	M	121152

phonec

EmpID	Phone
121150	+61(2)5555-1795
121152	+61(2)5555-1667
121153	+61(2)5555-1348

```
data empsauc;
   merge empsau phonec;
   by EmpID;
run;
```

Reads that observation into the PDV.

PDV

First	Gender	EmpID	Phone
Kylie	F	121151	

114

...

Execution

empsau

First	Gender	EmpID
Togar	M	121150
Kylie	F	121151
Birin	M	121152

phonec

EmpID	Phone
121150	+61(2)5555-1795
121152	+61(2)5555-1667
121153	+61(2)5555-1348

```
data empsauc;
   merge empsau phonec;
   by EmpID;
run;
```

Implicit OUTPUT;
Implicit RETURN;

PDV

First	Gender	EmpID	Phone
Kylie	F	121151	

115

...

Execution

empsau

First	Gender	EmpID
Togar	M	121150
Kylie	F	121151
Birin	M	121152

phonec

EmpID	Phone
121150	+61(2)5555-1795
121152	+61(2)5555-1667
121153	+61(2)5555-1348

```
data empsauc;
   merge empsau phonec;
   by EmpID;
run;
```

Do the **EmpID** values match?

Yes

PDV

First	Gender	EmpID	Phone
Kylie	F	121151	

116   ...

Execution

empsau

First	Gender	EmpID
Togar	M	121150
Kylie	F	121151
Birin	M	121152

phonec

EmpID	Phone
121150	+61(2)5555-1795
121152	+61(2)5555-1667
121153	+61(2)5555-1348

```
data empsauc;
   merge empsau phonec;
   by EmpID;
run;
```

Did **EmpID** change?

Yes

PDV

First	Gender	EmpID	Phone
Kylie	F	121151	

117   ...

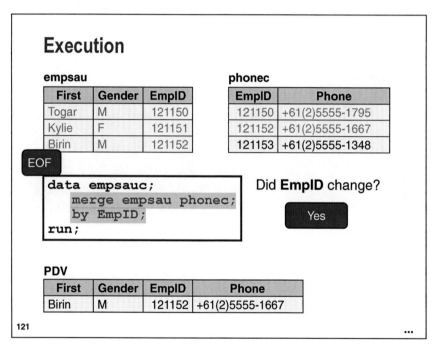

Execution

empsau

First	Gender	EmpID
Togar	M	121150
Kylie	F	121151
Birin	M	121152

phonec

EmpID	Phone
121150	+61(2)5555-1795
121152	+61(2)5555-1667
121153	+61(2)5555-1348

EOF

Reinitialize PDV

```
data empsauc;
   merge empsau phonec;
   by EmpID;
run;
```

PDV

First	Gender	EmpID	Phone
		.	

122   ...

Execution

empsau

First	Gender	EmpID
Togar	M	121150
Kylie	F	121151
Birin	M	121152

phonec

EmpID	Phone
121150	+61(2)5555-1795
121152	+61(2)5555-1667
121153	+61(2)5555-1348

EOF

```
data empsauc;
   merge empsau phonec;
   by EmpID;
run;
```

Reads the observation into the PDV.

PDV

First	Gender	EmpID	Phone
		121153	+61(2)5555-1348

123   ...

Final Results

empsauc

First	Gender	EmpID	Phone
Togar	M	121150	+61(2)5555-1795
Kylie	F	121151	
Birin	M	121152	+61(2)5555-1667
		121153	+61(2)5555-1348

The final results include both matches and nonmatches.

126

10.06 Short Answer Poll

Consider the data set **empsauc** created by the program in the previous example. Which input data sets contributed information to the last observation?

a. empsau
b. phonec
c. both empsau and phonec
d. There is insufficient information.

empsauc

First	Gender	EmpID	Phone
Togar	M	121150	+61(2)5555-1795
Kylie	F	121151	
Birin	M	121152	+61(2)5555-1667
		121153	+61(2)5555-1348

127

Business Scenario

An Orion Star manager requested three phone inventory reports.

- employees with company phones
- employees without company phones
- phones with an invalid employee ID

130

IN= Data Set Option

The *IN= data set option* creates a variable that indicates whether the data set contributed to building the current observation.

> **MERGE** *SAS-data-set* (**IN=***variable*) ...

variable is a temporary numeric variable that has two possible values:

0	Indicates that the data set did **not** contribute to the current observation.
1	Indicates that the data set **did** contribute to the current observation.

131

IN= Data Set Option

MERGE statement examples:

```
merge empsau(in=Emps)
      phonec(in=Cell);
```

```
merge empsau(in=E)
      phonec(in=P);
```

```
merge empsau(in=AU)
      phonec;
```

132

Execution

empsau

First	Gender	EmpID
Togar	M	121150
Kylie	F	121151
Birin	M	121152

phonec

EmpID	Phone
121150	+61(2)5555-1795
121152	+61(2)5555-1667
121153	+61(2)5555-1348

```
data empsauc;
   merge empsau(in=Emps)
         phonec(in=Cell);
   by EmpID;
run;
```

match

PDV

First	Gender	EmpID	Emps	Phone	Cell
Togar	M	121150	1	+61(2)5555-1795	1

133

p110d08
...

10.07 Short Answer Poll

What are the values of **Emps** and **Cell**?

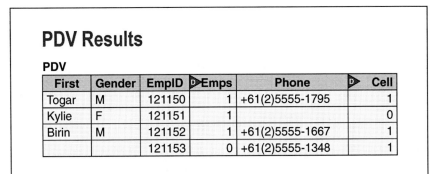

empsau

First	Gender	EmpID
Togar	M	121150
Kylie	F	121151
Birin	M	121152

phonec

EmpID	Phone
121150	+61(2)5555-1795
121152	+61(2)5555-1667
121153	+61(2)5555-1348

EOF

```
data empsauc;
   merge empsau(in=Emps)
         phonec(in=Cell);
   by EmpID;
run;
```

PDV

First	Gender	EmpID	Emps	Phone		Cell
		121153		+61(2)5555-1348		

136

PDV Results

PDV

First	Gender	EmpID	Emps	Phone		Cell
Togar	M	121150	1	+61(2)5555-1795		1
Kylie	F	121151	1			0
Birin	M	121152	1	+61(2)5555-1667		1
		121153	0	+61(2)5555-1348		1

The variables created with the IN= data set option are available only during DATA step execution.

- They are not written to the SAS data set.
- Their value can be tested using conditional logic.

138

Matches Only

Add a subsetting IF statement to select the employees that have company phones.

```
data empsauc;
   merge empsau(in=Emps)
         phonec(in=Cell);
   by EmpID;
   if Emps=1 and Cell=1;
run;
```

empsauc

First	Gender	EmpID	Phone
Togar	M	121150	+61(2)5555-1795
Birin	M	121152	+61(2)5555-1667

139   p110d08

Nonmatches from empsau

Select the employees that do not have company phones.

```
data empsauc;
   merge empsau(in=Emps)
         phonec(in=Cell);
   by EmpID;
   if Emps=1 and Cell=0;
run;
```

empsauc

First	Gender	EmpID	Phone
Kylie	F	121151	

140   p110d08

Nonmatches from phonec

Select the phones associated with an invalid employee ID.

```
data empsauc;
   merge empsau(in=Emps)
         phonec(in=Cell);
   by EmpID;
   if Emps=0 and Cell=1;
run;
```

empsauc

First	Gender	EmpID	Phone
		121153	+61(2)5555-1348

141   p110d08

All Nonmatches

```
data empsauc;
   merge empsau(in=Emps)
         phonec(in=Cell);
   by EmpID;
   if Emps=0 or Cell=0;
run;
```

empsauc

First	Gender	EmpID	Phone
Kylie	F	121151	
		121153	+61(2)5555-1348

⚠ Use the OR operator, not the AND operator.

142   p110d08

Alternate Syntax

When checking a variable for a value of *1* or *0* as in the previous scenario, you can use the following syntax:

Instead of	You can use
if Emps=1 and Cell=1;	if Emps and Cell;
if Emps=1 and Cell=0;	if Emps and not Cell;
if Emps=0 and Cell=1;	if not Emps and Cell;
if Emps=0 or Cell=0;	If not Emps or not Cell;

143

Alternate Syntax

Both programs create a report of employees without cell phones.

```
data empsphone;
   merge empsact(in=inEmps)
         phoneact(in=inCell);
   by EmpID;
   if inEmps=1 and inCell=0;
run;
```

```
data empsphone;
   merge empsact(in=inEmps)
         phoneact(in=inCell);
   by EmpID;
   if inEmps and not inCell;
run;
```

144   p110d09

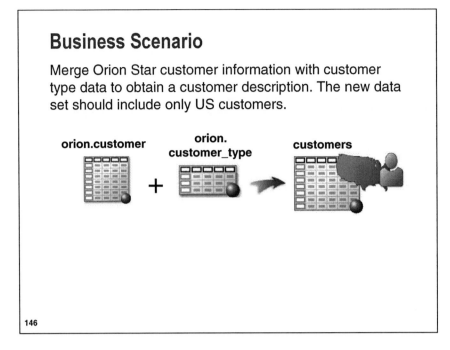

Business Scenario

Merge Orion Star customer information with customer type data to obtain a customer description. The new data set should include only US customers.

orion.customer   orion. customer_type   customers

146

Considerations

The **orion.customer** data set is not sorted by **Customer_Type_ID**, the common variable. The subsetting variable, **Country**, is defined in only one data set.

orion.customer

Customer_ ID	Country	Customer_ Name	...	Birth_ Date	Customer_Type_ ID
			...		

orion.customer_type

Customer_ Group	Customer_Group_ ID	Customer_ Type	Customer_Type_ ID

147

10.08 Short Answer Poll

Open and submit **p110a03**. Correct the program and resubmit. What change is needed to correct the error?

```
proc sort data=orion.customer
          out=cust_by_type;
   by Customer_Type_ID;
run;

data customers;
   merge cust_by_type orion.customer_type;
   by Customer_Type_ID;
   where Country='US';
run;
```

148

Subsetting IF

Use a subsetting IF statement when the subsetting variable is not in all data sets that are named in the MERGE statement.

```
proc sort data=orion.customer
          out=cust_by_type;
   by Customer_Type_ID;
run;

data customers;
   merge cust_by_type  orion.customer_type;
   by Customer_Type_ID;
   if Country='US';
run;
```

150   p110a03s

Viewing the Output

Partial SAS Log

```
407   proc sort data=orion.customer
408            out=cust_by_type;
409      by Customer_Type_ID;
410   run;
NOTE: There were 77 observations read from the data set ORION.CUSTOMER.
NOTE: The data set WORK.CUST_BY_TYPE has 77 observations and 12 variables.

411
412   data customers;
413      merge cust_by_type orion.customer_type;
414      by Customer_Type_ID;
415      if Country='US';
416   run;

NOTE: There were 77 observations read from the data set WORK.CUST_BY_TYPE.
NOTE: There were 8 observations read from the data set ORION.CUSTOMER_TYPE.
NOTE: The data set WORK.CUSTOMERS has 28 observations and 15 variables.
```

151

WHERE versus Subsetting IF Statement

Step and Usage	WHERE	IF
PROC step	Yes	No
DATA step (source of variable)		
SET statement	Yes	Yes
assignment statement	No	Yes
INPUT statement	No	Yes
SET/MERGE statement (multiple data sets)		
Variable in ALL data sets	Yes	Yes
Variable not in ALL data sets	No	Yes

152

Exercises

If you restarted your SAS session since the last exercise, open and submit the **libname.sas** program that can be found in the data folder.

Level 1

7. Merging Using the IN= Option

a. Retrieve the starter program **p110e07**. Add a DATA step after the PROC SORT step to merge **work.product** and **orion.supplier** by **Supplier_ID** to create a new data set, **work.prodsup**.

b. Submit the program and confirm that **work.prodsup** was created with 556 observations and 10 variables.

c. Modify the DATA step to output only those observations that are in **work.product** but not **orion.supplier**. A subsetting IF statement that references IN= variables listed in the MERGE statement must be added.

d. Submit the program and confirm that **work.prodsup** was created with 75 observations and 10 variables.

e. Submit the PROC PRINT step to create the report below. The results should contain 75 observations.

> Supplier information is missing in the output.

Obs	Product_ID	Product_Name	Supplier_ID	Supplier_Name
1	210000000000	Children	.	
2	210100000000	Children Outdoors	.	
3	210100100000	Outdoor things, Kids	.	
4	210200000000	Children Sports	.	
5	210200100000	A-Team, Kids	.	

Level 2

8. Merging Using the IN= and RENAME= Options

a. Write a PROC SORT step to sort **orion.customer** by **Country** to create a new data set, **work.customer**.

b. Write a DATA step to merge the resulting data set with **orion.lookup_country** by **Country** to create a new data set, **work.allcustomer**.

In the **orion.lookup_country** data set, rename **Start** to **Country** and rename **Label** to **Country_Name**.

Include only four variables: **Customer_ID**, **Country**, **Customer_Name**, and **Country_Name**.

c. Create the report below. The results should contain 308 observations.

Partial PROC PRINT Output

Obs	Customer_ID	Country	Customer_Name	Country_Name
1	.	AD		Andorra
2	.	AE		United Arab Emirates
...				
306	3959	ZA	Rita Lotz	South Africa
307	.	ZM		Zambia
308	.	ZW		Zimbabwe

d. Modify the DATA step to store only those observations that contain both customer information and country information. A subsetting IF statement that references the IN= variables in the MERGE statement must be added.

e. Submit the program to create the report below. The results should contain 77 observations.

Partial PROC PRINT Output

Obs	Customer_ID	Country	Customer_Name	Country_ Name
1	29	AU	Candy Kinsey	Australia
2	41	AU	Wendell Summersby	Australia
3	53	AU	Dericka Pockran	Australia
4	111	AU	Karolina Dokter	Australia
5	171	AU	Robert Bowerman	Australia

Challenge

9. **Merging and Creating Output in Multiple Data Sets**

    a. Write a PROC SORT step to sort **orion.orders** by **Employee_ID** to create a new data set, **work.orders**.

    b. Write a DATA step to merge **orion.staff** and **work.orders** by **Employee_ID** and create two new data sets: **work.allorders** and **work.noorders**.

    - The **work.allorders** data set should include all observations from **work.orders**, regardless of matches or nonmatches from the **orion.staff** data set.

    - The **work.noorders** data set should include only those observations from **orion.staff** that do not have a match in **work.orders**.

    - Both new data sets should include only **Employee_ID**, **Job_Title**, **Gender**, **Order_ID**, **Order_Type**, and **Order_Date**.

    c. Submit the program and confirm that **work.allorders** was created with 490 observations and six variables and **work.noorders** was created with 324 observations and six variables.

    d. Create a detailed listing report for each new data set with an appropriate title.

10.5 Solutions

Solutions to Exercises

1. **Concatenating Like-Structured Data Sets**

    How many observations in **work.thirdqtr** are from **orion.mnth7_2011**? **10 observations**

    How many observations in **work.thirdqtr** are from **orion.mnth8_2011**? **12 observations**

    How many observations in **work.thirdqtr** are from **orion.mnth9_2011**? **10 observations**

```
data work.thirdqtr;
   set orion.mnth7_2011 orion.mnth8_2011 orion.mnth9_2011;
run;


proc print data=work.thirdqtr;
run;
```

2. **Concatenating Unlike-Structured Data Sets**

   What are the names of the two variables that are different in the two data sets?

orion.sales	orion.nonsales
First_Name	First
Last_Name	Last

```
proc contents data=orion.sales;
run;

proc contents data=orion.nonsales;
run;

data work.allemployees;
   set orion.sales
       orion.nonsales(rename=(First=First_Name Last=Last_Name));
   keep Employee_ID First_Name Last_Name Job_Title Salary;
run;

proc print data=work.allemployees;
run;
```

3. **Concatenating Data Sets with Variables of Different Lengths and Types**

   a. Open **p110e03**. Submit the PROC CONTENTS steps or explore the data sets interactively to complete the table below. Fill in attribute information for each variable in each data set.

	Code		Company		ContactType	
	Type	Length	Type	Length	Type	Length
orion.charities	Char	6	Char	40	Char	10
orion.us_suppliers	Char	6	Char	30	Char	1
orion.consultants	Char	6	Char	30	Num	8

```
proc contents data=orion.charities;
run;
proc contents data=orion.us_suppliers;
run;
proc contents data=orion.consultants;
run;
```

```
data work.contacts;
   set orion.charities orion.us_suppliers;
run;
proc contents data=work.contacts;
run;

data work.contacts2;
   set orion.us_suppliers orion.charities;
run;
proc contents data=work.contacts2;
run;

data work.contacts3;
   set orion.us_suppliers orion.consultants;
run;
```

c. Submit a PROC CONTENTS step to examine **work.contacts**. From which input data set were the
    variable attributes assigned? **the first data set in the set statement, orion.charities**

e. Submit a PROC CONTENTS step to examine **work.contacts2**. From which input data set were
    the variable attributes assigned? **the first data set in the set statement, orion.us_suppliers**

f. Write a DATA step to concatenate **orion.us_suppliers** and **orion.consultants**, and creating a
    temporary data set, **contacts3**.

    Why did the DATA step fail? **ContactType was defined as both character and numeric.**

4. **Merging Two Sorted Data Sets in a One-to-Many Merge**

```
proc contents data=orion.orders;
run;

proc contents data=orion.order_item;
run;

data work.allorders;
   merge orion.orders
         orion.order_item;
   by Order_ID;
   keep Order_ID Order_Item_Num Order_Type
      Order_Date Quantity Total_Retail_Price;
run;

proc print data=work.allorders noobs;
   where Order_Date between '01Oct2011'd and '31Dec2011'd;
run;

  /* alternate solution */
proc print data=work.allorders noobs;
   where Order_Date>='01Oct2011'd and Order_Date<='31Dec2011'd;
run;

proc print data=work.allorders noobs;
   where qtr(Order_Date)=4 and year(Order_Date)=2011;
run;
```

5. Merging a Sorted Data Set and an Unsorted Data Set in a One-to-Many Merge

```
proc sort data=orion.product_list
          out=work.product_list;
   by Product_Level;
run;

data work.listlevel;
   merge orion.product_level work.product_list ;
   by Product_Level;
   keep Product_ID Product_Name Product_Level Product_Level_Name;
run;

proc print data=work.listlevel noobs;
   where Product_Level=3;
run;
```

6. Using the MERGENOBY Option

a. What is the purpose of this option and why is it used? **This option is used to issue a warning or an error when a BY statement is omitted from a merge. Performing a merge without a BY statement merges the observations based on their positions. This is almost never done intentionally and can lead to unexpected results.**

b. Complete the following table to include the values that this option can assume.

Value	Description	Default (Y/N)
NOWARN	Performs the positional merge without warning.	N
WARN	Performs the positional merge but writes a warning message to the log.	Y
ERROR	Writes an error message to the log and the DATA step terminates.	N

7. Merging Using the IN= Option

```
proc sort data=orion.product_list
          out=work.product;
   by Supplier_ID;
run;

data work.prodsup;
   merge work.product(in=P)
         orion.supplier(in=S);
   by Supplier_ID;
   if P=1 and S=0;
run;

proc print data=work.prodsup;
   var Product_ID Product_Name Supplier_ID Supplier_Name;
run;
```

8. Merging Using the IN= and RENAME= Options

```
proc sort data=orion.customer
          out=work.customer;
   by Country;
run;

data work.allcustomer;
   merge work.customer(in=Cust)
         orion.lookup_country(rename=(Start=Country
                                      Label=Country_Name) in=Ctry);
   by Country;
   keep Customer_ID Country Customer_Name Country_Name;
   if Cust=1 and Ctry=1;
run;

proc print data=work.allcustomer;
run;
```

9. Merging and Creating Output in Multiple Data Sets

```
proc sort data=orion.orders
          out=work.orders;
   by Employee_ID;
run;

data work.allorders work.noorders;
   merge orion.staff(in=Staff) work.orders(in=Ord);
   by Employee_ID;
   if Ord=1 then output work.allorders;
   else if Staff=1 and Ord=0 then output work.noorders;
 /* alternate statement */
 /* else output work.noorders; */
   keep Employee_ID Job_Title Gender Order_ID Order_Type Order_Date;
run;

proc print data=work.allorders;
run;

proc print data=work.noorders;
run;
```

Solutions to Student Activities (Polls/Quizzes)

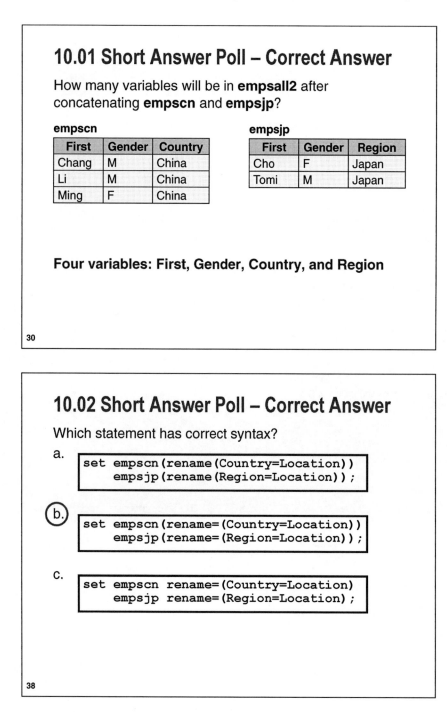

10.01 Short Answer Poll – Correct Answer

How many variables will be in **empsall2** after concatenating **empscn** and **empsjp**?

empscn

First	Gender	Country
Chang	M	China
Li	M	China
Ming	F	China

empsjp

First	Gender	Region
Cho	F	Japan
Tomi	M	Japan

Four variables: First, Gender, Country, and Region

30

10.02 Short Answer Poll – Correct Answer

Which statement has correct syntax?

a.
```
set empscn(rename(Country=Location))
    empsjp(rename(Region=Location));
```

(b.)
```
set empscn(rename=(Country=Location))
    empsjp(rename=(Region=Location));
```

c.
```
set empscn rename=(Country=Location)
    empsjp rename=(Region=Location);
```

38

10.03 Multiple Choice Poll – Correct Answer

Which of the following BY statements correctly sorts
by descending **salary** within **gender**?

a. by descending salary within gender;
b. by descending salary gender;
c. by gender descending salary;
d. by gender salary descending;

**The keyword "descending" is placed
before the variable to which it applies.**

52

10.04 Short Answer Poll – Correct Answer

What are the modified, completed statements?

```
proc sort data=orion.employee_payroll
          out=work.payroll;
   by Employee_ID;
run;

proc sort data=orion.employee_addresses
          out=work.addresses;
   by Employee_ID;
run;

data work.payadd;
   merge work.payroll work.addresses;
   by Employee_ID;
run;
```

59

p110a01s

10.05 Short Answer Poll – Correct Answer

In a one-to-many merge, does it matter which data set is listed first in the MERGE statement?

- Open **p110a02** and submit the program.
- Reverse the order of the data sets and submit it again.
- Observe the results. How are they different?

The results are the same, but the order of the variables is different.

96

10.06 Short Answer Poll – Correct Answer

Consider the data set **empsauc** created by the program in the previous example. Which input data sets contributed information to the last observation?

a. empsau
b. phonec
c. both empsau and phonec
d. There is insufficient information.

empsauc

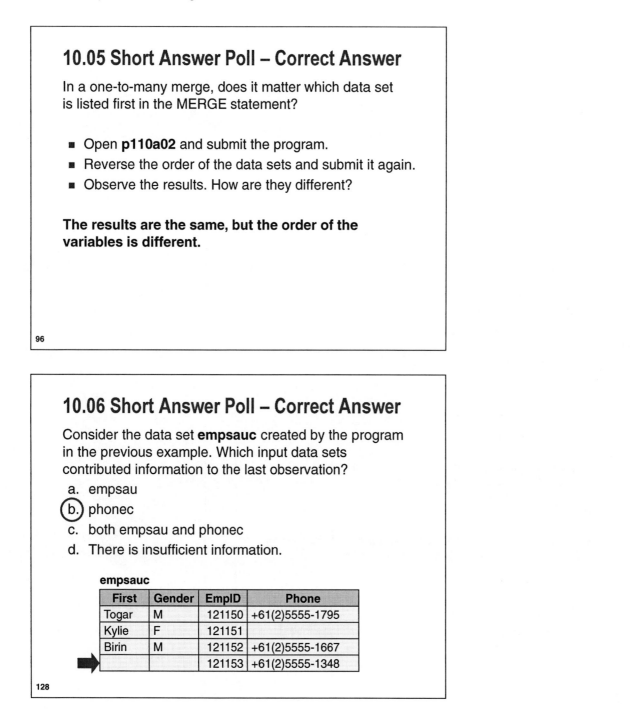

First	Gender	EmpID	Phone
Togar	M	121150	+61(2)5555-1795
Kylie	F	121151	
Birin	M	121152	+61(2)5555-1667
		121153	+61(2)5555-1348

128

10.07 Short Answer Poll – Correct Answer

What are the values of **Emps** and **Cell**?

empsau

First	Gender	EmpID
Togar	M	121150
Kylie	F	121151
Birin	M	121152

EOF

phonec

EmpID	Phone
121150	+61(2)5555-1795
121152	+61(2)5555-1667
121153	+61(2)5555-1348

```
data empsauc;
   merge empsau(in=Emps)
         phonec(in=Cell);
   by EmpID;
run;
```

nonmatch

PDV

First	Gender	EmpID	Emps	Phone	Cell
		121153	0	+61(2)5555-1348	1

137

10.08 Short Answer Poll – Correct Answer

What change is needed to correct the error?

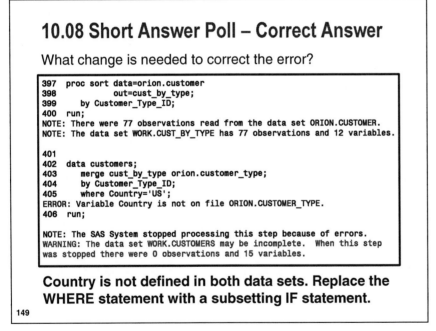

```
397  proc sort data=orion.customer
398          out=cust_by_type;
399     by Customer_Type_ID;
400  run;
NOTE: There were 77 observations read from the data set ORION.CUSTOMER.
NOTE: The data set WORK.CUST_BY_TYPE has 77 observations and 12 variables.

401
402  data customers;
403     merge cust_by_type orion.customer_type;
404     by Customer_Type_ID;
405     where Country='US';
ERROR: Variable Country is not on file ORION.CUSTOMER_TYPE.
406  run;

NOTE: The SAS System stopped processing this step because of errors.
WARNING: The data set WORK.CUSTOMERS may be incomplete.  When this step
was stopped there were 0 observations and 15 variables.
```

Country is not defined in both data sets. Replace the WHERE statement with a subsetting IF statement.

149

Chapter 11   Creating Summary Reports

11.1   The FREQ Procedure

Objectives

- Produce one-way and two-way frequency tables with the FREQ procedure.
- Enhance frequency tables with options.
- Use PROC FREQ to validate data in a SAS data set.

3

Business Scenario

Orion Star management wants to know the number of male and female sales employees in Australia.

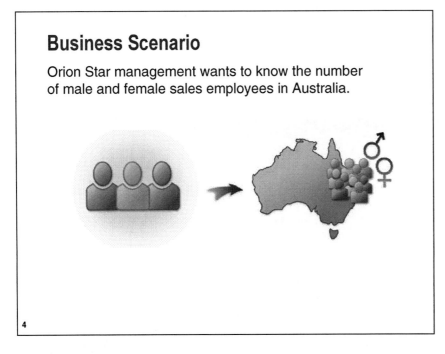

4

Considerations

Use the FREQ procedure to analyze the **Gender** variable in a subset of **orion.sales**.

```
              The FREQ Procedure

     Gender     Frequency      Percent

     F              XX          XX.XX
     M              XX          XX.XX
```

5

FREQ Procedure

The FREQ procedure produces a one-way frequency table for each variable named in the TABLES statement.

```
proc freq data=orion.sales;
   tables Gender;
   where Country='AU';
run;
```

PROC FREQ DATA=*SAS-data-set*;
    <TABLES *variable(s)* </ *options*>>;
RUN;

⚠ If the TABLES statement is omitted, a one-way frequency table is produced for *every* variable in the data set. This can produce a large amount of output and is seldom preferred.

6   p111d01

PROC FREQ displays a report by default. The output can be saved in a SAS data set.

The procedure can compute the following:

- chi-square tests for one-way to *n*-way tables
- tests and measures of agreement for contingency tables
- tests and measures of association for contingency tables and more

Viewing the Output

A one-way frequency table was created for **Gender**.
It lists the discrete values found in the data set and
the number of observations in which the variable
has that value.

```
                        The FREQ Procedure

                                     Cumulative    Cumulative
  Gender    Frequency    Percent     Frequency      Percent

  F               27      42.86            27         42.86
  M               36      57.14            63        100.00
```

The default output includes frequency and percentage
values, including cumulative statistics.

7

Options to Suppress Statistics

Use options in the TABLES statement to suppress
the display of selected default statistics.

TABLES *variable(s) / options* ;

Option	Description
NOCUM	Suppresses the cumulative statistics.
NOPERCENT	Suppresses the percentage display.

8

Cumulative frequencies and percentages are useful when there are at least three levels of a variable in an
ordinal relationship. When this is not the case, the NOCUM option produces a simpler, less confusing
report.

Options to Suppress Statistics

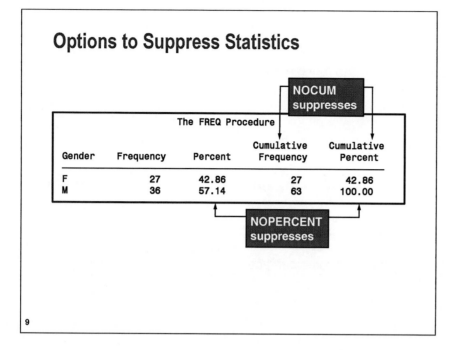

11.01 Short Answer Poll

Open and submit **p111a01**. Review the log to determine
the cause of the error. Correct and resubmit the program.
What change was needed?

```
proc freq data=orion.sales;
   tables country nocum nopercent;
run;
```

Idea Exchange

This step creates a table for every variable in the data set:

```
proc freq data=orion.sales;
run;
```

- **Employee_ID**
- **First_Name**
- **Last_Name**
- **Gender**
- **Salary**

- **Job_Title**
- **Country**
- **Birth_Date**
- **Hire_Date**

Which variables are most appropriate for a frequency analysis? Why?

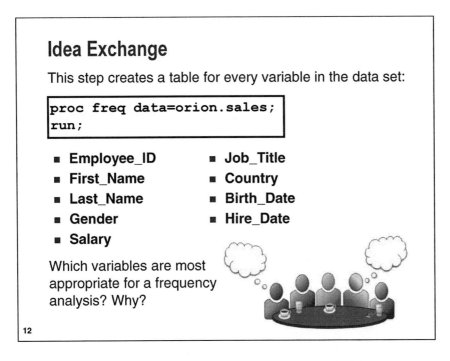

12

Business Scenario

Orion Star management wants to know how many sales employees are in each country, as well as the count of males and females.

14

TABLES Statement

You can list multiple variables in a TABLES statement.
A separate table is produced for each variable.

```
proc freq data=orion.sales;
   tables Gender Country;
run;
```

PROC FREQ Output

The FREQ Procedure

Gender	Frequency	Percent	Cumulative Frequency	Cumulative Percent
F	68	41.21	68	41.21
M	97	58.79	165	100.00

Country	Frequency	Percent	Cumulative Frequency	Cumulative Percent
AU	63	38.18	63	38.18
US	102	61.82	165	100.00

15   p111d02

BY Statement

The BY statement is used to request separate analyses
for each BY group.

```
proc sort data=orion.sales out=sorted;
   by Country;
run;

proc freq data=sorted;
   tables Gender;
   by Country;
run;
```

The data set must be sorted or indexed by the variable
(or variables) named in the BY statement.

16   p111d02

Viewing the Output

Each group appears on a separate page with a BY line.

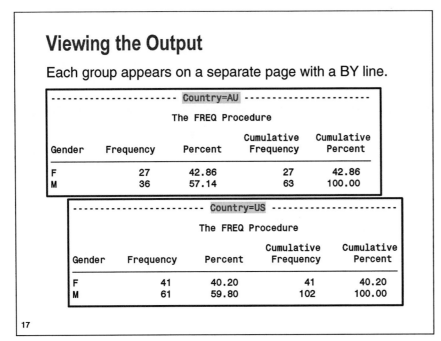

```
---------------------- Country=AU ----------------------

                     The FREQ Procedure

                                    Cumulative    Cumulative
Gender    Frequency      Percent     Frequency       Percent

F                27        42.86            27         42.86
M                36        57.14            63        100.00
```

```
---------------------- Country=US ----------------------

                     The FREQ Procedure

                                    Cumulative    Cumulative
Gender    Frequency      Percent     Frequency       Percent

F                41        40.20            41         40.20
M                61        59.80           102        100.00
```

17

Crosstabulation Table

An asterisk between two variables generates a two-way frequency table, or *crosstabulation table*.

```
proc freq data=orion.sales;
   tables Gender*Country;
run;
                  rows    columns
```

A two-way frequency table generates a single table with statistics for each distinct combination of values of the selected variables.

p111d02

18

Viewing the Output

PROC FREQ Output

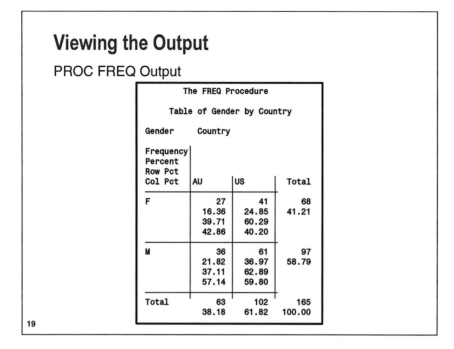

19

Options to Suppress Statistics

Use options in the TABLES statement to suppress
the display of selected default statistics.

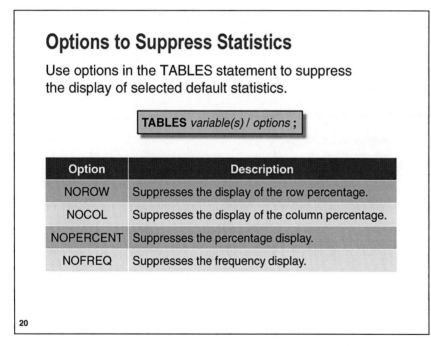

TABLES *variable(s)* / *options* ;

Option	Description
NOROW	Suppresses the display of the row percentage.
NOCOL	Suppresses the display of the column percentage.
NOPERCENT	Suppresses the percentage display.
NOFREQ	Suppresses the frequency display.

20

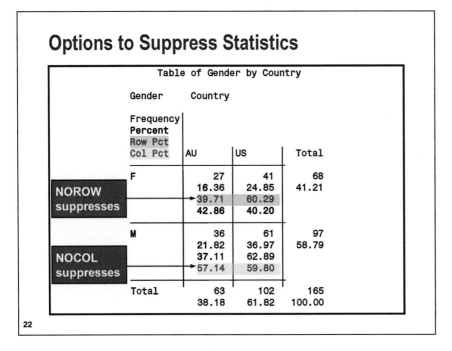

LIST and CROSSLIST Options

You can use the LIST and CROSSLIST options in the TABLES statement to "flatten" the output.

Gender	Country	Frequency	Percent	Cumulative Frequency	Cumulative Percent
F	AU	27	16.36	27	16.36
F	US	41	24.85	68	41.21
M	AU	36	21.82	104	63.03
M	US				

LIST option

CROSSLIST option

Table of Gender by Country

Gender	Country	Frequency	Percent	Row Percent	Column Percent
F	AU	27	16.36	39.71	42.86
	US	41	24.85	60.29	40.20
	Total	68	41.21	100.00	
M	AU	36	21.82	37.11	57.14
	US	61	36.97	62.89	59.80
	Total	97	58.79	100.00	
Total	AU	63	38.18		100.00
	US	102	61.82		100.00
	Total	165	100.00		

23

Business Scenario

A new data set, **orion.nonsales2**, must be validated. It contains information about non-sales employees and might include invalid and missing values.

Partial **orion.nonsales2**

Employee_ ID	First	Last	Gender	Salary	Job_Title	Country
120101	Patrick	Lu	M	163040	Director	AU
120104	Kareen	Billington	F	46230	Admin Mgr	au
120105	Liz	Povey	F	27110	Secretary I	AU
120106	John	Hornsey	M	.	Office Asst II	AU
120107	Sherie	Sheedy	F	30475	Office Asst II	AU
120108	Gladys	Gromek	F	27660	Warehouse Asst II	AU

25

Considerations

Use the FREQ procedure to screen for invalid, missing, and duplicate data values.

Requirements of non-sales employee data:

- **Employee_ID** values must be unique and not missing.
- **Gender** must be *F* or *M.*
- **Job_Title** must not be missing.
- **Country** must have a value of *AU* or *US.*
- **Salary** values must be in the numeric range of 24000 to 500000.

26

11.02 Short Answer Poll

What problems exist with the data in this partial data set?

Employee_ID	First	Last	Gender	Salary	Job_Title	Country
120101	Patrick	Lu	M	163040	Director	AU
120104	Kareen	Billington	F	46230	Administration Manager	au
120105	Liz	Povey	F	27110	Secretary I	AU
120106	John	Hornsey	M	.	Office Assistant II	AU
120107	Sherie	Sheedy	F	30475	Office Assistant III	AU
120108	Gladys	Gromek	F	27660	Warehouse Assistant II	AU
120108	Gabriele	Baker	F	26495	Warehouse Assistant I	AU
120110	Dennis	Entwisle	M	28615	Warehouse Assistant III	AU
120111	Ubaldo	Spillane	M	26895	Security Guard II	AU
120112	Ellis	Glattback	F	26550		AU
120113	Riu	Horsey	F	26870	Security Guard II	AU
120114	Jeannette	Buddery	G	31285	Security Manager	AU
120115	Hugh	Nichollas	M	2650	Service Assistant I	AU
.	Austen	Ralston	M	29250	Service Assistant II	AU
120117	Bill	Mccleary	M	31670	Cabinet Maker III	AU
120118	Darshi	Hartshorn	M	28090	Cabinet Maker II	AU

Hint: There are seven data problems.

27

FREQ Procedure for Data Validation

The FREQ procedure lists all discrete values
for a variable and reports missing values.

```
proc freq data=orion.nonsales2;
    tables Gender Country / nocum nopercent;
run;
```

29   p111d03

Viewing the Output

PROC FREQ Output

```
The FREQ Procedure

Gender      Frequency
-------------------------
F                 110
G                   1
M                 123

Frequency Missing = 1


Country     Frequency
-------------------------
AU                 33
US                196
au                  3
us                  3
```

30

NLEVELS Option

The *NLEVELS option* displays a table that provides the number of distinct values for each analysis variable.

```
proc freq data=orion.nonsales2 nlevels;
   tables Gender Country / nocum nopercent;
run;
```

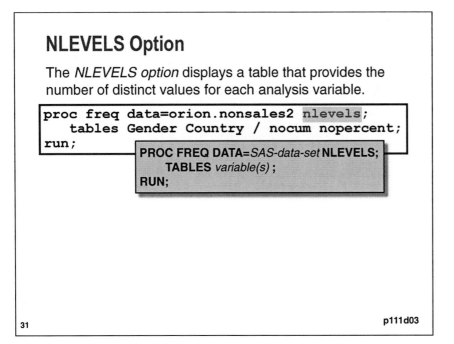

PROC FREQ DATA=*SAS-data-set* **NLEVELS;**
    TABLES *variable(s)* ;
RUN;

31   p111d03

Viewing the Output

PROC FREQ Output

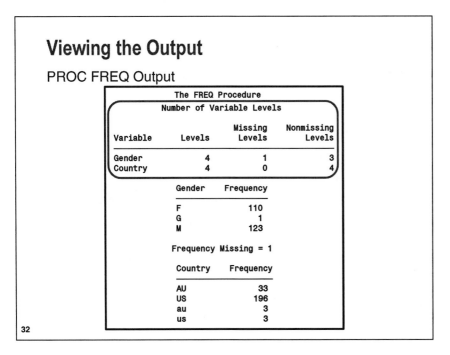

```
                The FREQ Procedure
             Number of Variable Levels

                              Missing    Nonmissing
Variable          Levels       Levels        Levels

Gender                 4            1             3
Country                4            0             4

            Gender      Frequency
            _____
            F                 110
            G                   1
            M                 123

         Frequency Missing = 1

            Country     Frequency
            _____
            AU                 33
            US                196
            au                  3
            us                  3
```

32

Check for Uniqueness

The values of **Employee_ID** must be unique and not
missing. PROC FREQ can be used to check for duplicate
or missing values.

```
proc freq data=orion.nonsales2 order=freq;
   tables Employee_ID / nocum nopercent;
run;
```

The ORDER=FREQ option displays the results
in descending frequency order.

33   p111d04

Viewing the Output

Partial PROC FREQ Output

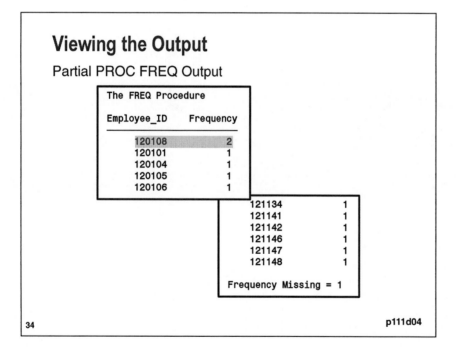

```
The FREQ Procedure

Employee_ID    Frequency
─────────────────────────
  120108          2
  120101          1
  120104          1
  120105          1
  120106          1

          121134          1
          121141          1
          121142          1
          121146          1
          121147          1
          121148          1

     Frequency Missing = 1
```

34   p111d04

NLEVELS Option

NLEVELS can also be used to identify duplicates, when the number of distinct values is known.

```
proc freq data=orion.nonsales2 nlevels;
    tables Employee_ID / noprint;
run;
```

This example uses the NOPRINT option to suppress the frequency table. Only the Number of Variable Levels table is displayed.

35   p111d04

Viewing the Output

Partial PROC FREQ Output

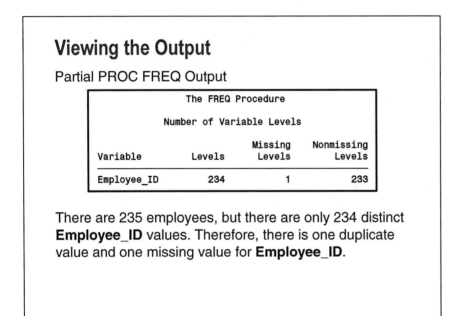

The FREQ Procedure			
Number of Variable Levels			
Variable	Levels	Missing Levels	Nonmissing Levels
Employee_ID	234	1	233

There are 235 employees, but there are only 234 distinct **Employee_ID** values. Therefore, there is one duplicate value and one missing value for **Employee_ID**.

36

NLEVELS Option

The _ALL_ keyword with the NOPRINT option displays the number of levels for all variables without displaying frequency counts.

```
proc freq data=orion.nonsales2 nlevels;
   tables _all_ / noprint;
run;
```

p111d04

Viewing the Output

PROC FREQ Output

```
                  The FREQ Procedure
                Number of Variable Levels

                              Missing      Nonmissing
     Variable      Levels     Levels         Levels

     Employee_ID     234        1             233
     First           204        0             204
     Last            228        0             228
     Gender            4        1               3
     Salary          230        1             229
     Job_Title       125        1             124
     Country           4        0               4
```

No frequency tables were displayed.

11.03 Short Answer Poll

Modify **p111a02** to analyze **Job_Title**. Display the NLEVELS table listing the frequency counts in decreasing order.

How many unique, nonmissing job titles exist?
Which job title occurs most frequently?
What is the frequency of missing job titles?

39

Identifying Observations with Invalid Data

PROC FREQ uncovered the existence of invalid data values for **Gender**, **Country**, and **Employee_ID**. Use PROC PRINT to display the observations with invalid values.

```
proc print data=orion.nonsales2;
   where Gender not in ('F','M') or
         Country not in ('AU','US') or
         Job_Title is null or
         Employee_ID is missing or
         Employee_ID=120108;
run;
```

41

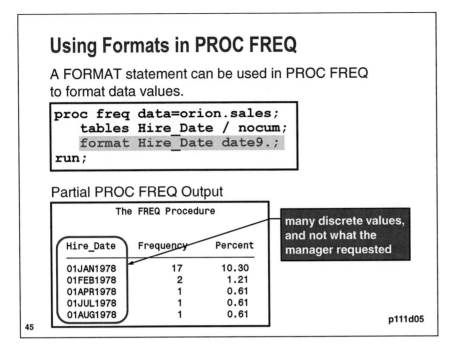

Using Formats in PROC FREQ

A FORMAT statement can be used in PROC FREQ
to format data values.

```
proc freq data=orion.sales;
   tables Hire_Date / nocum;
   format Hire_Date date9.;
run;
```

Partial PROC FREQ Output

```
                The FREQ Procedure


     Hire_Date     Frequency      Percent

     01JAN1978        17          10.30
     01FEB1978         2           1.21
     01APR1978         1           0.61
     01JUL1978         1           0.61
     01AUG1978         1           0.61
```

many discrete values, and not what the manager requested

45   p111d05

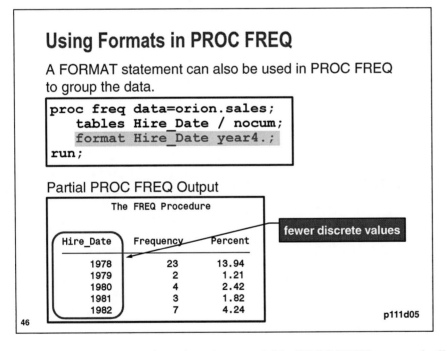

Using Formats in PROC FREQ

A FORMAT statement can also be used in PROC FREQ
to group the data.

```
proc freq data=orion.sales;
   tables Hire_Date / nocum;
   format Hire_Date year4.;
run;
```

Partial PROC FREQ Output

```
                The FREQ Procedure


     Hire_Date     Frequency      Percent

          1978        23          13.94
          1979         2           1.21
          1980         4           2.42
          1981         3           1.82
          1982         7           4.24
```

fewer discrete values

46   p111d05

If a format is permanently assigned to a variable, PROC FREQ automatically groups
the report by the formatted values.

11.04 Short Answer Poll

Open and submit **p111a03** and view the output.
Add a statement to apply the TIERS format to **Salary**
and resubmit the program.

Can user-defined formats be used to group data?

47

FORMAT Statement

User-defined formats can also be used to display levels
with alternate text in a frequency table.

```
proc freq data=orion.sales;
   tables Gender*Country;
   format Country $ctryfmt.
          Gender $gender.;
run;
```

49   p111d06

Viewing the Output

Partial PROC FREQ Output

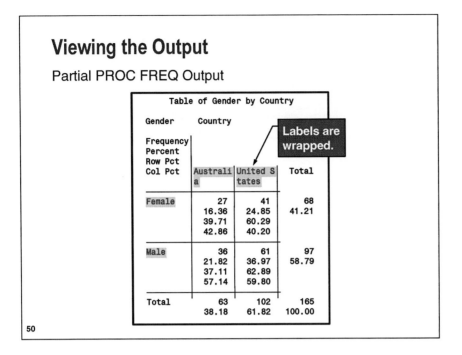

The default format for cell statistics is 8.*d*, where *d* is 0 for frequencies and 2 for percentages. Eight print positions are sometimes not enough for column headings.

FORMAT= Option

Use the *FORMAT= option* in the TABLES statement to format the frequency value and to change the width of the column.

```
proc freq data=orion.sales;
   tables Gender*Country / format=13.;
   format Country $ctryfmt.
          Gender $gender.;
run;
```

p111d06

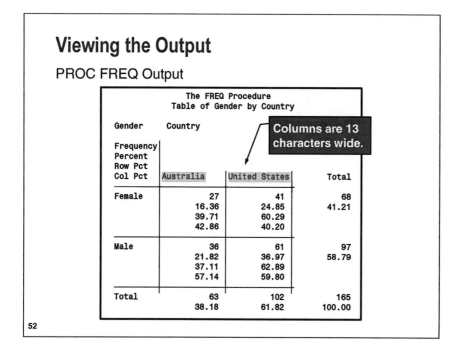

The FREQ Procedure
Table of Gender by Country

```
Gender    Country

Frequency
Percent
Row Pct
Col Pct   Australia       United States       Total

Female          27              41             68
             16.36           24.85          41.21
             39.71           60.29
             42.86           40.20

Male            36              61             97
             21.82           36.97          58.79
             37.11           62.89
             57.14           59.80

Total           63             102            165
             38.18           61.82         100.00
```

52

The FORMAT= option applies only to the frequency. Percentage values are always displayed with two decimal places.

Exercises

If you restarted your SAS session since the last exercise, open and submit the **libname.sas** program that can be found in the data folder.

Level 1

1. **Counting Levels of a Variable with PROC FREQ**

   a. Retrieve the starter program **p111e01**.

   b. Submit the program without making changes to analyze **Customer_ID** and **Employee_ID** in **orion.orders**. Would you expect to see frequencies of 1 for customers and sales employees? _____

   c. Modify the program to produce two separate reports.

      1) Display the number of distinct levels of **Customer_ID** and **Employee_ID** for retail orders.

         a) Use a WHERE statement to limit the report to retail sales (**Order_Type=1**).

         b) Do not display the frequency count tables.

         c) Display the title **Unique Customers and Salespersons for Retail Sales**.

         d) Submit the program to produce the following report:

PROC FREQ Output

```
Unique Customers and Salespersons for Retail Sales

                    The FREQ Procedure

                 Number of Variable Levels

    Variable        Label            Levels
    ---------------------------------------------
    Customer_ID     Customer ID        31
    Employee_ID     Employee ID       100
```

2) Display the number of distinct levels for **Customer_ID** for catalog and Internet orders.

   a) Use a WHERE statement to limit the report to catalog and Internet sales by selecting observations with **Order_Type** values other than *1*.

   b) Specify an option to display the results in decreasing frequency order.

   c) Specify an option to suppress the cumulative statistics.

   d) Display the title **Catalog and Internet Customers**.

   e) Submit the program to produce the following report:

Partial PROC FREQ Output

```
              Catalog and Internet Customers

                    The FREQ Procedure

                       Customer ID

    Customer_ID    Frequency      Percent
    -------------------------------------------
            16          15          6.52
            29           9          3.91
             5           8          3.48
           ...
         26148           1          0.43
         70059           1          0.43
```

2. **Validating orion.shoes_tracker with PROC FREQ**

   a. Retrieve the starter program **p111e02**.

   b. Complete the PROC FREQ step to create one-way frequency tables for **Supplier_Name** and **Supplier_ID** in **orion.shoes_tracker**. Include the NLEVELS option.

   The data in **orion.shoes_tracker** should meet the following requirements:
- **Supplier_Name** must be *3Top Sports* or *Greenline Sports Ltd.*
- **Supplier_ID** must be *2963* or *14682*.

   What invalid data exists for **Supplier_Name** and **Supplier_ID**? _____

Level 2

3. Producing Frequency Reports with PROC FREQ

a. Retrieve the starter program **p111e03**.

b. Add statements to the PROC FREQ step to produce three frequency reports.

1) Number of orders in each year: Apply a format to the **Order_Date** variable to combine all orders within the same year.

2) Number of orders of each order type: Apply the ORDERTYPES. format that is defined in the starter program to the **Order_Type** variable. Suppress the cumulative frequency and percentages.

3) Number of orders for each combination of year and order type: Suppress all percentages that normally appear in each cell of a two-way table.

c. Submit the program to produce the following output:

PROC FREQ Output

```
                       Order Summary by Year and Type

                           The FREQ Procedure

                    Date Order was placed by Customer

                                            Cumulative      Cumulative
         Order_Date    Frequency    Percent    Frequency       Percent
         ─────────────────────────────────────────────────────────────
               2007         104      21.22          104         21.22
               2008          87      17.76          191         38.98
               2009          70      14.29          261         53.27
               2010         113      23.06          374         76.33
               2011         116      23.67          490        100.00


                               Order Type

                    Order_
                      Type    Frequency     Percent
                    ───────────────────────────────
                    Retail          260       53.06
                    Catalog         132       26.94
                    Internet         98       20.00
```

```
                    Table of Order_Date by Order_Type

             Order_Date(Date Order was placed by Customer)
                      Order_Type(Order Type)

          Frequency Retail   Catalog  Internet   Total

             2007      45       41       18       104

             2008      51       20       16        87

             2009      27       23       20        70

             2010      67       33       13       113

             2011      70       15       31       116

             Total    260      132       98       490
```

4. **Validating orion.qtr2_2011 with PROC FREQ**

   Write a PROC FREQ step to validate the data in **orion.qtr2_2011**.

   a. Create frequency tables for **Order_ID** and **Order_Type**. Include the **Number of Variable Levels** table.

   b. Submit the program.

      The data in **orion.qtr2_2011** should meet the following requirements:
      - **Order_ID** must be unique (36 distinct values) and not missing.
      - **Order_Type** must have a value of *1*, *2*, or *3*.

      What invalid data exists for **Order_ID** and **Order_Type**? _____

Challenge

5. **Creating an Output Data Set with PROC FREQ**

   Write a program to perform a frequency analysis on **Product_ID** in **orion.order_fact**.

   a. Create an output data set that contains the frequency counts based on **Product_ID**. Explore the SAS Help Facility or online documentation for information about creating an output data set of counts from PROC FREQ results.

   b. Combine the output data set with **orion.product_list** to obtain the **Product_Name** value for each **Product_ID** code. Output only those products that were ordered.

   c. Sort the combined data so that the most frequently ordered products appear first in the resulting data set. Print the first five observations—that is, those that represent the five products ordered most often. Use the OBS= data set option to limit the number of observations that are displayed.

   d. Submit the program to produce the following report:

PROC PRINT Output

```
                     Top Five Products by Number of Orders

                    Product
        Orders      Number      Product

          6       230100500056   Knife
          6       230100600030   Outback Sleeping Bag, Large,Left,Blue/Black
          5       230100600022   Expedition10,Medium,Right,Blue Ribbon
          5       240400300035   Smasher Shorts
          4       230100500082   Lucky Tech Intergal Wp/B Rain Pants
```

11.2   The MEANS and UNIVARIATE Procedures

Objectives

- Calculate summary statistics and multilevel summaries with the MEANS procedure.
- Enhance summary tables with options.
- Identify extreme and missing values with the UNIVARIATE procedure.

56

Business Scenario

The payroll manager would like to see the average salary for all employees.

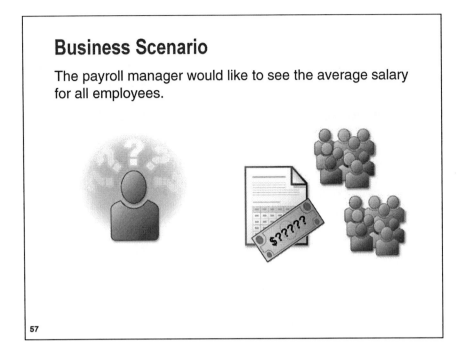

57

MEANS Procedure

The MEANS procedure produces summary reports with descriptive statistics.

```
proc means data=orion.sales;
run;
```

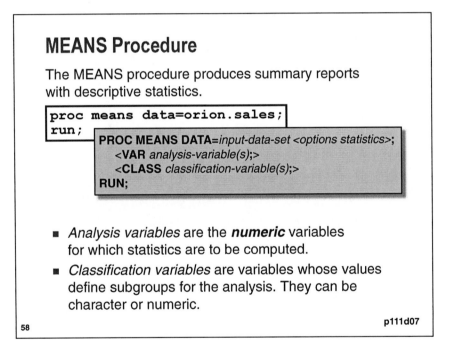

PROC MEANS DATA=*input-data-set <options statistics>*;
   <**VAR** *analysis-variable(s)*;>
   <**CLASS** *classification-variable(s)*;>
RUN;

- *Analysis variables* are the **numeric** variables for which statistics are to be computed.
- *Classification variables* are variables whose values define subgroups for the analysis. They can be character or numeric.

58   p111d07

Viewing the Output

PROC MEANS Output

```
                    The MEANS Procedure

Variable        N        Mean        Std Dev        Minimum        Maximum

Employee_ID    165    120713.90    450.0866939    120102.00    121145.00
Salary         165     31160.12     20082.67       22710.00    243190.00
Birth_Date     165      3622.58      5456.29       -5842.00     10490.00
Hire_Date      165     12054.28      4619.94        5114.00     17167.00
```

Default statistics are displayed for all numeric variables.

59

VAR Statement

The VAR statement identifies the analysis variable
(or variables) and their order in the output.

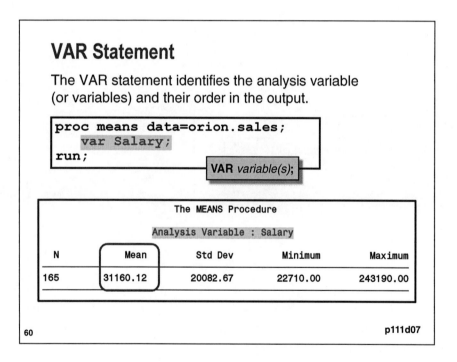

```
proc means data=orion.sales;
    var Salary;
run;
                              VAR variable(s);
```

```
                The MEANS Procedure

            Analysis Variable : Salary

    N        Mean        Std Dev     Minimum      Maximum

   165     31160.12     20082.67    22710.00    243190.00
```

60   p111d07

Business Scenario

Analyze **Salary** by **Country** within **Gender**.

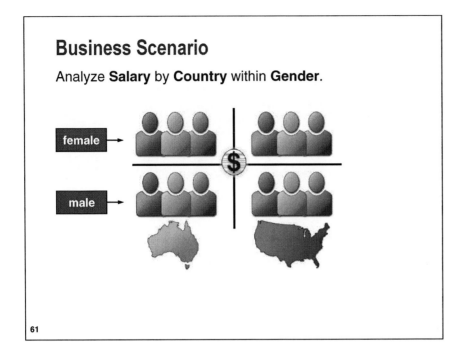

61

CLASS Statement

The *CLASS statement* identifies variables whose values define subgroups for the analysis.

```
proc means data=orion.sales;
    var Salary;
    class Gender Country;
run;
```

CLASS *classification-variable(s)*;

- Classification variables are character or numeric.
- They typically have few discrete values.
- The data set does **not** need to be sorted or indexed by the classification variables.

62   p111d08

Viewing the Output

Statistics are produced for each combination of values
of the classification variables.

```
                       The MEANS Procedure
                    Analysis Variable : Salary

                     N
Gender Country      Obs     N       Mean     Std Dev    Minimum    Maximum

F        AU          27     27    27702.41    1728.23   25185.00   30890.00

         US          41     41    29460.98    8847.03   25390.00   83505.00

M        AU          36     36    32001.39   16592.45   25745.00  108255.00

         US          61     61    33336.15   29592.69   22710.00  243190.00
```

- *N Obs* – the number of observations with each unique
  combination of class variables
- *N* – the number of observations with nonmissing values
  of the analysis variable (or variables)

63

11.05 Short Answer Poll

For a given data set, there are 63 observations with
a **Country** value of *AU*. Of those 63 observations,
only 61 observations have a value for **Salary**.
Which output is correct?

```
a. Analysis Variable : Salary          b. Analysis Variable : Salary

                    N                                      N
      Country      Obs      N                Country      Obs      N

      AU            63      61               AU            61      63
```

64

Business Scenario

Analyze **Salary** by **Country** within **Gender**. Generate a report that includes the number of missing **Salary** values, as well as the minimum, maximum, and sum of salaries.

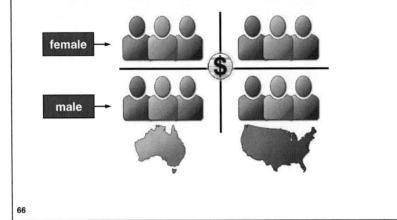

66

PROC MEANS Statistics

Use options in the PROC MEANS statement to request specific statistics.

```
proc means data=orion.sales nmiss min max sum;
   var Salary;
   class Gender Country;
run;
```

The requested statistics override the default statistics.

67   p111d09

PROC MEANS Statistics

The statistics are displayed in the order in which they are requested.

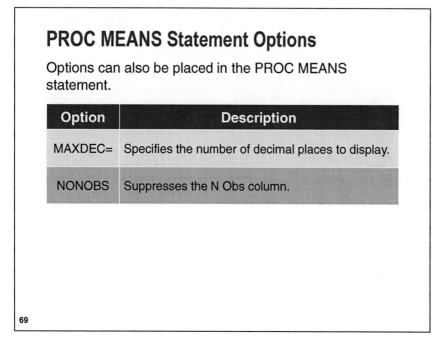

68

PROC MEANS Statement Options

Options can also be placed in the PROC MEANS statement.

Option	Description
MAXDEC=	Specifies the number of decimal places to display.
NONOBS	Suppresses the N Obs column.

69

MAXDEC= Option

MAXDEC=0

```
                    The MEANS Procedure
                  Analysis Variable : Salary

           N
Country   Obs    N       Mean      Std Dev     Minimum      Maximum

AU         63    63      30159      12699       25185        108255

US        102   102      31778      23556       22710        243190
```

MAXDEC=1

```
                    The MEANS Procedure
                  Analysis Variable : Salary

           N
Country   Obs    N       Mean      Std Dev     Minimum      Maximum

AU         63    63     30159.0    12699.1      25185.0      108255.0

US        102   102     31778.5    23555.8      22710.0      243190.0
```

70   p111d10

NONOBS Option

N Obs included by default

```
                    The MEANS Procedure
                  Analysis Variable : Salary

           N
Country   Obs    N       Mean      Std Dev     Minimum      Maximum

AU         63    63     30158.97   12699.14     25185.00     108255.00

US        102   102     31778.48   23555.84     22710.00     243190.00
```

NONOBS option

```
                    The MEANS Procedure
                  Analysis Variable : Salary

Country    N          Mean       Std Dev      Minimum      Maximum

AU         63       30158.97    12699.14      25185.00     108255.00

US        102       31778.48    23555.84      22710.00     243190.00
```

71   p111d10

Other PROC MEANS Statistics

Descriptive Statistic Keywords				
CLM	CSS	CV	LCLM	MAX
MEAN	MIN	MODE	N	NMISS
KURTOSIS	RANGE	SKEWNESS	STDDEV	STDERR
SUM	SUMWGT	UCLM	USS	VAR

Quantile Statistic Keywords				
MEDIAN | P50	P1	P5	P10	Q1 | P25
Q3 | P75	P90	P95	P99	QRANGE

Hypothesis Testing Keywords				
PROBT	T			

72

Idea Exchange

Which PROC MEANS statistics would you request when you are validating numeric variables?

73

Business Scenario

Validate salary data in **orion.nonsales2**. **Salary** must be in the numeric range of 24000 to 500000.

Partial **orion.nonsales2**

Employee _ID	First	Last	Gender	Salary	Job_Title	Country
120101	Patrick	Lu	M	163040	Director	AU
120104	Kareen	Billington	F	46230	Admin Mgr	au
120105	Liz	Povey	F	27110	Secretary I	AU
120106	John	Hornsey	M	.	Office Asst II	AU
120107	Sherie	Sheedy	F	30475	Office Asst II	AU
120108	Gladys	Gromek	F	27660	Warehouse Asst II	AU

75

UNIVARIATE Procedure

PROC UNIVARIATE displays extreme observations, missing values, and other statistics for the variables included in the VAR statement.

```
proc univariate data=orion.nonsales2;
   var Salary;
run;
```

PROC UNIVARIATE DATA=_SAS-data-set_;
    <**VAR** _variable(s)_;>
RUN;

If the VAR statement is omitted, PROC UNIVARIATE analyzes all numeric variables in the data set.

76   p111d11

Viewing the Output: Extreme Observations

The *Extreme Observations* section includes the five lowest and five highest values for the analysis variable and the corresponding observation numbers.

Partial PROC UNIVARIATE Output

```
                  Extreme Observations

      -----Lowest----        -----Highest----

      Value      Obs         Value       Obs

       2401       20        163040         1
       2650       13        194885       231
      24025       25        207885        28
      24100       19        268455        29
      24390      228        433800        27
```

✎ Obs is the observation number, not the count of observations with that value.

77

NEXTROBS= Option

The *NEXTROBS= option* specifies the number of extreme observations to be displayed.

```
proc univariate data=orion.nonsales2
               nextrobs=3;
    var Salary;
run;
```

Partial PROC UNIVARIATE Output

```
          The UNIVARIATE Procedure
             Variable:  Salary

           Extreme Observations

      -----Lowest----     -----Highest----

     Value      Obs        Value      Obs

      2401       20        207885       28
      2650       13        268455       29
     24025       25        433800       27
```

78   p111d11

The default value for NEXTROBS= is 5, and *n* can range between 0 and half the maximum number of observations. You can specify NEXTROBS=0 to suppress the table of extreme observations.

ID Statement

The *ID statement* displays the value of the identifying variable (or variables) in addition to the observation number.

```
proc univariate data=orion.nonsales2;
   var Salary;
   id Employee_ID;
run;                              ID variable(s);
```

p111d11

79

Viewing the Output

Partial PROC UNIVARIATE Output

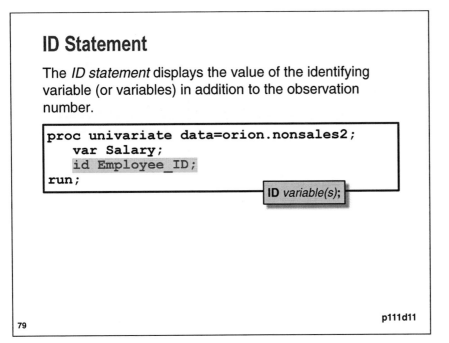

```
                     The UNIVARIATE Procedure
                        Variable:  Salary

                      Extreme Observations

-----------Lowest----------         -----------Highest----------

  Value    Employee_ID    Obs         Value    Employee_ID    Obs

   2401        120191      20        163040       120101        1
   2650        120115      13        194885       121141      231
  24025        120196      25        207885       120260       28
  24100        120190      19        268455       120262       29
  24390        121132     228        433800       120259       27
```

80

Viewing the Output: Missing Values Section

The *Missing Values* section displays the number and percentage of observations with missing values for the analysis variable.

Partial PROC UNIVARIATE Output

		Missing Values	
Missing Value	Count	-----Percent Of-----	
		All Obs	Missing Obs
.	1	0.43	100.00

81

11.06 Short Answer Poll

PROC UNIVARIATE identified two observations with **Salary** values less than 24,000.

What procedure can be used to display the observations that contain the invalid values?

82

 Exercises

If you restarted your SAS session since the last exercise, open and submit the **libname.sas** program that can be found in the data folder.

Level 1

6. **Creating a Summary Report with PROC MEANS**

   a. Retrieve the starter program **p111e06**.

   b. Display only the SUM statistic for the **Total_Retail_Price** variable.

   c. Add a CLASS statement to display separate statistics for each combination of **Order_Date** and **Order_Type**.

   d. Apply the ORDERTYPES format so that the order types are displayed as text descriptions. Apply the YEAR4. format so that order dates are displayed as years.

   e. Submit the program to produce the following report:

   Partial PROC MEANS Output

   ```
                          Revenue from All Orders

                            The MEANS Procedure

       Analysis Variable : Total_Retail_Price Total Retail Price for This Product

                  Date
                 Order
                   was
                placed
                    by    Order      N
              Customer    Type      Obs          Sum
             ─────────────────────────────────────────
                  2007    Retail     53       7938.80

                          Catalog    52      10668.08

                          Internet   23       4124.05

                  2008    Retail     63       9012.22

                          Catalog    23       3494.60

                          Internet   22       3275.70
   ```

7. **Validating orion.price_current with the UNIVARIATE Procedure**

   a. Retrieve the starter program **p111e07**.

   b. Add a VAR statement to analyze **Unit_Sales_Price** and **Factor** and submit the program.

   c. View the Extreme Observations output.

      How many values of **Unit_Sales_Price** are over the maximum of 800? _____

      How many values of **Factor** are under the minimum of 1? _____

      How many values of **Factor** are over the maximum of 1.05? _____

Level 2

8. **Analyzing Missing Numeric Values with PROC MEANS**

   a. Retrieve the starter program **p111e08**.

   b. Display the number of missing values and the number of nonmissing values present in the **Birth_Date**, **Emp_Hire_Date**, and **Emp_Term_Date** variables.

   c. Add a CLASS statement to display separate statistics for each value of **Gender**.

   d. Suppress the column that displays the total number of observations in each classification group.

   e. Submit the program to produce the following report:

   PROC MEANS Output

   ```
                    Number of Missing and Non-Missing Date Values

                              The MEANS Procedure

        Employee                                                   N
        Gender      Variable      Label                         Miss        N

        F           Birth_Date    Employee Birth Date              0      191
                    Emp_Hire_Date Employee Hire Date               0      191
                    Emp_Term_Date Employee Termination Date      139       52

        M           Birth_Date    Employee Birth Date              0      233
                    Emp_Hire_Date Employee Hire Date               0      233
                    Emp_Term_Date Employee Termination Date      169       64
   ```

9. **Validating orion.shoes_tracker with the UNIVARIATE Procedure**

   a. Write a PROC UNIVARIATE step to validate **Product_ID** of **orion.shoes_tracker**. A valid **Product_ID** value must have exactly 12 digits.

   b. Submit the program and view the Extreme Observations output.

   How many values of **Product_ID** are too small? _____

   How many values of **Product_ID** are too large? _____

Challenge

10. **Creating an Output Data Set with PROC MEANS**

   a. Retrieve the starter program **p111e10**.

   b. Modify the PROC MEANS step to create an output data set that contains the sum of **Total_Retail_Price** values for each value of **Product_ID**. (Creating an output data set from PROC MEANS results is discussed in the SAS Help Facility and in the online documentation.)

   c. Combine the output data set with **orion.product_list** to obtain the **Product_Name** value for each **Product_ID** code.

d. Sort the combined data so that the products with higher revenues appear at the top of the resulting data set.

e. Apply the OBS= data set option in a PROC PRINT step to display the first five observations—that is, those that represent the five products with the most revenue.

f. Display the revenue values with a leading euro symbol (€), a period that separates every three digits, a comma that separates the decimal fraction, and two decimal places.

g. Submit the program to produce the following report:

PROC MEANS Output

```
                          Top Five Products by Revenue

                                   Product
         Obs     Revenue            Number     Product

          1      €3.391,80       230100700009   Family Holiday 6
          2      €3.080,30       230100700008   Family Holiday 4
          3      €2.250,00       230100700011   Hurricane 4
          4      €1.937,20       240200100173   Proplay Executive Bi-Metal Graphite
          5      €1.796,00       240200100076   Expert Men's Firesole Driver
```

11. Selecting Only the Extreme Observations Output from the UNIVARIATE Procedure

a. Write a PROC UNIVARIATE step to validate **Product_ID** in **orion.shoes_tracker**.

b. Before the PROC UNIVARIATE step, add the following ODS statement:

```
ods trace on;
```

c. After the PROC UNIVARIATE step, add the following ODS statement:

```
ods trace off;
```

d. Submit the program and notice the trace information in the SAS log.

What is the name of the last output added in the SAS log? _____

e. Add an ODS SELECT statement immediately before the PROC UNIVARIATE step to select only the Extreme Observation output object. Documentation about the ODS TRACE and ODS SELECT statements can be found in the SAS Help Facility and in the online documentation.

f. Submit the program to create the following PROC UNIVARIATE report:

```
                         The UNIVARIATE Procedure
                    Variable:  Product_ID  (Product ID)

                            Extreme Observations

             --------Lowest-------        -------Highest------
                 Value       Obs             Value       Obs

              2.20200E+10      4          2.2020E+11       6
              2.20200E+11      1          2.2020E+11       7
              2.20200E+11      2          2.2020E+11       9
              2.20200E+11      3          2.2020E+11      10
              2.20200E+11      5          2.2020E+12       8
```

11.3   Using the Output Delivery System

Objectives

- Define the Output Delivery System and ODS destinations.
- Create HTML, PDF, RTF, and LISTING files with ODS statements.
- Use the STYLE= option to specify a style template.
- Create files that can be viewed in Microsoft Excel.

87

Business Scenario

Generate reports in various formats for distribution within Orion Star.

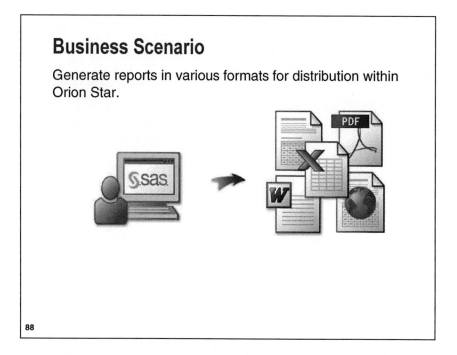

88

Interactive Method

Each SAS interface creates a specific report format by default and has an interactive method for changing the type of report format.

	Default Report Formats	Interactive Method for Changing Report Format	Possible Interactive Report Formats
SAS Studio	HTML, PDF, and RTF	More Application Options ⇨ Preferences ⇨ Results	HTML, PDF, and RTF
SAS Enterprise Guide	SASREPORT	Tools ⇨ Options ⇨ Results General ⇨ Results	SASREPORT, HTML, PDF, RTF, and LISTING (text)
SAS Windowing Environment	HTML	Tools ⇨ Options ⇨ Preferences ⇨ Results	HTML and LISTING (text)

89

SAS Studio:

- creates HTML output based on HTML5.
- creates PDF and RTF output in addition to HTML output. The PDF and RTF output is not visible on the Results tab. A download button must be clicked so that you can see the PDF or RTF output.

SAS Enterprise Guide:

- creates HTML output based on HTML4.

SAS windowing environment:

- creates HTML output based on HTML4.
- Prior to SAS 9.3, the SAS windowing environment created LISTING (text) output.

Programming Method

Alternatively, a user can add ODS statements to a SAS program to control the report formats that are created.

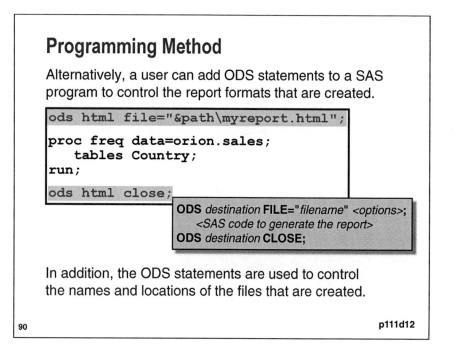

```
ods html file="&path\myreport.html";

proc freq data=orion.sales;
    tables Country;
run;

ods html close;
```

> **ODS** *destination* **FILE="***filename***"** *<options>*;
> *<SAS code to generate the report>*
> **ODS** *destination* **CLOSE;**

In addition, the ODS statements are used to control the names and locations of the files that are created.

90   p111d12

Output Delivery System (ODS)

Use the Output Delivery System to create different report formats by directing output to various ODS destinations.

ODS destinations and statements can be used regardless of the operating environment, processing mode, or SAS interface.

91

ODS Destinations

The following are some of the common ODS destinations:

Destination	Type of File	Extension	Viewed In
HTML	Hypertext Markup Language	.html	Web browser such as Internet Explorer
PDF	Portable Document Format	.pdf	Adobe product such as Adobe Reader
RTF	Rich Text Format	.rtf	Word processor such as Microsoft Excel
LISTING	Text	.txt	Text editor such as Notepad
SASREPORT	Extensible Markup Language	.xml	SAS product such as SAS Enterprise Guide

92

ODS Statements

With ODS statements, output from multiple procedures can be sent to multiple ODS destinations.

```
ods html file="&path\example.html";
ods pdf file="&path\example.pdf";
ods rtf file="&path\example.rtf";

proc freq data=orion.sales;
   tables Country;
run;
proc means data=orion.sales;
   var Salary;
run;

ods html close;
ods pdf close;
ods rtf close;
```

93   p111d13

ODS Statements

ALL can be used in the ODS CLOSE statement
to close all open destinations.

```
ods html file="&path\example.html";
ods pdf file="&path\example.pdf";
ods rtf file="&path\example.rtf";

proc freq data=orion.sales;
   tables Country;
run;
proc means data=orion.sales;
   var Salary;
run;

ods _all_ close;
ods html;
```

A good habit is to open a destination such as HTML after you close all destinations.

94   p111d13

11.07 Short Answer Poll

What is the problem with this program?

```
ods listing file="&path\myreport.txt";

proc print data=orion.sales;
run;

ods close;
```

95   p111a05

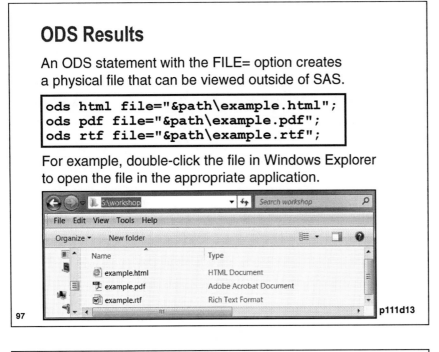

ODS Results

An ODS statement with the FILE= option creates
a physical file that can be viewed outside of SAS.

```
ods html file="&path\example.html";
ods pdf file="&path\example.pdf";
ods rtf file="&path\example.rtf";
```

For example, double-click the file in Windows Explorer
to open the file in the appropriate application.

ODS Results

In addition, the SAS interface can be used to access
the file that was created with ODS statements.

To access the ODS file, do the following:

- In SAS Enterprise Guide, click the download button on the Results tab.
- In SAS Studio, double-click the file in the Folders section of the navigation pane.
- In the SAS windowing environment, double-click the file in the expanded Results window.

STYLE= Option

Use a STYLE= option in the ODS statement to specify a style template.

> **ODS** *destination* **FILE="***filename***"**
>   **STYLE=***style-template***;**

- A *style template* sets presentation aspects including colors and fonts.

✎ STYLE= has no effect in the LISTING destination.

99

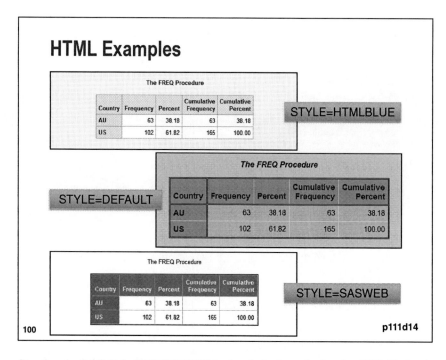

HTML Examples

STYLE=HTMLBLUE

STYLE=DEFAULT

STYLE=SASWEB

100   p111d14

Starting in SAS 9.3, HTMLBLUE is the default style for the HTML destination.

Prior to SAS 9.3, DEFAULT is the default style for the HTML destination.

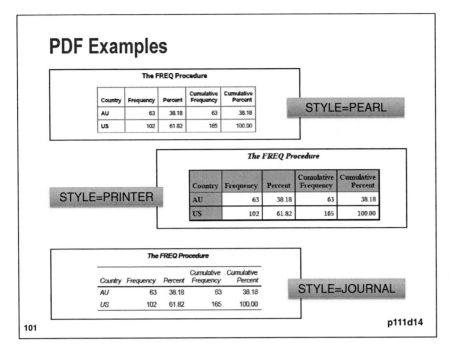

Starting in SAS 9.4, PEARL is the default style for the PDF destination.

Prior to SAS 9.4, PRINTER is the default style for the PDF destination.

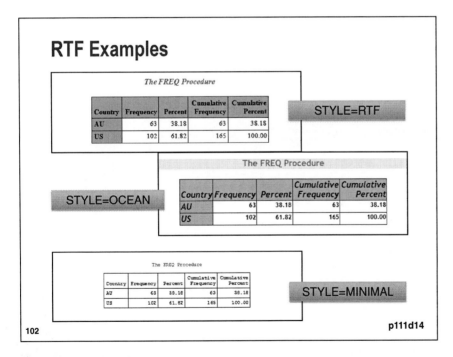

RTF is the default style for the RTF destination.

Available Styles

Use the TEMPLATE procedure to see a list of the available styles.

```
proc template;
   list styles;
run;
```

Partial Output

```
Listing of: SASHELP.TMPLMST
Path Filter is: Styles
Sort by: PATH/ASCENDING

Obs   Path                       Type

 1    Styles                     Dir
 2    Styles.Analysis            Style
 3    Styles.BarrettsBlue        Style
 4    Styles.BlockPrint          Style
 5    Styles.DTree               Style
 6    Styles.Daisy               Style
 7    Styles.Default             Style
```

103   p111d14

Business Scenario

Create SAS reports that can be opened in Microsoft Excel. Use the CSVALL, MSOFFICE2K, and EXCELXP destinations.

105

ODS Destinations Used with Excel

The following ODS destinations are used to create files that can be opened in Excel:

Destination	Type of File	Extension	Viewed In
CSVALL	Comma-Separated Value	.csv	Text Editor or Microsoft Excel
MSOFFICE2K	Hypertext Markup Language	.html	Microsoft Word or Microsoft Excel
TAGSETS. EXCELXP	Extensible Markup Language	.xml	Microsoft Excel

106

11.08 Short Answer Poll

Complete the ODS statements below to send the output to a CSVALL destination.

```
ods _____  file="&path\myexcel.____";

proc freq data=orion.sales;
   tables Country;
run;

proc means data=orion.sales;
   var Salary;
run;

ods _____  close;
```

107

CSVALL Destination

CSVALL does not include any style information.

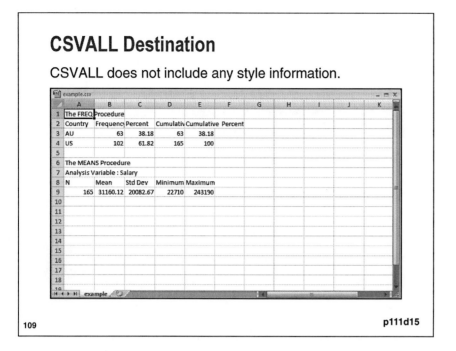

109   p111d15

MSOFFICE2K Destination

MSOFFICE2K keeps the style information, including spanning headers.

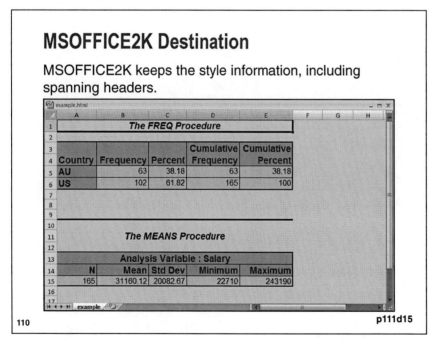

110   p111d15

EXCELXP Destination

EXCELXP keeps the style information. Output from each procedure is on a separate sheet.

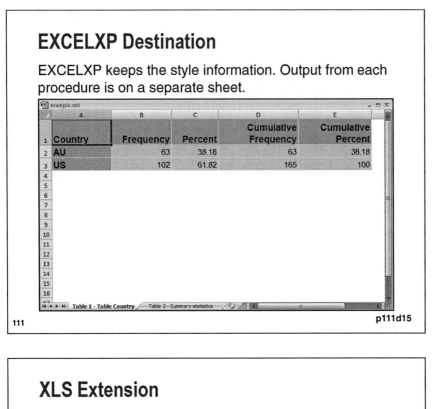

111   p111d15

XLS Extension

An XLS extension can be used in place of the CSV, HTML, or XML extension in order to open the file in Excel from within SAS.

```
ods csvall file="&path\myexcela.xls";
ods msoffice2k file="&path\myexcelb.xls";
ods tagsets.excelxp file="&path\myexcelc.xls";
```

Excel warns you that the file is not an XLS file.

112

Using the Output Delivery System

Creating HTML, PDF, and RTF Files

1. Open and submit **p111d16**.

```
options nodate nonumber;
title; footnote;

ods listing; /* Output window in SAS Windowing Environment */
ods html file="&path\myreport.html";
ods pdf file="&path\myreport.pdf";
ods rtf file="&path\myreport.rtf";

title 'Report 1';
proc freq data=orion.sales;
   tables Country;
run;

title 'Report 2';
proc means data=orion.sales;
   var Salary;
run;

title 'Report 3';
proc print data=orion.sales;
   var First_Name Last_Name
       Job_Title Country Salary;
   where Salary > 75000;
run;

ods _all_ close;
ods html; /* SAS Windowing Environment */
```

2. View the HTML, PDF, and RTF files in the appropriate application outside of your SAS session. The LISTING file can be viewed in the Output window of the SAS windowing environment.

Creating CSV, HTML, and XML Files That Open in Excel

1. Open and submit **p111d17**.

```
options nodate nonumber;
title; footnote;

ods csvall file="&path\myexcela.xls";
ods msoffice2k file="&path\myexcelb.xls";
ods tagsets.excelxp file="&path\myexcelc.xls";

title 'Report 1';
proc freq data=orion.sales;
   tables Country;
run;

title 'Report 2';
proc means data=orion.sales;
   var Salary;
run;
```

```
title 'Report 3';
proc print data=orion.sales;
    var First_Name Last_Name
        Job_Title Country Salary;
    where Salary > 75000;
run;

ods _all_ close;
ods html; /* SAS Windowing Environment */
```

2. View the CSV, HTML, and XML files in Microsoft Excel. Select **Yes** to open the files when you are prompted about the file format and extension not matching.

 Exercises

Level 1

12. Directing Output to PDF and RTF Destinations

a. Retrieve the starter program **p111e12**.

b. Add ODS statements to create a PDF file with the following naming convention:

Windows	"&path\p111e12.pdf"
UNIX	"&path/p111e12.pdf"

c. Submit the program and view the PDF output in Adobe Reader.

d. Add additional ODS statements to create an RTF file with the following naming convention:

Windows	"&path\p111e12.rtf"
UNIX	"&path/p111e12.rtf"

e. Submit the program and view the RTF output in Microsoft Word.

f. Add the STYLE= option to the ODS PDF statement to use the Curve style template, and add the STYLE= option to the ODS RTF statement to use the Journal style template.

g. Submit the program and view the output in Adobe Reader and Microsoft Word.

Level 2

13. Directing Output to the EXCELXP Destination

a. Retrieve the starter program **p111e13**.

b. Add ODS statements to create an XML output with the following naming convention:

Windows	"&path\p111e13.xls"
UNIX	"&path/p111e13.xls"

   c. Add the STYLE= option to the ODS statement to use the Listing style template.

   d. Submit the program and view the XML output in Microsoft Excel. Select **Yes** to open the files when you are prompted about the file format and extension not matching.

Challenge

14. Adding Options to the EXCELXP Destination

   a. Retrieve the starter program **p111e14**.

   b. Submit the program and view the XML output in Microsoft Excel. Select **Yes** to open the files when you are prompted about the file format and extension not matching.

   c. In the log, view the documentation for the EXCELXP destination.

   d. Add EMBEDDED_TITLES= and SHEET_NAME= options to create the following output:

	Obs	Customer_Type_ID	Customer_Type	Customer_Group_ID	Cust
			Customer Type Definitions		
4	1	1010	Orion Club members inactive	10	Orion
5	2	1020	Orion Club members low activity	10	Orion
6	3	1030	Orion Club members medium activity	10	Orion
7	4	1040	Orion Club members high activity	10	Orion
8	5	2010	Orion Club Gold members low activity	20	Orion
9	6	2020	Orion Club Gold members medium activity	20	Orion
10	7	2030	Orion Club Gold members high activity	20	Orion
11	8	3010	Internet/Catalog Customers	30	Intern

11.4 Solutions

Solutions to Exercises

1. Counting Levels of a Variable with PROC FREQ

Would you expect to see frequencies of 1 for customers and sales employees? **No. This file contains all customer orders, and the ID of the employee who helped with the sale. Employee_ID is likely to have higher frequency counts, as would frequent customers.**

```
title1 'Unique Customers and Salespersons for Retail Sales';
proc freq data=orion.orders nlevels;
   where Order_Type=1;
   tables Customer_ID Employee_ID / noprint;
run;
title;
title1 'Catalog and Internet Customers';
proc freq data=orion.orders order=freq;
   where Order_Type ne 1;
   tables Customer_ID / nocum;
run;
```

```
title;
```

2. Validating orion.shoes_tracker with PROC FREQ

```
proc freq data=orion.shoes_tracker nlevels;
    tables Supplier_Name Supplier_ID;
run;
```

What invalid data exists for **Supplier_Name** and **Supplier_ID**?

- **two observations with invalid values for Supplier_Name (*3op Sports*)**
- **one observation with a missing value for Supplier_ID**

3. Producing Frequency Reports with PROC FREQ

```
proc format;
    value ordertypes
          1='Retail'
          2='Catalog'
          3='Internet';
run;

title 'Order Summary by Year and Type';
proc freq data=orion.orders;
    tables Order_Date;
    tables Order_Type / nocum;
    tables Order_Date*Order_Type / nopercent norow nocol;
    format Order_Date year4. Order_Type ordertypes.;
run;
title;
```

4. Validating orion.qtr2_2011 with PROC FREQ

```
proc freq data=orion.qtr2_2011 nlevels;
    tables Order_ID Order_Type;
run;
```

What invalid data exists for **Order_ID** and **Order_Type**?

- **two observations with missing values for Order_ID**
- **one observation with a value of *0* for Order_Type**
- **one observation with a value of *4* for Order_Type**

5. Creating an Output Data Set with PROC FREQ

```
proc freq data=orion.order_fact noprint;
    tables Product_ID / out=product_orders;
run;

data product_names;
    merge product_orders orion.product_list;
    by Product_ID;
    keep Product_ID Product_Name Count;
run;

proc sort data=product_names;
    by descending Count;
```

```
run;

title 'Top Five Products by Number of Orders';
proc print data=product_names(obs=5) label noobs;
    var Count Product_ID Product_Name;
    label Product_ID='Product Number'
          Product_Name='Product'
          Count='Orders';
run;
title;
```

6. Creating a Summary Report with PROC MEANS

```
proc format;
    value ordertypes
        1='Retail'
        2='Catalog'
        3='Internet';
run;

title 'Revenue from All Orders';
proc means data=orion.order_fact sum;
    var Total_Retail_Price;
    class Order_Date Order_Type;
    format Order_Date year4. Order_Type ordertypes.;
run;
title;
```

7. Validating orion.price_current with the UNIVARIATE Procedure

```
proc univariate data=orion.price_current;
    var Unit_Sales_Price Factor;
run;
```

Find the Extreme Observations output.

- How many values of **Unit_Sales_Price** are over the maximum of 800? **one (*5730*)**

- How many values of **Factor** are under the minimum of 1? **one (*0.01*)**

- How many values of **Factor** are over the maximum of 1.05? **two (*10.20* and *100.00*)**

8. Analyzing Missing Numeric Values with PROC MEANS

```
title 'Number of Missing and Non-Missing Date Values';
proc means data=orion.staff nmiss n nonobs;
    var Birth_Date Emp_Hire_Date Emp_Term_Date;
    class Gender;
run;
title;
```

9. Validating orion.shoes_tracker with the UNIVARIATE Procedure

```
proc univariate data=orion.shoes_tracker;
    var Product_ID;
run;
```

How many values of **Product_ID** are too small? **one (*2.20200E+10*)**

How many values of **Product_ID** are too large? **one (*2.2020E+12*)**

10. **Creating an Output Data Set with PROC MEANS**

```
proc means data=orion.order_fact noprint nway;
   class Product_ID;
   var Total_Retail_Price;
   output out=product_orders sum=Product_Revenue;
run;

data product_names;
   merge product_orders orion.product_list;
   by Product_ID;
   keep Product_ID Product_Name Product_Revenue;
run;

proc sort data=product_names;
   by descending Product_Revenue;
run;

title 'Top Five Products by Revenue';
proc print data=product_names(obs=5) label;
   var Product_Revenue Product_ID Product_Name;
   label Product_ID='Product Number'
         Product_Name='Product'
         Product_Revenue='Revenue';
   format Product_Revenue eurox12.2;
run;
title;
```

11. **Selecting Only the Extreme Observations Output from the UNIVARIATE Procedure**

```
ods trace on;
ods select ExtremeObs;
proc univariate data=orion.shoes_tracker;
   var Product_ID;
run;

ods trace off;
```

What is the name of the last output added in the SAS log? **ExtremeObs**

12. **Directing Output to PDF and RTF Destinations**

```
ods pdf file="&path\p111e12.pdf" style=curve;
ods rtf file="&path\p111e12.rtf" style=journal;

title 'July 2011 Orders';
proc print data=orion.mnth7_2011;
run;

ods pdf close;
ods rtf close;
```

13. Directing Output to EXCELXP Destination

```
ods tagsets.excelxp file="&path\p111e13.xls" style=Listing;

title 'Customer Type Definitions';
proc print data=orion.customer_type;
run;

title 'Country Definitions';
proc print data=orion.country;
run;

ods tagsets.excelxp close;
```

14. Adding Options to the EXCELXP Destination

```
ods tagsets.excelxp file="&path\p111e14.xls"
                    style=Listing
                    options(doc='help'
                            embedded_titles='yes'
                            sheet_name='First Report');

title 'Customer Type Definitions';
proc print data=orion.customer_type;
run;

ods tagsets.excelxp options(sheet_name='Second Report');

title 'Country Definitions';
proc print data=orion.country;
run;

ods tagsets.excelxp close;
```

Solutions to Student Activities (Polls/Quizzes)

11.01 Short Answer Poll – Correct Answer

What change was needed? **A slash is required before the options in the TABLES statement.**

```
31    proc freq data=orion.sales;
32        tables country nocum nopercent;
ERROR: Variable NOCUM not found.
ERROR: Variable NOPERCENT not found.
33    run;
```

```
proc freq data=orion.sales;
    tables country / nocum nopercent;
run;
```

```
The FREQ Procedure
Country      Frequency

AU                  63
US                 102
```

p111a01s

11

11.02 Short Answer Poll – Correct Answer

What problems exist with the data in this partial data set?

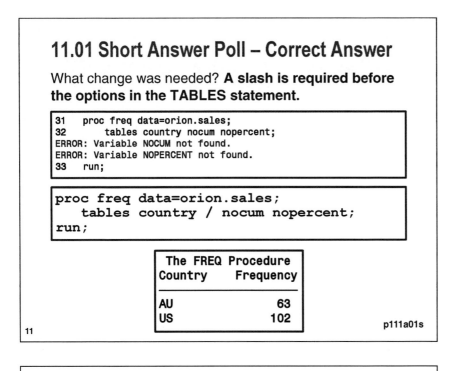

Employee_ID	First	Last	Gender	Salary	Job_Title	Country
120101	Patrick	Lu	M	163040	Director	AU
120104	Kareen	Billington	F	46230	Administration Manager	au
120105	Liz	Povey	F	27110	Secretary I	AU
120106	John	Hornsey	M		Office Assistant II	AU
120107	Sherie	Sheedy	F	30475	Office Assistant III	AU
120108	Gladys	Gromek	F	27660	Warehouse Assistant II	AU
120108	Gabriele	Baker	F	26495	Warehouse Assistant I	AU
120110	Dennis	Entwisle	M	28615	Warehouse Assistant III	AU
120111	Ubaldo	Spillane	M	26895	Security Guard II	AU
120112	Ellis	Glattback	F	26550		AU
120113	Riu	Horsey	F	26870	Security Guard II	AU
120114	Jeannette	Buddery	G	31285	Security Manager	AU
120115	Hugh	Nichollas	M	2650	Service Assistant I	AU
	Austen	Ralston	M	29250	Service Assistant II	AU
120117	Bill	Mccleary	M	31670	Cabinet Maker III	AU
120118	Darshi	Hartshorn	M	28090	Cabinet Maker II	AU

Hint: There are seven data problems.

28

11.03 Short Answer Poll – Correct Answer

How many unique, nonmissing job titles exist? **124**

Which job title occurs most frequently? **Trainee**

What is the frequency of missing job titles? **1**

```
proc freq data=orion.nonsales2 nlevels
          order=freq;
   tables Job_Title /nocum nopercent;
run;
```

p111a02s

11.04 Short Answer Poll – Correct Answer

Can user-defined formats be used to group data? **yes**

			Cumulative	Cumulative
Salary	Frequency	Percent	Frequency	Percent
Tier1	1	0.61	1	0.61
Tier2	158	95.76	159	96.36
Tier3	4	2.42	163	98.79
Tier4	2	1.21	165	100.00

The FREQ Procedure

p111a03s

11.05 Short Answer Poll – Correct Answer

For a given data set, there are 63 observations with
a **Country** value of *AU*. Of those 63 observations,
only 61 observations have a value for **Salary**.

Which output is correct?

65

11.06 Short Answer Poll – Correct Answer

PROC UNIVARIATE identified two observations
with **Salary** values less than 24,000.

What procedure can be used to display the observations
that contain the invalid values? **PROC PRINT**

```
proc print data=orion.nonsales2;
   where Salary<24000;
run;
```

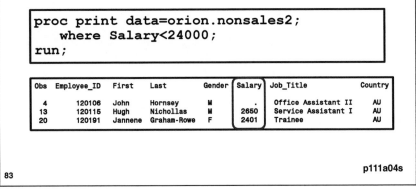

83   p111a04s

11.07 Short Answer Poll – Correct Answer

What is the problem with this program?

```
ods listing file="&path\myreport.txt";

proc print data=orion.sales;
run;

ods listing close;
```

96   p111a05s

11.08 Short Answer Poll – Correct Answer

Complete the ODS statements below to send the output
to a CSVALL destination.

```
ods csvall file="&path\myexcel.csv";

proc freq data=orion.sales;
   tables Country;
run;

proc means data=orion.sales;
   var Salary;
run;

ods csvall close;
```

108   p111a06s

Chapter 12   Learning More

12.1 Introduction

Objectives

- Identify the areas of support that SAS offers.
- Identify the next steps after the completion of this course.

2

Customer Support

SAS provides a variety of resources to help customers.

http://support.sas.com/resourcekit/

3

Education

SAS Education provides comprehensive training, including

- more than 200 course offerings
- world-class instructors
- multiple delivery methods
- worldwide training centers.

http://support.sas.com/training/

4

SAS Global Certification Program

SAS Education also provides
- globally recognized certifications
- preparation materials
- practice exams.

A World of Opportunity

http://support.sas.com/certify/

5

The following icons are identified from top left to right, and then bottom left to right:

Twitter, RSS, Myspace, YouTube, Facebook, Technorati, and sasCommunity.org

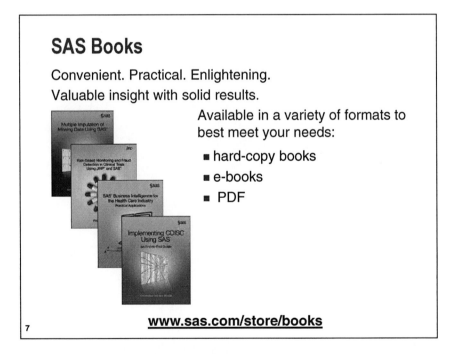

Beyond This Course

To grow your SAS skills, remember to activate the *extended learning page* for this course.

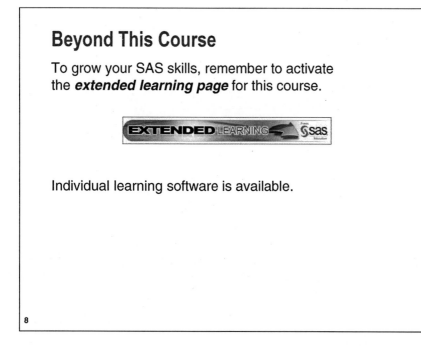

Individual learning software is available.

8

Next Steps

To learn more about this:	Enroll in this course:
Programming techniques, including DATA and PROC steps to manipulate data	SAS® Programming 2: Data Manipulation Techniques
How to use SQL to manipulate and merge data files	SAS® SQL 1: Essentials
Creating reports using the REPORT and TABULATE procedures, plus the Output Delivery System (ODS)	SAS® Report Writing 1: Essentials
Performing statistical analysis using SAS/STAT software	Statistics 1: Introduction to ANOVA, Regression, and Logistic Regression
How to use many of the most popular SAS functions	SAS® Functions by Example
A variety of techniques to find errors in your data	Data Cleaning Techniques

9